THE DISSOLUTION OF MIND

A Fable of How Experience
Gives Rise to Cognition

VIBS

Volume 128

Robert Ginsberg
Founding Editor

Peter A. Redpath
Executive Editor

A volume in
Cognitive Science
CS
Oscar Vilarroya, Editor

THE DISSOLUTION OF MIND

A Fable of How Experience Gives Rise to Cognition

Oscar Vilarroya

Amsterdam – New York, NY 2002

The paper on which this book is printed meets the requirements of "ISO 9706:1994, Information and documentation - Paper for documents - Requirements for permanence".

ISBN: 90-420-1370-2
©Editions Rodopi B.V., Amsterdam – New York, NY 2002
Printed in The Netherlands

To Joe, for being my *alter ego*
To Lluis, for being the *alter ego*
To Cristina, for being Cristina

Somewhere in the heart of experience there is an order and a coherence which we might surprise if we were attentive enough, loving enough, or patient enough. Will there be time?

Lawrence Durrell, *Justine*

CONTENTS

LIST OF ILLUSTRATIONS

EDITORIAL FOREWORD

This book is the first volume in the VIBS's Special Series in Cognitive Science (henceforth, CS). The aim of CS is to provide an original corpus of scholarly work that makes explicit the import of cognitive science for philosophical analyses of knowledge and mind.

Cognitive science appeared in the 1960s at the intersection of disciplines such as neuroscience, philosophy of mind, psychology, linguistics, and computer science. This convergence occurred because researchers in those fields realized that they shared a common conceptual and methodological framework for understanding, explaining, and reproducing the cognitive abilities of brains and other intelligent artifacts.

At present, cognitive science enjoys good academic health generally, but its significance for modern philosophical analysis has yet to be fully realized. Two reasons account for this situation. The first is the continued lack of communication between the different branches of cognitive science. The second is the reluctance of the philosophical mainstream to accept psychological, neuroscientific, and computational research as a source of inspiration for the study of the mind.

The challenge, then, is to develop and articulate a multidisciplinary perspective within cognitive science while maintaining an integrated view of cognition and knowledge.

CS seeks to fulfill three fundamental objectives: (1) establish an explicit link between the theoretical and empirical foundations of cognitive science and philosophy; (2) strengthen the cross-disciplinary conceptual and methodological coherence among the cognitive-science disciplines, and (3) promote cognitive science within philosophy and the humanities in general.

I could not end this section without mentioning Robert Ginsberg. His vision, encouragement, and enthusiasm have made it possible to begin this enterprise. I look forward to witnessing the growth and success of CS in the years to come. It should be an exciting enterprise.

Oscar Vilarroya
Editor, Cognitive Science

GUEST FOREWORD

A Brain Submerged Within the World

Our time must be special since many scientists seem to feel highly compelled to attempt a serious assault on one of the oldest and most challenging questions: how humans get their knowledge of themselves and about the world? This venerable and exclusive domain of philosophical inquiry has been permeated lately by bold and nontrivial incursions from the scientific ranks. Once discounted the legitimate rewards paid by publishing houses that flood the market with products carrying labels as promising as *How the mind works?*, *The feeling of what happens*, *Consciousness explained*, *Images of mind*, and so on, I suspect that perseverance in building viable and systematic explanations of the mindful secretions of brain workings must respond to other impulses.

The flourishing of Neurobiology in recent decades, and of Cognitive Neuroscience in particular, appears as the most plausible force behind most of these efforts. It is a rule that new businesses need territory to conquer, and thus claim, at the start, as much of this territory as they can foresee warranting credit, ownership and potential revenues. So it is not strange that once the program was launched to describe the mindful properties of neural systems, the urge to produce rough sketches or provisional maps of the whole endeavor abounds, especially given the seminal signals of progress emerging at a quickening pace from different research front lines.

In this book Oscar Vilarroya takes us on a especially inspiring trip through the subtleties of the brain/mind world. By virtue of his privileged link with an omniscient "K," who is in possession of a fully detailed description of how humans (or analogue creatures) feel, think, and behave, Vilarroya advances a tantalizing and encompassing conjecture about how the brain may build up a fanciful, though entirely physical, piece of machinery (the "cognitive system") that contains all the necessary keys to decipher the singularities of the preposterous tapestry that was once called the "human spirit."

The hub of the proposal is experience. Or better still, "instants of experience." This is the nodal point of the whole scaffolding: human brains would not produce feelings or thoughts, desires or beliefs, if they had not the ability to detect, engrave, and accumulate "instants of experience" that stem from their most virginal interactions with the external or the inner world. These spontaneous, synchronous, vivid, and evocable "instants of life" would function as the units of workable material that discern the crucial layers and relationships within intimate events in the brain/mind world.

On his way to explaining the ultimate roots and core processes of cognition, Vilarroya demolishes a series of artifacts erected by a centuries-old tradition of inquiries concerning the nature of human understanding: from perceptual objects to concepts, and from representations to communicative tools, the classical domains, or modules, of the brain/mind recede towards the "instants of experience" connected through evocative paths. Using the traditional way of referring to psychological processes, I guess that Vilarroya's conjecture could be stated as follows: the neural tissue forming a given net extending from sensors to effectors, all with different attentional and memory capabilities, will create the "instants of life" that result in cognitive events. All the rest are additions to this elementary circuit.

During a week-long feast of teatime dialogues between Alice and her Non-Professor, we are taken through a fascinating and demanding exploration, punctuated with a never-ending flow of candid anecdotes, lucid examples, and startling aphorisms in a continuous shuttling from Arkadia (a metaphorical experiment to illustrate the functioning of Vilarroya's tools of thought dissection) to Earthland. We visit the frontiers of contemporary Cognitive Science with the assistance of the perfect guide, one that combines charm, ingenuity, curiosity, and enthusiasm in the service of the perplexities of a brain entangled within an ever-changing world.

I would have preferred to find, occasionally at least, incursions that contrast the ideas advanced here with what we already know about the properties of neural systems in order to see if the anchorage is feasible or if insurmountable gaps still exist. And I also would have liked to have seen specific suggestions about the minimal requirements of an "instant of life" and how to devise measures of them. But this comes from my point of view (read: "background," in Vilarroya's terms), which is more inclined to search for substrates, and which is obviously a task for future developments. I do invite you to detect errors, inconsistencies, difficulties, or contrivances in a scenario that seems robust and fragile at the same time.

I have the opportunity of sharing with Vilarroya, for an hour once a week, the marvels of debate on science topics. To me the combination of the apparent fragility with the robustness and sharpness of his suggestions and elaborations is pretty familiar. I am happy that with this book he has moved to initiate work on his hypothesis and views within the science of the brain/mind so that they may be scrutinized by wide and challenging audiences. I am sure he will have all kinds of returns, from skeptical to critical or praising, but always delighted to participate in a wonderful intellectual exercise.

Adolf Tobeña
Professor of Psychiatry, Universitat Autònoma de Barcelona

PREFACE

This book has taken me two years to write, but I have been composing its contents since I first had the use of reason. In all this time I have been trying to understand the marvel of a highly organized mass of organic matter that is capable of knowing. Unfortunately, all the accounts I have found of it are unsatisfying in some way or another. This book is a sketch of how my account would have to look like.

The core of the hypothesis, and the starting point of the book, is what I believe to be an original approach to the notion of *experience*, understood as the way in which the brain processes and registers the activity of the sensory systems. This approach allows me to attempt two things. First, I explore how experience gives rise to cognition, that is, how the brain acquires, organizes, and applies knowledge in its interactions with the rest of the world. Secondly, I employ this notion of experience to reread some central issues in epistemology, linguistics, and philosophy of mind.

I cannot deny that my sketch appears suspiciously ambitious. I pretend nothing less than putting concepts and word meaning within the scope of experiential processing, bridging the divide between rationalist and empiricist approaches to knowledge, as well as providing a possible way out to the mind/body problem that does not require a supernumerary of substances, nor of properties. Appearances notwithstanding, I do not take myself to have constructed a new philosophical system. If anything, my accomplishment is only speculative. I merely probe what would happen if we threw the notion of experience down a different slope of cognition than the one normally chosen. Here I report the consequences. If these consequences are significant, the reason is that experience carries its momentum.

My proposal does not come out of the blue. It is the result of spending long hours with neurobiological research, as well as current trends in cognitive science. In this sense, I have been especially influenced by lines of research such as cognitive neuroscience, situated cognition, connectionism, evolutionary biology, perceptual theories of knowledge, cognitive linguistics, and artificial life. I must also acknowledge the influence of authors such as Lawrence W. Barsalou, Elizabeth A. Bates, Rodney A. Brooks, Patricia S. Churchland, Paul M. Churchland, Andy Clark, Francis Crick, Stanislas Dehaene, Daniel Dennett, Merlin Donald, Hubert L. Dreyfus, Gerald Edelman, Jeffrey L. Elman, Michael S. Gazzaniga, Richard Gregory, Stevan Harnad, Douglas Hofstadter, Mark L. Johnson, Philip Johnson-Laird, Daniel Kahneman, Eric R. Kandel, George Lakoff, Rodolfo Llinás, Ruth G. Millikan, Katherine Nelson, Pasko Rakic, Vilayanur S. Ramachandran, Robert C. Richardson, David E. Rumelhart, Terrence Sejnowski, Herbert A. Simon, Elliott Sober, Esther Thelen, Francisco J. Varela, Lofti A. Zadeh, and Semir Zeki. The reader should not blame any of these schools and authors for the book's shortcomings.

Despite such influences, I believe that my proposal cannot be comfortably placed under any particular paradigm, nor can it be conceived as one of their possible developments. Instead, I have use these lines of research to feed my alternative. Much of the originality of the present hypothesis may stem from breaking with certain assumptions maintained by mainstream accounts of experience. I like to think of these assumptions as magician's tricks that nearly all accounts utilize.

The first magician's trick is the point of departure of nearly all epistemological texts. "Four elements exist in perception: (1) the subject, the 'I' who perceives; (2) the sensory experience; (3) the object, or thing perceived, and (4) the relation between object and the subject." I have always thought that the "I" is a rabbit that we pull out of our philosophical hats. In my opinion, we do not have any justification for distinguishing between the sensory experience and the "I"; it is not an ingredient that we can add or subtract from the perceptual process. To be sure, the "I" is unavoidable when we speak of perceiving, thinking, knowing, but it cannot be segregated from such processes.

The second magician's trick is that of granting the mind the capability to be aware of what properties and elements constitute its experiences. By contrast, I think that the mind has not yet earned the right to say, "Provided that I know that this is a bouncing red ball, then my experience is constituted by the elements: bouncing, red, and ball." For all I know, the mind has a crucial role to play in the interactions of organisms with the world; this need not include being aware of what their experiences are made of.

The third magician's trick is performed so extensively that it is almost impossible to detect. It concerns the belief that in order to use past experiences to analyze new ones, the analysis needs to "go beyond" the concreteness of past experiences. In my opinion, until we have not comprehensively explored the power of a vast and rich systematization of concrete experiences, we need not create spurious objects or properties, such as abstractions. This is not to say that we are incapable of abstracting, but merely that abstractions do not exist as autonomous objects of mind.

I am sure that I will not convince everybody that the next trick is a trick, but allow me the benefit of the doubt. Perception is traditionally understood as a mediation process between an "external reality" and an intelligent characterization of such a reality. Many accounts of perception exist, but nearly all of them explain such a process as an analysis of the external information by a system. Where is the trick?, you may ask. In my opinion, it consists of confining the perceptual process to the present, that is, to the temporal window in which the piece of external reality is there. By contrast, I believe that we have underestimated the role of the past in perception; not the past as a mere source of information for the present perceptual process, but the past also as an active modeler of perceptual processing.

The last magician's trick is the most difficult to undo, because it has been with us since the moment (of evolutionary time) in which the conscious mind became self-conscious. This trick is based on the "need" to copy external reality (that is, the realm of objects, states of affairs or events), into the realm of the mind. What if such a duplication were a *trompe-l'oeil*? Again, I do not see why we do have to populate the world with spurious realities on the basis of dualistic prejudices, unless we have explored all the possibilities of the reality we already know.

Enough about the proposal. Let me now briefly talk about the book. *The Dissolution of Mind* introduces the basics and scope of my proposal concerning experience, and develops some of its possible psychological and philosophical consequences. It is not a classical academic text, nor a popularization. Instead, the book should be seen as an initial exploration of this hypothesis, both for me and for any reader who may be interested in cognition. Thus, I have tried to appeal to the prephilosophical intuitions of a reader who has no technical background in cognitive science.

With such a reader in mind, I have avoided the use of technical language, notes and bibliographic references, even if I list, chapter by chapter, at the end of the book those references that can help the reader to identify the sources of the proposals made in the book. Secondly, I have selected a dialogue format between two characters: Alice, who represents the voice of common sense, and Non-Professor O, who speaks on my behalf. The dialogue takes place in an imaginary place, Arkadia, whose inhabitants are characterized according to the proposed hypothesis. The dialogue presents the proposal in the following way: "if things were *like X* then *Y* would happen..." I think that this may help to eliminate the magician's tricks mentioned above. Thirdly, I introduce some neologisms and certain typographic conventions that allow me to reduce the connotations of the terms that I want to modify.

The first and most important neologism is "slife," which I use as a shorthand for my proposal of experience. The term is a fused form of slice-of-life. Slife seemed to me a good translation for the Spanish term *vivencia*, which was the word that I first thought of when I sketched the proposal presented herein. The aim of introducing this neologism is rhetorical: in using this neologism, I want to emphasize that I am referring to experience according to my approach. Since everything I say about slifes should corresponds to experience, I may not employ the term beyond the context of the book.

I also introduce the neologism "panception," which could be seen as an alternative for perception. However, here the question of correspondence is a bit less clear than in the case of slife. For one thing, I understand perception as including emotional and conceptual processing. This would not be seen as belonging to the domain of perceptual processing proper by mainstream cognitive science, but many theorists continue to use the term perception even if they conceive perception as a conceptual process.

Perhaps the only neologism that could have a place outside this book is "memogram." A memogram could be understood as an engram, that is, a memory trace, of a complete experience. Thus, if something like the memory trace of an experience exists, then "memogram" could be used as a new term.

The word "satisficing" may be considered to be a neologism by some readers. However, the term was fathered by Herbert Simon, and is now widely used in the field of economics and ecology. The notion of surrogate cognition could also appear to be a new coinage. Yet, my contribution here is only in the choice of the term "surrogate," since the notion that it refers to has been analyzed and developed by many authors before me; Andy Clark, for example, employs the term "scaffolded mind" in a similar fashion.

Finally, in order to avoid inflating the text with neologisms, I have introduced the typographic convention of employing the letter "k" to mark all those terms that I use in a non-standard way.

The Dissolution of Mind is organized into nine chapters. The first chapter, "Alice's Perplexities," helps to set the stage, presenting Alice as the voice of common sense, and introducing the "rules of the game" that I want the reader to be aware of. The second chapter consists of a list of aphorisms, by which I hope to predispose the reader toward the issues discussed in the book.

In chapter Three ("Monday"), I lay out my proposal of a mental architecture based on what I have called slife. The main task is to show how the processes of sensation, perception and cognition are to be accounted for by this proposal of slife. Chapter Four ("Tuesday") explores how a mental architecture based exclusively on slife units can explain human conceptual abilities. Subsequently, in Chapter Five ("Wednesday"), I present the theory of knowledge that is derived from a slife-based cognition. Firstly, I analyze how a slife can be considered knowledge and how it can be true and justified. Secondly, I examine how the theory of slifes compares to the two main traditions in epistemology, namely, rationalism and empiricism, in that slife knowledge depends not only on the inherent cognitive capacities of the brain, but also on its experience in interacting with the world.

The implications for linguistics, in general, and semantics, in particular, are explored in the sixth chapter ("Thursday"). The particular theory of communication that the proposal entails is presented in Chapter Seven ("Friday"). The slife hypothesis has particular consequences for the theory of mind, which are presented in Chapter Eight ("Saturday"). Here I explore how the properties of thoughts are instantiated by slifes, and how my proposal allows an empirical characterization of the mind, while accounting for conscious experience. The last chapter ("Sunday") reviews, from Alice's point of view, the main theses of the book, relating them to Non-Professor O's aphorisms presented at the beginning of the work.

As a final note I would like to emphasize the fact that *The Dissolution of Mind* contains an empirical hypothesis. As such, the book should not be seen as a finished project, but merely its beginning. Continuing this project will require setting up a research program aimed at testing the proposals that I present. I must admit that some of these proposals cannot be proved or disproved yet, as they are still too far down the line to be able to be feasibly tested. However, I envisage many experimental paths that can be explored to test the theory. So, the best that could happen to this book is that it might induce the development of a new line of research. As Fodor's Auntie would say, "To say the right things is fine, but to say and to prove them is even better."

Oscar Vilarroya
Barcelona, 1 December 2001

ACKNOWLEDGMENTS

In the preface, I confess to have been composing the contents of this book since I had use of reason. To be fair, then, I should list here all the people who have helped in some way or other during all these years. However, this would take more space than the book itself, so I will just mention those who have been mostly directly concerned with the writing of the book.

First, I am tremendously indebted to Adolf Tobeña, as teacher, colleague, and friend. His intellectual stimulus and professional guidance have a lot to do with my undertaking this project, and with my publishing it (even if I know that he is not going to be happy until I take the proposal into a lab!).

I would also like to mention Antoni Gomila, whose uncompromising and thorough analyses of my work have much improved my philosophical argumentation. David Casacuberta has also been crucial for the outcome of this enterprise. His keen reaction to an initial version of the book, and his insightful comments gave me the stimulus to finish the "last mile." Eva Juarros and I have maintained a long-standing friendship, full of enriching discussions and mutual support. Her intelligent reading has also allowed me to improve the text.

I am also thankful to Leonardo Valencia, whose tireless enthusiasm and warm friendship have helped me in the most difficult moments of this enterprise. Many of his suggestions have also improved the text (sorry, Leonardo, for not keeping your suggestion for the title: Alice in Arkadia). I appreciate the effort made by my friends Martí Carandell and Magda Rossende for reading an initial draft of the book. They provided me with quite useful observations, regardless of their lack of familiarity with the book's contents. I also want to thank Walter Meyerstein for his rigorous and intelligent comments, which have helped me to keep my feet on the ground. My friends Alfredo Martínez and Joan Carles Soliva also merit a place here. I value much more the intellectual honesty with which they analyzed the book, than the bad night I went through. I must also mention the help received by Harmonía Carmona, Albert Gassull, Vicenç del Hoyo, Emma Sans, Rubes Editorial, and my family.

I would also like to acknowledge the critical role that Judith Alexis Weninger and Adlinguam have played in composing the English version of this book. The Biblioteca de Catalunya and their personnel also deserve a mention here, since they have let me work in an uncomparable gothic setting.

Joe Hilferty is one of those friends everybody should have. It is not enough for him to be there when I need him: he has managed to make me a better writer and a better thinker. I hope that this does not give an indication to Carmina and Javier about the time I have kept Joe away from his dissertation. (Joe, I am sorry, but you will have to put up with "slife" instead of your proposal of "experiogram").

Lluis Fontanals is the person who has helped me the most in shaping this book. We have spent many long hours over the years talking about its contents.

He has witnessed the birth and growth of these ideas, and has helped me to sharpen them. He would merit more than a simple acknowledgment. I may even repay him a beer some time.

My parents, Tomás Vilarroya and Consuelo Oliver, also deserve their share of recognition. I can easily summarize it by saying that everything I have obtained would have not been possible without their support and good example.

My companion Cristina Durisotti has been able to put up with me and the book for a long time, aided nevertheless by her exquisite blend of indifference and irony. Nonetheless, I am sure that she is as happy as I am with this publication.

I could not end this section without showing my gratitude to Robert Ginsberg. First, I am sure that this book would not have been published if it were not for his open-mindedness and intuition. I want also to thank him for his endless enthusiasm and encouragement. Last, but not least, I want to express my appreciation to him for the time he took to transform this work into a publishable text. Credit should be given to him for many textual improvements.

One

ALICE'S PERPLEXITIES

My name is Alice, even if my friends call me Miss Common Sense. I cannot remember how old I am, although I feel like I have been living for a long time. I lost track of my age the day a rabbit convinced me to celebrate my non-birthday. I like pancakes with syrup, the number 25 and the bluish-green color that some lakes have. I live in a cold, damp country. Sometimes I like it, and sometimes I do not.

Do not worry. I am not going to write about my likes and dislikes, or about my country. So about what am I going to write? A Buddhist saying is that when the wise man points to the moon, the fool looks at his finger. This book is a description of the Buddhist's finger. But I have an excuse for the foolishness: a good friend told me that I will never understand a juggler if I look at the balls the juggler tosses into the air.

The fact is that since I have had use of reason, whatever that may be, I keep a notebook where I write down anecdotes that leave me perplexed and for which I cannot find an explanation. The notebook's title is "Perplexities." What sort of anecdotes does the notebook contain? I will tell you some of them throughout this book.

One day, I showed the notebook to a professor, who was a good friend until she recommended a book to me, or what she believed to be a book. She told me that "a kind of professor, or not, whose name begins with O...," had written a book some time ago that was called "Slifes." The problem is that it was a pirated edition and soon became impossible to find.

I do not think a library exists anywhere, public or private, or a book store, be it old, new, or forgotten that does not know my face and my resignation. Nothing. Not a trace. Until a week ago. I was wandering one spring Sunday through a flea market, when I found myself looking at a chest of drawers that was exactly like my grandmother's. I opened the second drawer and there it was, dusty, old, and worn out.

I did not understand a thing. And then I got angry. I had spent quite a few years looking for the damned book, and now it turns out that the Buddhist was right. The work, if something with only one page of original text can be called that, consisted of a list of aphorisms and a series of bibliographical sources. The aphorisms were incomprehensible or impossible. But the strangest thing was the sources. An endless catalogue of autobiographies, diaries, and chronicles written in the first person. Thousands of them.

I spent a few hours of insomnia tossing and turning in bed, my spirits ruffled, my thoughts weighed down with reproaches. You may say that I was going too far, that it was not such a big deal, that no perplexities exist, and especially not mine, that warrant such a reaction. You are right. It is not worth all that, but that is the way I am. Somebody must have passed through my child-hood and sprinkled me with windows where paradoxes happily peep out. And life appears to cultivate them like flowers in a cemetery; they spring up with no effort.

Since I could not get to sleep, I decided to go out. I wandered the streets of my city for a few hours. I suppose it was the time of day. That moment of the dawn is the time I like most, and the time I enjoy the least. It appears like the city belongs to me. The air barely has consistency, and you can still name the sounds. I felt something, went home, and I went to bed, barely seeing my bed. Then one of those strange things occurred that happen to me sometimes. When I woke up, I was in a different world. Do not ask me how I did it. I do not know why, or how, or when.

The fact of the matter is that this "world" where I landed is a kind of archipelago. Its residents call it Arkadia, which makes them Arkadians. I was awakened by what appeared a fellow disguised as a rabbit who introduced me to the famous stranger, this non-professor O, who was exactly like I had imagined him to be. He was short and had a nasal voice, smoked a pipe and scratched his head a lot, and I had tea with him for a week. Now that I think about it, all I did was have tea. The fact is that the first day I got up at teatime. The fellow dis-guised as a rabbit took me to the terrace where Non-Professor O was smoking a pipe, and we talked all afternoon, until the sun disappeared below the horizon. Then everyone went to bed. Strangely enough, the next day, the rabbit woke me up again, and strangely enough, it was tea-time again. That is how the whole week went by.

I am telling you this because Non-Professor O convinced me that in order to understand his aphorisms it would be good for me to get to know the Arka-dians. Arkadians seem to be different to human beings, he told me. The differ-ences mainly have to do with their way of perceiving the world, of understand-ing it, of thinking it, if such a thing can be said. It is not very different from the human way, although it works slightly differently.

I am not sure that Arkadia has helped me to explain my perplexities, but it has allowed me to look at them from a different perspective. This book is an attempt to share that perspective with you. I do not know if you have perplexi-ties, but I can lend you mine, because the panorama is definitely worth the trip.

The first thing I will do is present Non-Professor O's list of aphorisms. I think that will help you. I will continue with the transcriptions of my conversa-tions with Non-Professor O on the seven days that I was in Arkadia, and I will finish by showing you how Arkadia helped me figure out the meaning of the aphorisms.

Before starting, I should caution you about two things. The differences between Arkadians and human beings are extremely slippery, and sometimes appear trivial. My effort has been aimed at stressing the differences. Many of the readings will not appreciate them, and others cannot do so. Which is a pity. Secondly, the only thing that can be derived from this book is a perspective on a landscape, not a detailed description of it. Thus, everything that is in the landscape remains to be explored.

Therefore, in the best of cases, this book can only be considered the "tap-tap" that we give to a compass so that it loosens its lazy needle and effectively points north. I do not deny that it is perhaps the north of my lunacy. But I bet that it will not be easy for you to find out the truth.

Two

NON-PROFESSOR O'S APHORISMS

1.   The slife is the unit of knowledge, not the concept.
2.   Knowledge is a virtual world that fills in our experiences.
3.   Knowledge requires being lived.
4.   Conceptualizing something is not a matter of representation, but of creation.
5.   Every slife is prisoner of its time.
6.   To understand is to notice the past that explains the present.
7.   An abstraction is an understanding that has forgotten its past.
8.   A metaphor is an understanding that has not forgotten its past.
9.   Words are evocative, not symbolic.
10. Language can handle truth, but it cannot tell it.
11. To communicate consists of manipulating points of view, not of transmitting messages.
12. Information is not a thing, but an act.
13. Words are incapable of going beyond knowledge.
14. Texts do not codify contents, but readings.
15. Imagination is not creative, but re-creative.
16. Learning is not an acquisition, but an adaptation.
17. To educate consists of constraining particular experiences.
18. Reason is a logic without truth.
19. The cause of a behavior is not a reason, but its history.
20. Free will is a form of singularity, not of indetermination.
21. The nature of a sensation is the weight of its past.
22. A thought is a look at the present through one's whole life.
23. To reason is the word's journey through its virtual world.
24. The mind is the present of a past.

Three

MONDAY
On How No Superfluous Experiences Exist

The time has come for me to explain my visit to Arkadia. As I told you, one Sunday a week ago I went to sleep with all my perplexities. I woke up in a room that was not mine, and in a house that I had never seen before. In front of me a person disguised as a rabbit kept talking to me.

"Quick, quick."

I looked around me, trying to remember if I had disappeared in the middle of a party and could not quite remember where it had taken place. I could hardly understand any of what was happening, but I was not frightened.

"Come on, come on, we are late for tea."

I was bewildered. It was the bedroom of a child, and I would even say that it belonged to a little girl. The room was spacious, although it had only one window, through which an intense light streamed in.

"Come on, come on, we are late for tea."

I looked in the full-length mirror that was in a corner of the room. I was wearing a ridiculous little white dress.

"What tea?"

"*The* tea of course. What other tea would it be?"

The rabbit talked with that cheerful tone that can only irritate. I stared at him. He reminded me of someone, but I could not quite remember who.

"Who are you? Why are you dressed as a rabbit?"

"Is that one question or two?"

We looked at each other like two children on their first day of school.

"What do you mean is that one question or two?"

"'Who are you?' and 'Why are you dressed as a rabbit?' Is that one question or two?"

"Two, of course."

"Oh! In that case, I cannot answer you, because I can only answer one question at a time."

The rabbit was starting to make me nervous. To calm down, I looked around the room again, just in case my friends were playing a joke on me.

"Answer whichever one you want."

"Oh, no. I cannot choose the questions. Anyway, it is getting late. We have to go and have tea."

"Why are you dressed as a rabbit?"

"I am not dressed as a rabbit. I am a hare."

The ridiculous little white dress appeared to be much too small for me. I was quite amused.

"Why are you dressed as a hare?"

"Because I am a hare."

I walked around the room, and I realized that it all looked familiar to me. Very familiar.

"Where am I?"

"Well where do you think you are? In Arkadia."

"Arkadia? What is Arkadia?"

"What do you think it is? An archipelago. It is getting very late for tea."

I could not quite remember where I had seen that face, that room, those books, that little dress.

"Where is this archipelago?"

"Where do you think it is? In Arkadia. You ask some very strange questions. I am rushing off to tea."

"Wait a minute."

I went up to the closet. I opened the door a little nervously, in case I were to find two tortoises playing croquet.

"It is getting very late."

"Do not worry, it will not take me long."

The inside of the wardrobe was quite similar to one I had a few years ago. Then I found myself looking through it as if I did so every day.

"It is getting very late for tea."

"Who lives in this archipelago?"

"Who do you think lives here? The Arkadians. I have never heard such boring questions."

I found some pants and a sweater very similar to ones I used to have, and I changed in front of the rabbit.

"Quick, quick."

"The tea is not going to get cold."

"But we are late all the same."

As soon as I was ready, the rabbit opened the door and started hopping down the stairs, singing softly.

"We are going to have tea, we are going to have tea...."

The whole house was white stucco, with little furniture, walls that were almost bare, and a faint smell of the sea. Something was familiar about it. Suddenly, the rabbit stopped and gave me a funny look.

"You know the tea rules, don't you?"

"Are there rules for tea in Arkadia?"

"Of course there are."

"What are they?"

"The last rule is that you have to add the letter 'k' to everything that is different."

"The letter 'k?'"

"Of course, what other letter would it be?"

"I do not quite understand that rule."

He looked away and started hopping awkwardly, as if it were the first time he imitated a rabbit.

"Quick, quick."

"What a bothersome rabbit."

"The second to last rule is that you have to hang the concept of 'concept' on the hook before going in for tea."

"What kind of rule is that! How am I supposed to hang up the concept of 'concept.'"

"Well how do you think? By hanging it. Really, you ask very boring questions."

He was really trying my patience. Then, suddenly, he started hopping toward what appeared to be a large window opening onto a terrace.

"The third to last rule is that you have to hang the concept of 'thought' on the hook before going in for tea."

Then he stopped next to a door, and adopted the gestures of a valet introducing a dance.

"The fourth to last rule is that you have to hang the concept of 'knowledge' on the hook before going in for tea."

"Just where is the damned hook?"

"Where do you think it is? There."

The rabbit stopped and pointed to a section of wall as white and clean as freshly fallen snow.

"The fifth to last rule is that you have to hang the concept of 'language' on the hook before going in for tea."

"The poor hook."

I looked around, searching for something in the house that would give me back my memory.

"Do you want me to continue reminding you of the rules?"

"As far as I am concerned you can go straight to the first rule; I have already forgotten the ones you just told me."

"Well the first rule is that you have to put on the glasses of objectivity before going in for tea."

"Where can I find these glasses of objectivity?"

"Well where do you think. Right here."

He handed me a piece of air.

"Goodness gracious are you boring!"

Just when I was about to go out on the terrace, the rabbit interrupted me again.

"Oh, do not forget the purpose of having tea."

"The purpose of having tea?"

"Yes."

"And what may that be?"

"To discover who Non-Professor O is talking about."

"Wow! Non-Professor O! Where can I find him? I have been looking for him for quite a while."

"Well where do you think he is? Here."

Then he opened the door for me. I went through it to a large terrace edged with a balustrade. The house looked out over a village, and it had been built almost parallel to the coast. On both sides, a line of hills extended out, covered with a skin of grass and few trees. In the middle of the terrace was a round table, and next to it sat a man in a rocking chair, smoking a pipe and looking toward the sea.

"Oh, hello Alice. I have been waiting for you."

He looked just as he had in my imagination. How strange! The same face, the same gestures, and the same warm and familiar voice.

"Wow! You even know my name. You are hard to find, you know."

"You only had to ask for me. Sit down."

Still surprised, and amused, I sat down in front of him.

"Ask for you.... If I did not have a million questions to ask you, I had take this chair and hit you with it."

"Do not say that. Sometimes questions take time."

I took two deep breaths.

"Tell me, what is all this stuff about Arkadia? I have never heard of a place like this."

"We cannot always be in places that we have heard of, can we?"

"That is not the question."

"You are right; that is not the question."

"Look, for a while now I have been noting down in a notebook paradoxes that obsess me, and a professor told me that your little book could help me. The truth is, I do not know what she was thinking, because in addition to making me waste my time and lose my patience, your book has not helped me at all."

"I would not be so sure that it has not helped you at all."

"What I mean is I did not understand a thing."

"Ah! That is a different question. Tell me some of your perplexities."

"For example, one that I remember happened in a hot and boring summer afternoon. I turned on the television. A documentary was on about the wild animals living in the savannas of Africa. It looked like just another nature program about lions and elephants and the like. The program told about the life of a litter of cheetahs starting from birth. Everything occurs as expected, but not quite. The mother decides that she has had enough. She does not want to hunt any more for her lazy offspring. Time for emancipation. So after a hunt, the mother refuses to share her prey, and this causes a few days of doubt and incomprehension, but then the young realize that they had better get a move on. They try to hunt on their own, with disastrous results. And then comes D-day. The siblings choose a victim, nothing less than a male gazelle, why not aim for the best? Everything occurs as always, and the gazelle starts to run ahead of the young cheetahs. But then something unusual happens. The gazelle does not try to escape from the young hunters, but it charges another male gazelle. Without the slightest worry about the cheetahs, the two gazelles are clinched in battle. 'All the better for the cheetahs,' I thought, 'now they will have two dinners for the price of one.' But much to my surprise, once they reach the gazelles, the cheetahs stop in their tracks, astonished, not knowing what to do, watching the gazelles give free rein to their hormones. 'But you were supposed to run and we had to catch you,' the young cheetahs thought. Their dinner is not a gazelle, but instead a gazelle-that-runs-and-tries-to-avoid-being-caught. Could you tell me why?"

"I think that I have an answer."

"That would surprise me."

"I am convinced that if you let me tell you about how the Arkadians are, you will understand my little book, as you call it, and you will be able to figure out the answers to perplexities as the one you have just told me."

I stood up and went toward the balustrade. It seemed like a typical Mediterranean village, with its white-washed houses, narrow streets, a church in the highest part, and the afternoon silence broken by barks and the laughter of children. However, something was in the air that I had never felt in a Mediterranean village, something that could as easily be a memory of tropical heat as the aroma of an arctic cold.

"Then, tell me about how the Arkadians are, and we will see if I am able to figure my doubts out."

At that moment, I turned and saw that a tray was on the table, with tea and crackers, and a fruit bowl with apples in it. I sensed a little empty place in my stomach.

"Come, sit down. Have some tea and then we will talk."

I did as he suggested, and it was just what I needed. There were cookies like the ones my grandmother used to buy for me. They were delicious. While I ate, Non-Professor O prepared his pipe.

"To begin, I have to tell you that it appears the Arkadians are not like human beings."

"We are off to a fine start."

"They are not like human beings, but they are similar to human beings. They are so similar that you would not be able to differentiate between them. To help you see the differences, I am going to take an indirect route, full of analogies and partial approximations. So, my description will be, by definition, imprecise, until its development has been completed."

"And the continuation is even better."

"I must warn you that I am going to take a liberty: I will speak on behalf of a kind of omniscient being, whom I will refer to from now on as K. K knows everything about the Arkadians, at all times, and more importantly, describes everything at a level that we can understand. When you go back home you will have to remember that I have used colloquial language, not the language that a future science of the Arkadians would allow us to explain them better."

"All right. Just go ahead."

"I will begin by quickly going over some of the most important basic elements of what I understand to be the Arkadian nature, especially something that I call, for lack of a better word, *slife*, which is a fused form of slice-of-life."

"Slife."

"You should understand the life of an Arkadian as the continuous and uninterrupted sequence of slifes, with each slife corresponding to a particular episode in space and time."

"Who decides what counts as a slife?"

"The brain of an Arkadian is in charge of dividing, from the moment of birth, their episodes into slifes, including all the episodes in an Arkadian's life, as insignificant as they may be, and this, from the time that the brain is minimally functional, which is around the fourth month of fetal life. Okay?"

"Go on, go on."

"Let us imagine an Arkadian, who from now on will spend quite a bit of time with us, and whose name is Katherine."

"Katherine?"

"Yes, Katherine. When Katherine was a baby, one of her first slifes was the hunger that she felt a couple of hours after being born. At that moment, her blood glucose level went down and a series of physiological processes brought on terrible pangs and an inconsolable crying. She felt the pangs when she was away from her mother, who heard her cries, picked her up, and starting nursing her. At that point, Katherine began to feel the warmth of her mother, with the pleasant touch, the breast and the milk stimulating her taste buds and creating a pleasurable emotion. The set of elements that intervened in this slife, including the hunger pangs, the sounds of the mother's voice, the warmth and the touch, are felt by the baby as a whole, and this is what defines the slife."

"So far nothing is strange in all that, is there?"

"So much the better. I would like to emphasize the fact that each moment in the life of an Arkadian is a slife. Slifes are not special situations in the life of an Arkadian. On the contrary, slifes correspond to any moment in the life of an Arkadian, as insignificant as it may appear. Precisely because the kognitive system...."

"Kognitive system?"

"It is a way to refer to the brain when I am talking about its capability to process information, to know, and to show intellectual abilities."

"If you say so, but why do you say 'kognitive system' with the letter 'k?'"

"I am following the last rule that the rabbit told you."

"I see."

"As I was saying, the kognitive system of the Arkadians is capable of registering and discerning among hundreds of thousands of slifes that they are able to understand and function in the world effectively. Some moments will be more important than others in the life of an Arkadian, and these will probably be remembered more often, but in general they all have the same kognitive weight. For example, when Katherine went up the stairs for the first time, the slife of going up the first step constituted an original slife, just as going up the second step did, and then the third, and the fourth, until the end of the stairs."

"That adds up to a lot of slifes."

"Do not worry about that now. As we will see tomorrow, after step number fifty or twenty, or whatever, Katherine's brain will possibly begin to confound each step, and after a time, Katherine will not be able to differentiate between the twelfth time she went up a step and the two hundred and twenty-fifth time, but she will differentiate between the first and the twelfth. In any case, she will not always confound them, because if a few days later Katherine trips on the stairs, this situation will constitute a particular slife, and with it she will establish the relationship between 'looking at mommy' and 'tripping on the stairs.' In this way, the slife that will be fixed in her brain could be characterized as 'what happens when I am going up the stairs and look at mommy.' Keep in mind that when I say that a slife corresponds to 'what happens when I am going up the stairs and look at mommy,' the description is from the point of view of K, not of Katherine."

"What do you mean that the description is made by K and not Katherine?"

"That the slife can be characterized by K and not by Katherine is funda-mental here. What is left in Katherine is only a relationship between elements, and as of now only K can give a characterization of these elements. So, for example, it may be that Katherine still does not know that what she is climbing is a 'stairway,' although she is familiar with many of its attributes, such as the regular steps, that it links her 'house' to the 'outside,' etc."

"Yes, but if I understand correctly, slifes appear to belong to one person, and should therefore be explained from the perspective of each person, right?"

"No. Nothing is further from a vision of slifes than comparing them with subjective structures. I am talking about situations that are lived and can be remembered, that are conscious, like going up the stairs, in order to help your comprehension of the concept, but slifes are not limited to those where pain is felt, or a stairway seen. Slifes encompass both conscious and unconscious elements. Because of this, a slife cannot be fully described by the Arkadian that has it. Introspection cannot reveal the relevant aspects in the specification of a slife, because that same individual cannot identify them. The perspective that we will adopt here is that of a third person, which is the process through which an external observer examines the activity of a brain in a given situation and puts together an exhaustive characterization of that slife. True, doing it is difficult. Only K is capable of achieving it completely and objectively."

"How can a slife be described objectively?"

"By making a description of those objects and properties noted by the Arkadian brain and about which we will talk more later. For this, we need a complete characterization of how the brain works, which we do not have at the moment, a description of that brain's activity at the time of the slife, and a catalogue of the Arkadian's past slifes."

"So, the individual who has the slife plays no role?"

"No, that is not it either. The idea is that the language that explains the slifes should distance itself, on the one hand, from a purely subjectivist description. This is because, although it may be a long and difficult task, accounting for the elements contained in the characterization of a slife is possible, but it should also include descriptions that we would call psychological, since perceptual, emotional, and conceptual factors also intervene in the characterization of a slife. So, for example, it can be determined that a slife in which Erik looks in the mirror and finds that he is ugly contains elements like the mirror and the disappointment he feels upon seeing his ugliness. Obviously, the most difficult point is to establish the way to present these elements in order to characterize what human beings would describe as 'Erik looks in the mirror and finds that he is ugly.' For the time being, more or less satisfactory explanations are made by K so that we understand him, although they are far from being a true science of slifes. We lack, I repeat, the theoretical and technical instruments necessary to identify the elements of the slifes in an objective, univocal, and agreed-upon way. However, ignorance of the details does not necessarily mean ignorance of the main points."

He was quiet for a moment while he lit his pipe, which had gone out. At that point, I noticed the sweet and aromatic smell of his tobacco.

"Who or what decides when a slife begins or ends?"

"Nobody or nothing. Each slife has a hazy beginning and end. Some overlap and share endings or beginnings, others are more or less parallel, such as the one that combines one slife, for example driving home from work, with another that is taking place, such as deciding where to go for vacation. However, as blurry as the limits may be, what is crucial is that a spatial-temporal context is established that is recorded in the brain, and along with it, the different elements that were noted. The time and space context is the most important part of the idea of slife. Therefore, slifes are like frozen moments, the components of which create a kind of small, private world."

"Do relationships among different slifes exist?"

"Yes, they do. Let us imagine the first time that Katherine rides a bike. To simplify the situation, say that this slife was preceded by the first time that Katherine sees a bike, and sees somebody ride a bike. That is, let us imagine that she has had no previous contact with those objects we call bikes and that she has never seen anybody riding one. This situation is full of particular slifes that will be related to each other. To begin with, we have her first visual and tactile contact with the bicycle. The second slife occurs when Erik explains to her how to ride a bike. And the third corresponds to Katherine's attempt to ride the bike, during which she feels, among other things, the gap between the sensation of ease felt when seeing Erik ride the bike, and how difficult it is to keep her balance, the sensation of frustration, of the position of each part of her body as regards the action of riding a bike, the relationship between one movement and another, her perceiving the mechanisms that make the bike work. Throughout all these slifes, which take place one after another in a specific period, Katherine's brain notes numerous elements that are incorporated in an articulated way to the complexity of each slife. In the first, these elements will be mainly perceptual, in the human sense, in the second, they will be verbal, and in the third, they will be motor and emotional. Only K can vaguely identify the limits that define each particular slife and place them in the description. However, that the limits are blurry does not prevent the brain from distinguishing among slifes."

The sun had hidden behind a cloud. I looked around. A road snaked through the hills to what appeared a lighthouse built on rocky cliffs. I had not realized it, but the village was located on the slope of a spectacular mountain.

"How is a slife created?"

"Let us say that the objective of the kognitive system is to 'give birth' to a slife and to do so it processes the information that it receives from the senses and combines it with what it has recorded in its memory. The most important thing is that this process is carried out before the slife takes place."

"What do you mean by 'before the slife?'"

"Let me explain the peculiarities, the structure, and functioning of the brain that help the Arkadian get along in the world. The kognitive system of the Arkadians appears to be similar to that of human beings, at least anatomically. They have the same sense organs, with nerves that travel to the brain and nerve centers like those of human beings. But, when we start talking about the functionality of this brain, things get a bit more complicated."

"That is?"

"The functional sequence that is normally attributed to the human brain is the following. A series of peripheral systems, the senses of sight, touch, hearing, smell, and taste are said to transmit information from the outside world to create what human beings call sensations. The central systems take responsibility for this information in order to carry out its analysis and higher processing, what we would normally call perception, and all the other higher processes, such as thought. Some motor systems also plan and control the body's activity, including the systems for linguistic production."

"Okay. Where is the problem?"

"Patience. A key aspect of how we human beings explain the way in which the information from the outside world is processed is by differentiating among the senses, perceptions, and concepts. To simplify, the data from the senses is the information that the sense organs contribute, the perceptions correspond to the organization of this data in unified and structured representations of the things we see, hear, touch, smell, and taste, while the concepts are the abstractions that the nervous system creates from these perceptions, or depending on how you look at it, that it imposes upon these perceptions. In this process, we differentiate between something that is called 'data from the senses,' which the perceptual representations form, colors, shapes, textures, intensity of light, on the one hand, and, on the other hand, all the other elements that already form part of the thought process, what are normally understood to be 'interpretations' of this perceptual information. Any higher process, such as that which interprets the perception of an apple as an example of the concept 'apple', comes after the sensorial systems have provided a perceptual representation that is more or less complete and appropriate."

"Can you explain this a bit more?"

"Suppose we want to explain how Catherine, human in this case, sees one of the apples that are on the table. Catherine's cognitive system receives a set of sensory data that contains information about color, shape, movement, smell, taste, touch. It organizes this data in such a way that it forms a representation of the apple in perceptual traits, and once the capability for abstraction has been acquired, the cognitive system can infer that this representation is an example of the concept 'apple.' In this way, when Catherine perceives an apple, it is as if she had a representation of an apple in her mind, which captures the properties of the apple, its shape, its color, a reminder of its flavor. When Catherine thinks about 'apples' and says things like, 'I do not like mealy apples,' she is not thinking about a specific apple, although images of apples are evoked, but instead she is thinking *with* the concept of apple."

"So?"

"The Arkadian brain appears to work differently. The crucial point is that analyzing it as if it had a well-established sequence involving sensation-perception-cognition is not adequate. The unit of brain function is the slife, and this occurs after all the processes —sensorial, perceptual, cognitive and emotional— have intervened. This does not mean that no different types of processing exist, but that the slife is subsequent to all of them. In other words, in Arkadians, there is not sensation and then judgment, but the slife contains both of them, and separating them is not possible, nor going to a state that is previous to the slife in order to identify the strictly perceptual or sensorial elements."

"I am still not quite sure of what you mean."

"Maybe you will understand it better with the help of an analogy that I often use: a musical instrument, the sound it produces, and the melody that is heard. When a clarinetist plays a piece, the clarinet produces sound, and the sound is heard as a melody. However, we cannot analyze the sounds as 'sounds' and then interpret them as 'components of the melody.' In other words, we cannot separate the sonorous contributions of the clarinet from its melodic contributions; one and the other are joined in time. No 'sound of the clarinet' and then 'clarinet notes in the melody' exist, but the sound and the note are created at the same time, and whoever hears it, if you will, cannot separate the musical meaning from the sonorous effect. In the same way, when a slife is created, everything, the sensations, the perceptions, the emotions, and the kognitions, are elements that make sense in the context of the slife, never before it. The kognitive activity of an Arkadian that is looking at this apple does not come from a sensorial state that is manipulated later by some perceptual system. Instead, the signal from the sense organs arrives at the same time to many areas and, before coming into the slife, it is treated along with the other signals from other organs, to finally establish its role in the slife. Getting back to the music analogy, the idea is that the role of a clarinet in the effect that an orchestra produces cannot be separated from the other instruments. While we can distinguish between the sound of the clarinet and that of the violin, we would not be capable of imagining the effect of the symphony if we listened to each instrument separately. We need them to play at the same time. Something like this is what happens to the kognitive system. When, let us say, Katherine's brain has an apple in front of it, we should consider that her senses, sight, touch, taste, do not send data from the senses that have already been interpreted, such as 'the color red,' 'sweet taste,' 'smooth to the touch,' to the kognitive system, but that they will only have this characterization when they appear in the slife."

"I was taught in school that the eyes are for seeing, the ears for hearing, and if an eye has something red in front of it, then it sends the information that the thing is red, isn't that right?"

"You are partly right. The Arkadian sense organs work in almost the same way as the human ones. That is, they codify the signals they pick up according to the energy that they receive: electromagnetic energy in the case of sight and hearing, chemical in the case of taste and smell, electrochemical and mechanic in the case of touch. The difference is that in order to better understand the Arkadians, you should not take the signals sent by the Arkadian sense organs as an interpretation of that energy until they are processed by the whole brain."

"Can you clarify that for me?"

"Let us see. Erik's eye connects his brain with the light that something emits, an apple, that is in front of him. However, that light does not become a part of the slife as 'red' until the brain relates it to the signal that it receives from around that apple and with other signals that it receives from other types of kognitive processing, including memory. What appears in the slife as 'red' is something that has gone through a process; it is not something given directly by the senses. Therefore, I prefer considering that the sensorial signals carried by the sensory nerves do not codify information about the surroundings, but that they connect an energy that is present in the surroundings to a part of the brain. To put it another way, the sensory nerves do not discharge information; what they do is tune the kognitive system into the world."

He stopped talking. The silence allowed me to notice the sounds of the village. From the port, a ship's siren sounded and a chorus of nervous barks answered it.

"Then what is the initial data that the Arkadian brain works with?"

"You have to imagine that no initial data exists, inasmuch as only final data exists. From its connection with the world through the senses, the kognitive system carries out a process that culminates in a slife. The 'redness' of an apple is not, for example, sensory data previous to the perception of the apple; instead, it shares, if you will, in the perceptual party in which other factors intervene. Nothing happens in this world that is sent by the Arkadian senses that does not receive, without mediation, an overall treatment by the brain. In other words, all of the relevant data, cognitive, emotional, perceptual, share the same rank in the kognitive processing, while maintaining their peculiarity in the global process-ing. As a result, since I cannot differentiate between the sensory, perceptual, and cognitive processes, I have to refer to the three processes under one name. What better name could there be than *panception*?"

"Panception?"

"Yes. From now on you should understand the kognitive system process as something that encompasses the perceptual, the emotional, and the strictly cognitive processing, and I will now call this process panception. Panception is the process of slifes. In fact, starting now we could use the terms panception and slife interchangeably, since the slife corresponds to the product of the panception process. But I will keep using the word slife because I like it better."

"As you wish."

"I will therefore use the term 'panceptual' to refer not just to what corre-sponds to the human sensory modalities, sight, touch, smell, hearing, taste, but to any aspect of what you would say is a slife, including the data regarding the state of the organism itself, and other properties that are normally considered cognitive in the human realm, in addition to emotions."

"Does this mean that Arkadian perception is more sophisticated than our perception?"

"Not exactly. What I am trying to say is before the end result, the slife, all the panceptual processes make their contributions, their functional specializations, which are similar to those of human beings."

I looked up. Four skimpy clouds battled against the wind.

"Nothing but slifes is in an Arkadian's head?"

"Slifes are the central elements of Arkadian brain activity and constitute the foundations upon which knowledge is built. However, even though it seems like a paradox, slifes are also complex structures, since they include an undetermined number of constituents and relationships among them."

"You are right. It seems like a paradox. What elements are you talking about?"

"I am referring to everything from sensory properties like 'redness,' to conceptual properties, like 'square,' including bodily sensations, like 'pain,' or the emotions, such as 'fear.' Obviously, these interpretations take place in the context of the slife and not before."

"What elements are included in a panception?"

"A slife includes the elements present in the surroundings and in the organism itself, which are noted by the kognitive system, and also the way in which they are noted. This generally includes any external object (that apple on the table) as well as internal (the feeling of hunger), and elements that are conscious (the sight of that apple) or unconscious (the association of this table with the feeling of hunger), sensory elements (the redness of the apple), perceptual elements (like the rounded shape of the apple), cognitive elements (like the concept of apple) and emotional elements (the happiness of discovering that there is an apple to eat), or any other relationship that can be established among the elements. Here I include as much concepts of natural types, like water, solid, red, as abstract concepts, like relationships of the contents/container type, and also a multitude of elements that are distinguished by the kognitive system at the unconscious level. To make things simpler, from now on I will use the word 'kontents' for all those elements that may form part of a slife. The kontents will therefore correspond to the set of elements that the kognitive system can discern in a slife, and that can in theory, but only in theory, partially correspond to human concepts. So, if an ordinary Arkadian, let us say Erik, is looking at this table and the apple grabs his attention because he's hungry, we can say that the slife includes [table], [fruit bowl], [apple], [feeling hungry], as well as [relationship between [apple] and [feeling hungry]]. If another Arkadian looks at the same thing, let us say Katherine, because she wants to paint the apple, especially the contrast of the green leaves and the red apple, then Katherine's slife includes the kontents [table], [apple] and [desire to paint], if such a thing exists, as well as the kontent [relationship between [colors] and [desire to paint]]."

"The desire to paint is also an element of the slife?"

"Yes. As I already said, a slife includes both kontents that human beings would call perceptual, as well as emotional and cognitive. Two slifes occurring in the same place, with the same objects, seen from the same point of view can be completely different. An example to help you understand this is what Erik would experience if he were here and on the table we had a glass urn with a snake sleeping in it. This slife would be completely different from what Erik would experience if he saw the same snake, but with the sole difference being that no glass between Erik and the snake existed. The slifes would be perceptually similar, but slifely quite different."

"You will have to explain more to me about a slife including both perceptual and cognitive elements."

At that point the professor went inside the house for a moment and came back with what appeared to be a picture, although he was carrying it backwards. After a few seconds, he turned it around.

"Oh, it is 'Self-portrait by Van Gogh with a pipe and a bandaged ear.'"

"Exactly."

"And?"

"Let us look at what just happened here. First you saw some blotches of color, but as soon as I turned it around those blotches began to make sense, take on a particular pattern, quite unmistakable, that you identified with a certain canvas painted by a specific artist. Something in your perception of the painting allows you to identify it as such painting. You do not know what it is, but a relationship exists among the different colors and shapes in the canvas that allows you to say that it is 'Self-Portrait with Pipe and Bandaged Ear,' and no other painting. The description of this relationship in an Arkadia slife has to include the different perceptual, emotional, and cognitive kontents that allow for the identification of the painting as 'Self-Portrait with Pipe and Bandaged Ear.'"

"Are you sure that identifying the painting is not something done after perceiving the painting?"

"No. It is integrated in the texture of the processes that give rise to the slife. This is essential in Arkadian thought."

"How is that possible?"

"Let us suppose that in Arkadia a violist named Kasal is famous for his 'silences,' which have been described as 'reflective moments that Kasal invites us to partake in, that make the pieces breathe and give us the vision of a landscape that opens up between the musical summits of each work.' That silence, which is what differentiates Kasal from other musicians, is anchored in the panception of the slifes in which this artist has been heard; it does not exist, it makes no sense, either before or after the sonorous perception of the silence. And if, later, Arkadians refer to 'the silences of Kasal,' they are referring exactly to those specific slifes in which they have experienced those silences. Those fractions of a second of delay by a musician between one note and the next are not, in the context of panception, fractions of a second of delay, but something more."

"Even something so abstract like, say, cause and effect can be integrated into a slife?"

"Even cause and effect."

"I do not see how that is possible."

"Let us suppose that Katherine has a slife in which she is playing a game of pool. Suppose that at a particular moment Katherine notes the way in which one ball causes another one to move, which brings about a sense of surprise that, depending on a lot of circumstances, translates into a relationship between the pool cue, the balls, and the table. This sensation is a phenomenon that is added to the mere vision, in the human sense, of the pool game. Katherine establishes a relationship that has a kind of 'slife weight' beyond the simple 'sensory weight' that can be attributed to it. And this slife 'weight' is the germ of what human beings call the abstract idea of cause and effect. A second example could be Katherine in another situation, when she sees her mother repeatedly putting in and taking the silverware out of a drawer in the kitchen. This slife, in which Katherine notices the relationship between silverware and the drawer could be characterized by K as a slife of the contents/ container relationship, which, in the future, she will connect with other slifes, like that of seeing a person getting in and out of a car, or that of noticing the relationship between a pair of shoes and their box, between water and the glass that holds it, etc. Naturally, this perceiving of the contents/container relationship does not have to occur the first time she sees her mother put silverware in a drawer; it may occur the second, the third, or the twentieth time. Furthermore, it does not have to take place when someone puts silverware in a drawer; it can occur at any moment, when she sees a dog go in and out of its doghouse, for instance. However, the important thing is that the Arkadian will register this relationship in the specific slife, and the later development of the application of these relationships will be determined by the slife. In the long run, with the repetition of the basis of the contents/container relationship in hundreds of different types of slifes, the original slife will have lost its uniqueness, although not its relevance."

"But the cause and effect relationship is a complex idea. How can only one slife allow it to be understood?"

"Just one slife is not enough. Katherine will need the subsequent activation of the cause and effect experienced in other situations, and the continued repetition of it in order for us to say, as we will see tomorrow, that Katherine is just as competent as a human being with the concept of cause and effect. In any case, we cannot underrate the wealth of a single Arkadia slife. Keep in mind that a detailed analysis of such a slife would probably require several months of study to be able to reveal all of its wealth. In every slife tons of kontents have been discerned, and their relationships with each other and with elements of other past slifes are extremely rich."

"Can we at least analyze each kontent independently?"

"No. Remember that I told you that the role of a signal sent by the senses appears at the end, in the slife. The same signal can have the role of 'red' in one slife, while in others that same energy may have the value of 'brown' or 'orange.'"

"Are you sure?"

"I am sure. To continue with the orchestra simile, one instrument can produce the same note in two different compositions, and its role may be perceived in a completely different way. The effect of an F sharp played by a clarinet in a symphony by Mozart is nothing like an F sharp in a piece by Stravinsky. In the same way, in the Arkadian brain, two identical signals produced by the optic nerve in two different slifes may play completely different roles depending on the sensory, perceptual, and cognitive context of the slife. When a signal arrives from the eyes and the ears, the kognitive system 'gives' the appropriate meaning to that signal along with the others. This means that when it starts appearing in Katherine's slifes, 'redness' will be linked to the slifes in which it appears, and it will not be an independent entity."

"How is it possible that 'redness' can exist in a slife without the Arkadian recognizing it as 'red?'"

"That is just how it is, and this point is crucial in understanding the Arkadians. A slife does not correspond to the set of kontents previously analyzed by the kognitive system. Quite the contrary, the kognitive system conceives the situation in the opposite way. For Arkadians, the nucleus, the basis, the most primitive part is the slife, and the constituents that intervene in each slife make sense because of their participation in a specific slife, or in a set of slifes. That is why the identification of the elements that play a part in the slife, their being constituted as recognizable elements, independent from their occurrence in that slife, takes place after their inclusion in one or more slifes. For example, the water that Katherine sees the first few times she notices her mother serving her water in a glass has meaning in the slife, and as we will see tomorrow, in the set of slifes in which, to put it simply, 'water is something that is served to satisfy one's thirst,' and not as an entity with certain characteristics, the odorless, colorless, tasteless liquid that it is, which are independent from its participation in the 'satisfy one's thirst' slifes. Similarly, the water that Katherine sees when she takes a bath and that comes out of the faucet has its characterization as part of the 'taking a bath' slifes, and not as an independent element with certain characteristics. And the water that Katherine sees in the sea has its characterization as part of the slifes that take place 'on the beach,' and not as an independent element. This does not mean that Katherine cannot establish links between the different elements in the slifes. It just means that at the beginning, each kontent that Katherine's brain notes has meaning only in the context of the slifes in which it participates."

"When Katherine is drinking water, does she have the concept of water or doesn't she?"

"If we are talking about baby Katherine, we cannot say that she has the concept of 'water.' To put it a better way, it does not make sense to attribute to the child the capability, whether conscious or unconscious, to categorize this liquid that it drinks as 'water.' We can, however, talk about the sensation produced in Katherine by a certain liquid that comes from a certain place, when a certain action is performed. We can also talk about the relationship formed, which is based on what she feels in all the slifes in which she drinks, takes a bath or looks at the waves, and she would even recognize in each of these slifes a kontent with similar properties. On some occasions, the water is transparent, on others it is a bluish green; sometimes it has no taste, and sometimes it is salty. In the long run, yes, this liquid will be recognized as being the same the more often it is experienced, and the more difficult it becomes to recognize a memory of water from one day as opposed to another."

"Does this mean that Katherine will never see an apple as being an example of the concept 'apple?'"

"No, that is not it either. The kognitive system is capable of identifying, individualizing kontents in slifes and creating an underlying relationship among the occurrences of the kontents in all of an individual's slifes. In this way, when language appears, the words are anchored in these kontents along with the slifes in which they occur. But that subject is for tomorrow. The crucial thing to keep in mind now is that Arkadia slifes are atomic, the basic units of Arkadian kognition, and that they are complex, as they are composed of elements that cannot be separated from their occurrence in the slife."

"And to top things off, I think I remember you saying that a slife also includes unconscious kontents, right?"

"They are not just included; they are the most important."

"Oh, wonderful."

"We human beings believe that everything in a perception are the objects, the properties and the relationships that are consciously entertained, that is, those elements that the mind is aware of. However, what is conscious in a slife is only a small part of the objects, properties, and relationships that an Arkadian brain notes. A slife comprises everything that is processed by the kognitive system even when it is not conscious, and this not being conscious applies especially to those kognitive processes that will never be accessible, such as the detection by your brain of the time lapse between the arrival of my voice to your left ear, which is closer, and its arrival to your right ear, which is further away. For all these reasons, a slife is not merely the description that an Arkadian might give of what is being experienced —seen, heard, tasted, smelled, touched—, but it includes many unconscious processes about which nothing can ever be said."

"Examples, please."

"Remember Katherine's slife when she is playing a game of pool. At that moment, she perceives everything that is relevant: the table, the balls, and the arrangement of the balls on the table, although we must include in her slife some conscious kontents and some unconscious kontents, since the conscious part does not include all of the aspects that are relevant. If Katherine makes a good shot, she can say to herself that it is because she perceived that the shot needed just that degree of strength, although the fact is that it may have been good because her brain was able to discriminate properties of that pool table, like calculating the exact angle in degrees and the precise distance between the balls in centimeters, that will never be conscious but that are still real slifely kontents. So, depending on the moment, the slife, and the context, the kontent created can be quite different."

I noticed a certain discomfort. I stood up and walked around the terrace, while Non-Professor O cleaned his pipe. Several mulberry trees rose up in front of the balustrade from an embankment below. However, the aroma that stood out was of orange blossom. A handful of swallows flitted and chirped just beyond the terrace. It was spring.

"How many different types of kontents can be in the description of a slife?"

"At this point we do not have the elements, the instruments and the techniques that would allow us to properly identify the kontents that comprise slifes. However, the progress in the science of the Arkadian brain will soon allow us to begin responding to these questions."

"Does a limit exist?"

"In theory no limit is to the kontents that a given Arkadian, or all Arkadians, past, present, and future, are capable of noting. In the configuration of a slife, we must consider that all the kontents that have been conceptualized by human beings intervene, plus many more, all those for which we, as theorists, do not yet have a label."

"How is that possible?"

"This is, apparently, another interesting difference between Arkadians and human beings. I will give you three examples from our world: Einstein, Darwin, and Schoenberg. If these three individuals had been Arkadians, we would have to say of them that they noted kontents that had never before been discerned: the theory of relativity, the theory of evolution, and atonality. And we would have to suppose that large sections of their brains were devoted to exploring the world, and that thanks to this work, and only thanks to this work, they managed to identify kontents that nobody else can identify."

"What I cannot quite manage to understand is how the kontents are created. Are they in the Arkadians' brains? Or are they in the world, and the Arkadians just have to observe them?"

"The kontents only make sense when they encompass both the world and the kognitive system. When I say world, I am referring both to the world outside the Arkadian individual, as well the body itself of the Arkadian, with its stomach, muscles, bones, etc. Keeping this in mind, the kontents come from the combination of the kognitive system, the world, and the previous slife background of that individual. The world provides the objects, and the kognitive system provides everything necessary to discern the relevant kontents in the slife. This means that discerning the kontent 'red' that Katherine sees in this apple comes simultaneously from the physical properties of the apple's surface, from the light it emits, from certain processes of the kognitive system, as well as from the reds that have been discerned in the past."

"I do not follow you."

"Imagine that the kognitive system is a sculptor, and that the world is a piece of clay. The kontent, the work created by the artist, is created through the combination of the clay, the sculptor's different instruments, and the artist is slife. And what is more important, the kontent does not exist without the action of the artist; as soon as the artist stops sculpting, the kontent disappears. In other words, the work of art only exists while the artist is using all the instruments; as soon as she stops working, the work comes undone. So, in the same way, in order for the kontent to exist, the world and the kognitive system are necessary. This is what happens with color. The color that an Arkadian panceives is not a property of the object to which the color is attributed; objects do not have the colors that the Arkadians or we human beings attribute to them. The apples are not 'red' but rather are seen red."

"I cannot believe that."

"That is the way it is. Color appears through the combination of three factors: the wavelengths of the light reflected by the objects, the lighting conditions, and the Arkadian brain. All objects reflect light off their surface according to a constant combination of different wavelengths. However, the specific wavelengths that are reflected are not constant; they depend on the lighting conditions. Thus, in the morning this apple may reflect different wavelengths than in the afternoon, although Katherine will still see the apple as being the same color. The reflectance, the combination of wavelengths, are not useful for determining a color either, since two different ones can be seen by Katherine as being the same color. Furthermore, the categories that Katherine, and all Arkadians, use to distinguish among colors follow strange patterns, in which different colors are 'important,' called the focal colors, like red, green, yellow, blue, etc., while the intermediate colors are panceived as variations of these focal colors, and not as different colors, which would be more fitting. To put it briefly, color as kontent comes from the combination of the kognitive system and the object. If no brain exists, no color exists."

"Then where are the kontents? Are they in the Arkadian brain? Are they in the world?"

"The kontents are not in the head or in the world. Like I said, kontents extend along the continuum between the world and the kognitive system."

"How can that be?"

"My grandfather began to have a bad memory when it came to telephone numbers, but he discovered a method to hold on to them: remembering the movement of the fingers when they dial the number on the phone. So, the particular combination of movement and the arrangement of the phone's dial create the telephone number. We cannot say that the telephone number is somewhere, but that it is in the conjunction between the dial and my grandfather's finger movement. In the same way, a slife corresponds to a complex unit that includes part of the world and the kognitive system. And that complex unit is the slife of the object."

He stopped.

"Do you follow me?"

"I do not know what to say."

"Let me put you another analogy, that of phantom limbs."

"Phantom limbs?"

"Yes. Phantom limbs. Following the amputation of an extremity, nearly all patients have the illusion that the missing limb is still present. This illusion can persist throughout the amputee's life and can often be reactivated by injury. Such phantom sensations are not limited to amputated limbs; phantom breasts following mastectomy, and phantoms of the entire lower body following spinal transection have also been reported."

"So?"

"We could say that the phantom-limb sensation is the rest of the kontent of the limb that was lost. When the patient had the limb, he or she had a complete kontent, that was part in the brain, and part in the limb. When the limb is sectioned, so it is the kontent."

"Whew!"

"The crucial thing is to keep in mind that the system does not do without the world that it has to perceive and in which it has to act; instead, what it does is contributing with everything necessary to discern the kontent that, for reasons we will explain later, it considers relevant to discern. One thing is true, it does need an effective kognitive system in order to discern many kontents that are not evident in the world."

"Do not Arkadians have a copy of the kontents in their head?"

"No, the Arkadian brain does not have a copy or a representation in mind. The kognitive system does not copy or represent reality in the head; it discerns kontents. When Katherine looks at the apple in the fruit bowl, her kognitive system will try to distinguish between the apple, the plate, and the table, without having a representation of the apple in her head. The processes that take place in the brain are aimed at connecting through the senses with that apple and that fruit bowl and trying to separate the elements."

"But does not Katherine have an image of the apple in the fruit bowl in her mind?"

"The fact that it seems to Katherine that she has an image of an apple in a fruit bowl on a table in her head, and that she believes that the image is a 'copy' or 'representation' of the apple and the fruit bowl does not mean that she has a copy of the apple. Arkadians cannot avoid the sensation that they see the apple just as it is. However, the transparency that they think they slife is deceptive, quite deceptive, because reality is not how they believe they see it. That apple seen by a bee is completely different from how the Arkadians see it."

"I will say."

"When you look at this view of the coastline you have the sensation that your mind has a kind of screen on which you are seeing the view, or the sensation that your eyes are true copyists of reality. Something like that also happens to the Arkadians, although it is not real. No such a screen exists, and the eyes are not copyists; instead, the conjunction between the world and the kognitive system creates that sensation, with its kontents included. Since every Arkadian has always received the same, or similar patterns of energy coming from fruit bowls with apples, they will be able to distinguish an apple from a pear, although the aspect, the nature of the sensation of apple will evolve along with the number of apples seen."

"Excuse me?"

"What I mean is that the nature of the sensation of apple does not depend only on the apple being looked at, but also on the apples that have been seen up to that point."

"When Katherine sees this apple, she will always see it as being red and round, right?"

"No, but yes, or yes, but no. When Katherine as a newborn looks at this apple, the baby does not see anything specific, only vague shapes and colors. After a few months, Katherine begins to see splashes of color, and more defined shapes, and as she gets older, she begins to see more things, until she becomes conceptually and linguistically competent and can say, 'What a round, red apple.' However, despite the fact that the kognitive system is the same in all these phases, what Arkadians see is not literally the same. They do not have perceptual sensations, as we human beings call them, that are the same in all these cases. Nothing is universal for an Arkadian individual in the perception of an apple, or of red and round. If Katherine and Erik look at this apple, they will see it in different ways, as they have different slife background. The slife is different in the two cases, and this is because the necessary elements for the slife's apprehension are incorporated into it."

"Can the past be so determinant?"

"Absolutely. Imagine that Erik's mother takes him for a walk in the park when he is barely eight months old. Suppose that Erik picks up a rock off the ground. For an Arkadian of this age, in this situation, and with this development, the kontent would be conditioned by the object, the situation and the surroundings, narrowing down an infinite number of possible situations to just a few in which the kontent would be 'thing to be bitten.' As time passes, the possible relationships become more and more complex. So, if we suppose that Erik has become a geologist, the kontent that is established between Erik and that same stone depends on the characteristics of the object, but also on numerous past slifes that have multiple connections with other slifes, in such a way that the kontent becomes 'quartz.' In any case, the crucial thing is that the nature of this relationship is the consequence of the characteristics of the object, the kognitive system, the relationship between the two, and past slifes."

"Could not you give me a clearer example?"

"Take for instance these figures that are diffi-cult to interpret because we cannot identify the object. The problem that the Arkadians have is that they cannot manage to activate the relevant past slifes, especially because the figures are not presented in the usual perspective. However, once they succeed in activating the relevant slifes, the Arkadians quickly see what it is. In the case of figure 1, if I tell an Arkadian that it is a Dalmatian, the ambiguity in the figure will probably disappear, since the vision of the Dalmatian is revived. There-fore, when they 'see something red and round' what the kognitive system does is connecting the stimu-

Figure 1. Can You See a Dalmatian?

lus that the senses tune in to with the memory of the previous slifes that are relevant. They do not see the apple as it is, but rather they see the apple 'super-imposed on all the apples they have seen before' and that is why it is seen as 'red and round.'"

The church bells rang.

"Does anything identify one slife in relation to all the other slifes?"

"The differential contribution, what makes the slife a particular slife, is something I am going to call *signifikance*. The signifikance of a slife determines what is original about a slife in relation to other types of past slife. The signifi-kance has a structure that can be put in objective terms, but for now only K can do it, by noting the elements that intervened in its generation, and that deter-mined a structure in the slife."

"How does K do it?"

"A signifikance can be broken down into a 'figure' and a 'ground.' The figure is what is emphasized, what is most focused on in the slife, while the ground is the context in which it occurs, although this use of the term 'context' should be considered a distant simile. Did you notice the volcano?"

"Volcano?"

"Yes. It is a dormant volcano and it is called Kuo."

As soon as he said it I saw that the mountain in front of me could not be anything but a volcano.

"If an Arkadian were to look at Kuo, she or he would see the silhouettes of the few trees there outlined against the slope. In this case, the trees are the figure and the slope serves as a ground. However, when a bird lands on one of the branches, the bird becomes the figure and the tree is now the ground. Therefore, the salient part of the scene is the figure, and the rest is the ground. We can apply this principle in order to understand how the meaning of a slife is structured. Let us imagine two slifes that occur in the bathroom, when Katherine looks in the mirror. In one slife, Katherine may note the image of herself that she sees reflected in the mirror, and that image is what will leave traces in the kognitive system, along with characteristics of the rest of the bathroom, her emotional state, even the feeling of breakfast in her digestive system, which shape the ground. On another occasion, also with Katherine in the bathroom looking at herself in the mirror, even just a minute before or after the first slife, Katherine does not notice her image but observes that the mirror is dirty, while the rest of the ground remains the same."

"I do not know if I follow what you are saying. What do the figure and ground correspond to?"

"The figure that identifies a slife can be of quite diverse nature. It can even correspond to abstract properties, like the properties of cause and effect and contents/container that we saw before."

"Could not the figure/ground of a slife be considered something like a human idea?"

"That would be a bad interpretation of what a slife signifikance is. In the occurrence, and in the reactivation of that slife and the elements that comprise it, the relationship is established, and that is how Katherine's kognitive system will use it. Katherine will not have to go back to the specific slife of the game of pool to detect the relationship in any reference to 'cause' or 'effect.' Katherine has probably had many slifes in which she discerns relationships similar to those that are established between the objects of the original slifes. In this way, the cause and effect relationship will always be anchored in the connection between the different specific occurrences that she has experienced, and in nothing more. That connection will not be independent of the slifes, and their kontents, in which it occurred."

"How do you know that the signifikance of a slife corresponds to the idea of cause and effect?"

"Katherine's kognitive system focuses these aspects on the relationship that is identified in the slife. In the case of cause and effect, 'contiguity' translates into the special attention paid to the contact between the two billiard balls, while 'temporality' focuses on the temporal sequence of the balls. In the case of the contents/container relationship, Katherine could have noticed the following properties:

(1) Contents are always either in or out.
(2) Containment is transitive: if one container is located inside another, the entity that is between the two is content.
(3) Contents are protected from external forces.
(4) Contents are subject to limits, such as movement, within the container.
(5) The contained entity has a fixed location.
(6) The container affects the panception of the content.

All these characteristics would be derived from the type of slifes that Katherine has had, but they could also be put into objective terms for Erik. The specific occurrence of slifes in which this relation is rooted can give different results. The previously mentioned characteristics are not always present in a slife or set of slifes that K describes as contents/container. If Katherine's mother had not closed the drawer, the slifes may not be associated with a protection type of sensation, and therefore those slifes would not have the characteristic (3)."

"Can that be proven?"

"That could be confirmed if we were to repeat the original slife and, by carrying out a complicated experiment, we changed the properties that Katherine had fixed in that slife."

"I suppose you can explain how that is to be done."

"Let us imagine that we show Katherine a game of pool in which we have manipulated the property of physical contiguity. We have made it so that when a ball gets close to another one, the impact of the balls is heard, and the consequence, that is, the stopping of one ball and the movement of the other, is seen but without there being physical contact between the balls. If Katherine has fixed the property of physical contiguity, this little magic trick will appear strange to her. Similarly, we could manipulate the property of temporality in our experiment, by making the ball receiving the impact start to roll before the first one arrives."

"But how is a slife in which these properties are fixed differentiated from another one in which Katherine is watching a game of pool and she notices, oh, say, the before and after relationship?"

"Let us take a look. The difference between the slife with a cause and effect figure/ground and another slife that detects the before and after relationship is not an extra-slife property, but a difference that can only be defined in that particular slife. It would appear that you could say that the slife was the same, since that figure/ground can also be established in a game of pool in a similar situation in which one ball hits another ball, and in which the temporal sequence fixed by the before and after relationship is the focus. However, for Katherine, the two slifes are different. In one, the impact, the reaction, the contiguity are the focus, as well as any other characteristics that serve to characterize it as a cause/effect slife; in the other slife, only the temporal sequence characterizes it. Therefore, although for a human being they would be perceptually indistinguishable, for Katherine they are completely different, since the figure/ground is different."

"Is not that an abstraction?"

"No. A figure/ground should not be interpreted as an abstract aspect; it is just another panceptual part of that slife. K does not see in that slife reflections about what it is to be cause or effect. What K sees is this special relationship that K interprets as the thing we human beings call 'the relationship of cause and effect.' As a consequence, if we had to characterize the knowledge that Katherine has of the cause and effect concept, we could only say that for her, it is the slife in which she saw how one billiard ball hit another one and pushed it along. Just as I told you, this first slife is probably followed by many others that fix similar properties, like the time that she saw a ball break a window pane, and to which she has transferred the relationship that we characterized as cause and effect in a game of pool."

"Where is this signifikance kept?"

"The signifikance of a slife is integrated into the slife that gave rise to it; it is a part of the slife, rooted in the slife, and it has no place outside of that specific slife, outside the kontents that have a place in that slife."

"Does the signifikance have a purpose?"

"Its basic function is to help understand. The signifikance is the structure that will later allow for the comprehension of what we human beings would call the idea of cause and effect, contents/container or even the idea of liberty, beauty...."

"Even beauty?"

"Yes, even beauty. Let us suppose that Erik sees an Arkadian woman, Nikole, for the first time, and when it happens he feels a certain sensation that is unlike any he has felt before. At that moment, in that slife, Erik fixes that sensation, which according to K includes a 'sensation of general admiration for the harmony of Nikole's face, the shine in her eyes, and her charming smile, bringing about spiritual delight.' Now let us suppose that Erik does not have that sensation again until one day, when he has already learned to talk, that he comes across the word 'beauty' and when he looks it up in the dictionary he discovers that the word means 'quality in a thing that makes us admire it and produces spiritual delight.' When Erik reads the definition of beauty in the dictionary his kognitive system transfers the signifikance of the Nikole slife, thus allowing him to quickly understand the new slife, that of reading the definition of 'beauty.' What that definition does is take him back to the sensation he had some time ago, so that from then on the word 'beauty' will always evoke that past slife. Therefore, understanding implies that the kognitive system transfers the signifikance of one slife to another, allowing for the analysis and the comprehension of new slifes. This description is obviously idealized, and to be fair we would have to incorporate a lot more of Erik's slifes related to faces, bodies, buildings, landscapes, etc. However, it is a useful example for the time being. The important thing is that for Erik nothing but that slife characterizes his knowledge of 'beauty.'"

"One thing that I do not understand is that if each slife is like an individual atom, then the head of an Arkadian is full of separate atoms, full of particular slifes with no connection to each other, like a pointillist painting, right?"

"No, the slife is particular, but the kognitive system is capable of setting up relationships between the elements of different slifes, and among the slifes in general, in such a way that through mechanisms that I will explain tomorrow, it superimposes and creates associations between slifes and elements of slifes according to certain criteria. As I said, Katherine's brain is capable of identifying the relationship of cause and effect in a slife but also of associating this figure/ground with many other slifes."

"Yes, but if the significance depends on the slife of each individual Arkadian, is it possible that Arkadian children end up acquiring the same cause and effect significance as any of their classmates do or that any adult may have? If each significance is a part of the slife of that Arkadian, then its meaning is private for that individual. We can never know if others have the same one."

"You are right in that this is a basic question in the understanding of what a slife means. You could add that for each situation that individuals might find themselves in, an infinite number of possibilities are available to note kontents, that is, many ways are available to establish the figure/ground relationship for a slife. The truth is that I do not have an easy or complete answer for your question, but at least we can look at some indicators."

"Go right ahead."

"To begin, imagine that the kognitive system is built in such a way that it restricts the characteristics of a slife. Just as a telescope reduces the point of view of a landscape, the architecture of the Arkadian brain restricts the kontents and the significance that can be experienced in a slife. This is what we could call the innate conditioning of slifes, which affects the kontents that can be noted, how they are noted, the connections established between the kontents, and how the significance can be transferred. To put it briefly, the brain of the Arkadians constrains the range of possible figures/backgrounds. That means that an Arkadian living is necessary to create some kontent, but the Arkadian must also be born with a brain."

"Examples, please."

"Let us suppose that the first time that baby Katherine sees the faces of Arkadians, she sees them in a room next to chairs, lamps, paintings, windows. In such a slife the structure of the face, because it is a 'facely' element, grabs our attention more than a chair does, and it becomes the center of that slife. In some certain standard slifes, such as seeing an Arkadian face for the first time after being born, all Arkadians, that is, the idealized or archetypal Arkadian, will note the face in a similar way. In short, each Arkadian individual has a common denominator with all other Arkadians, although the complete characterization of the slifes depends on particular characteristics, depending on that individual's specific constitution and past slifes. The kognitive system is born with a strong capability of conditioning the slifes of an individual. It does not come with the kontents 'face,' but it comes with the necessary tools to bring about such kontents. Without such tools no kontents exist either."

"So, each slife depends only on innate properties?"

"No. Innate constraints do not completely determine how a slife is to be structured in a figure/ground; instead, it sets general principles that, in the absence of other constraints, direct the attention of the Arkadian. Innate constraints are like tools provided by nature that will help in creating the relevant kontents, always counting on that certain brain-world situations will occur. In any case, the individual's slife background also affects how the kognitive systems apprehends each new slife. If, for example, Erik has learned that an apple satisfies his hunger, the next time he sees a fruit bowl with apples when he feels hungry, the figure/ground that is created will correspond to a smaller subclass of slifes than if he had not had this slife. In this sense, the slife ends up constraining the way in which future slifes are segmented into figures/grounds, which explains that the elements that an individual notes are also dependent upon the kontents that have previously been noted. This aspect of the slife background is directly related to the second reason for which a common ground of slifes is acquired. But we will talk about that tomorrow."

"Why not today?"

"We do not have time."

"Why not?"

"You will see."

"So what is it of the slifes, of the kontents, and the signifikance that remains in the brain when the slife fades?"

"What remains of a slife in the kognitive system is its memory, which I will call *memogram*. The memogram is the imprint of the slife in the kognitive system. Basically, a memogram is a record that preserves the activity of the kognitive system in the original slife. That is, turning the image of the sculptor inside out, now imagine that the kognitive system is the clay and that the world is what shapes it. Just as when we leave the imprint of our hand in the mud, the imprint in the mud has managed to discern the fingers of our hand, the Arkadian kognitive system works like a piece of clay that is imprinted by the world, including the states of the organism itself."

"Is not that a representation?"

"Strictly speaking no, since it is an imprint it is not a representation, just as when we see the tracks of an animal, they are not the representation of the animal. The kognitive system is so sophisticated and subtle that the imprints can correspond only to the kontent that produced that imprint, in the same way that the fossilized tracks of a dinosaur can correspond to only one type of dinosaur."

"Is that enough to preserve the properties of the kontent? How can Katherine get along in the world with only dinosaur imprints?"

"I wish I could explain that to you in simple terms. I cannot, but I will try to point you in the right direction. As I said, the kognitive system does not create a representation of the state of things. It does not set up a copy of the situation lived by the Arkadian; it just discerns contents. Going back to the sculptor, we said that the clay decomposes when the artist stops working. However, this does not mean that the work is lost: the artist can remember the movement that led to the molding. Not that the artist has the object in his or her head, although he or she has the 'memory of the object.' While the artist shapes the clay the sculpture exists, but when he or she stops working, he or she remembers the movements. Remember the analogy of the phantom limbs. Even if the patient loses the limb, and the kontent is sectioned, we could still say that, in a certain sense, the patient has the kontent's memory of the limb. The limb is not there, but the Arkadian remembers it, and he or she can say many things about such a kontent, and do many others. A patient with a phantom limb can describe the properties of his or her lost limb, without having it, such as how long it is. The same happens with all other kontents that an Arkadian discerns but disappear from the senses, such as an apple, a ball, or whatever you like. If the kognitive discrimination is reliable enough, it will not be necessary to represent the situation. As long as the kognitive system remembers the movement of the molding or the movement on the telephone dial, the kontent will still be discerned. That is why, if we were to change the properties of the world that correspond to the light reflected by, for instance, an apple, the Arkadian would not be able to panceive an apple correctly, just as my grandfather would lose the telephone number if we were to change the dial on the telephone. If the world were plagued by objects and things that changed their light-reflecting properties or if different objects showed similar energy behavior, or rocks or poisonous spiders reflected light the same way apples do, then perhaps Arkadians would not get by so well in this world, since they would confound apples with rocks or with poisonous spiders, with the dire consequences that this might bring about."

"Most definitely."

"Now, from what I have been able to see, the discerning capability of Arkadians is sharp, robust, and rich enough for identical objects to appear identical and for different objects to appear different. It is sharp enough because in normal situations that an Arkadian lives through relevant kontents are not confounded more than would be appropriate. In other words, Arkadians might confound a zucchini and a cucumber, but they will not confound an apple and a rock. Secondly, it is robust because the kognitive architecture always uses the same criteria to discern. And it is rich because the capability of the kognitive system to discern kontents is extraordinarily large. In a single slife, an Arkadian can discriminate among thousands of kontents at a time, and the quantity and quality of the discrimination that may take place throughout childhood, for example, would make the national library look small. Therefore, in a sense, we can say that just as dinosaur tracks indicate to the paleontologist the weight, height, and volume of the animal, and we do not need to recover the creature, or to have a copy of it, the kognitive system does not have to have a copy of the situation that gives rise to a slife in order to differentiate it from, or to assimilate it with, new slifes. Its imprint is enough. Upon reviving the slife, the kognitive system feels the weight, the height, and the volume of the slife. Also, the imprints of kognition are not fossils like those of a dinosaur; instead, they are dynamic and alive, and capable of associating with other imprints of other slifes."

"What happens when a memogram is activated?"

"When an imprint is reactivated in the kognitive system after being recorded, it is as if the Arkadian relived the moment in which the slife, the dinosaur, left the imprint. It is as if the kognitive system felt the weight of the dinosaur again, without the dinosaur being present. This, however, is enough for the kognitive purposes of the organism."

"Let me see if I am getting this straight. Suppose that each slife of an Arkadian, let us say Katherine, had a button that activated it. What would happen if we pushed the button?"

"Katherine would recreate the situation as she lived it in the original moment; the kognitive system would have recreated the conscious aspects of the situation as well as the unconscious ones."

"Like seeing a video of what happened?"

"No. Pushing the button of the slife is not like being shown a video of what happened in the original slife, or like reproducing a representation of it, but like reliving the impact of the original situation on the kognitive system. True, this time is without the chunk of world that gave rise to the slife. Upon reliving the imprint left by the world in the kognitive system, the weight of the world on the kognitive system is relived."

"So, a memogram is more or less the memory of a slife, isn't it?"

"No. Memograms are not memories in the human sense. Let us see why not. Human memories are defined by their subjectivity. A memory is a 'memory of somebody who remembers,' since its subjective nature as experienced by 'I' is precisely what defines it. Memograms, on the other hand, are objective elements describable from the position of a third person, since they are independent from the access that an individual may have to it."

"So they have nothing to do with each other?"

"Of course they do. A memory is a part of a memogram. Memories can also be described as the conscious recreation of an episode, that is, as the set of kontents experienced subjectively, while memograms comprise all the traces that the slife left, both conscious and unconscious. As a result, we can say that memories are the tips of the iceberg of memograms. And thanks to this property, Arkadians can deal with the world effectively. If they had to rely on subjective memory, they would be badly off."

"Even though memograms are not exactly memories, the most important capability of the Arkadians is their memory, right?"

"Yes."

"How is it different from human memory?"

"Human beings distinguish among different types of memory. To be more specific, human beings appear to have a short-term memory and a long term memory, a memory for autobiographical facts, another one for concepts, another one that records data, one that records abilities, etc. But Arkadians appear to have only one type of memory structure: the memogram. This does not mean that Arkadians do not have autobiographical memory or a memory for abilities. It means that the different types of memory are different ways of exploring the memogram."

"How?"

"Let us examine the situation in which Katherine was given her first bicycle. In the memogram, or memograms, that recorded the situation, we have the memory of the autobiographical fact, the one with data describing the bicycle and the one recording the ability to ride a bike, which also occurred that same day. To reveal each one of them separately we can adopt different exploration strategies that will give us each of the elements that make up the different types of human memory: the emotions felt, the movements involved in riding a bike, and the kontents describing the bike. That is why, supposing that she has not had any other slifes with bicycles, if Katherine were to lose the space and time axis of the bicycle gift memogram, then she would lose the ability to ride a bike and to understand what a bicycle is."

"If that is true, what happens when an Arkadian suffers amnesia? According to what you have told me so far, all intellectual capabilities would be lost when the memograms, or the access to them, are lost, right?"

"No. When Arkadians suffer a temporary amnesia, all of the properties of normal kognition are retained because the memograms are not lost. These people know how to do the same things as before, how to ride a bike, how to multiply, how to assess a syllogism, although they have lost the sensation of 'I,' of who they are, where they live, what they have done in the past, what relationships they have, etc. However that may be, it does not present a problem, because they have not actually lost their past, but only the ability to evoke the autobiographical context."

"How does the brain handle the slifes, their kontents and memograms to be able to deal with the world?"

"The brain's real work takes place at the time the slife is created. In this process, all the areas of the brain that have a functional specialization take responsibility for analyzing the data that comes from the senses and associating it with other data and with past data to create the slife. In this sense, the Arkadian brain is like a building containing numerous departments specialized in certain types of processes and that have as one thing in common that they work in the context of a slife."

"Are these systems known?"

"No. The whole set of capabilities that constitute Arkadian kognition is beginning to be understood, but the work is far from complete. As of now, Arkadian researchers have begun to break the brain down into several basic mechanisms that have functional properties. Among the ones that are already understood, it has been discovered that each basic kognitive process contributes to the satisfaction of general kognitive capabilities, in such a way that the system takes advantage of these operations in the activity of an operation. A large part of the kognitive processes take place without the Arkadian realizing it; that is, they are unconscious as well as automatic."

"Once the slifes exist, how does the kognitive system manage to manipulate the appropriate ones?"

"Once the slife is experienced, and is saved in the form of a memogram, the only thing the brain has to do is activating the past slifes, the memograms, that the current slife requires. So, if Katherine has to come up with the correct answer to a math problem, her brain will have to activate the slifes in which the required mathematical operations are rooted, and combine them in the right way."

"Is this the reason behind the fact that context is so crucial in Arkadia and for Arkadians?"

"Exactly. You must remember that the most important thing about slifes is that they are a set of kontents that are linked by a specific spatial and temporal context. Kontents are trapped in the slifes where they were born. So kontents are sort of prisoners of these contexts; they cannot escape them, although they can communicate with other elements imprisoned in other contexts. This is why Arkadians end up showing these capabilities in an extremely contextual way. And all this implies that the traces of kontents that are recorded in the brain, all the information, all the knowledge concerning colors, distances, angles, shadows, sounds, mathematical operations, etc. are linked to a context in space and time, and that their participation in any activity will never be separate from that context."

"Even colors, shapes and feelings?"

"Even colors, shapes and feelings. The specific knowledge of 'red' or 'right angle' or something like 'toothache' or 'beauty' will always be attached to other kontents and contexts, in which the knowledge was created. That is why Arkadians will always do addition in the Arkadian language that they learned to add in, and they will always need a context similar to the one in which they learned."

Non-Professor O gazed at the horizon for a few seconds.

"It is getting late...."

"Why?"

"You will see."

"When?"

"Soon. But now may be a good time to emphasize that everything that must be explained about the kognitive life of an Arkadian, including intellectual capabilities, from perception to reason, and including concepts and mental representation, as well as emotional capabilities, can only be understood as rooted in one or more slifes. The slifes and their records, the memograms, constitute the basis of the kognitive system's knowledge, which is nothing but a series of actions and states in a network of temporal, spatial, and causal connections, in which the traces of kontent discrimination associate with one another in a specific context in space and time. Memograms themselves, and the elements that form them, can, however, establish relationships with other memograms and with elements of memograms, which accounts for the conceptual capabilities of the Arkadians."

"So how do Arkadians get by in the world?"

"Arkadians get by in the world because they have their past available to them to understand and to act according to what has happened to them in the past. This way, at all times the individual has within reach the part of the past that can give meaning to what is happening at that moment. No need exists for mysterious and pitiful translations into fleeing mental languages, nor do we need to imagine mysterious mental structures floating around. But we will talk about that in the days to come."

And then, the sun disappeared.

"The sun has set. It is time to go to bed."

"What?"

"In Arkadia we go to bed when the sun sets."

"Always?"

"I do not know."

"But I am not sleepy."

"You will be soon."

"But I do not want to be sleepy. I have a lot of things to ask you!"

"We will have time."

"When?"

"Soon."

"You could do an exception, couldn't you?"

"Even if I wanted to do an exception, I would not be capable of changing anything. You will be sleepy anyway."

"We will see."

Non-Professor O slipped inside the house. Just then I started to feel incredibly tired, and I found my room as if by magic. I stretched out on the bed and fell asleep, barely aware of what was happening.

Four

TUESDAY
On How to Get by Without Concepts

Again, the rabbit woke me up. I saw him standing in the doorway, just as agitated as the day before.

"Quick, quick. We are late for tea!"

I rubbed my eyes. For a few seconds, I was bewildered again. I did not know where I was, or what I was doing there.

"Quick, quick. It is getting late!"

I slowly remembered Monday's scene with the rabbit, and the afternoon spent with Non-Professor O. I looked around the room, and found that nothing had changed, not even the light coming in through the window.

"What time is it?"

"What time do you think it is? It is tea time."

"How can it be the same time as yesterday?"

"How do you think it is? By being the same time. I have never been asked such boring questions."

I got up and went to the mirror. At least I was still wearing the same clothes as when I went to sleep.

"I am going."

The rabbit closed the door and disappeared. I went and stood by the window. The town was still there. Still sleepy, I came down the stairs and went toward the terrace. I opened the door and there was Non-Professor O, just as I saw him the first time.

"Hello, Alice. I hope that you slept well."

"Like a log. It seems like I slept all day, right?"

"I do not know."

The same tray with tea and crackers and the fruit bowl with an apple were on the table. I was ravenously hungry and devoured the crackers in a second. Non-Professor O prepared his pipe. Fortunately, we did not say anything for a few minutes.

"I was thinking about what you told me yesterday, and then I remembered another of my perplexities."

"Go ahead."

"Not long ago I was out to dinner with Laura. We were talking about why she has ended up doing what her father said she would do, something she always rejected. I mentioned destiny, which brought on a long discussion. Laura asked me why I say that destiny gives us signs. And then I remembered the story. 'There was a merchant in Baghdad who sent his servant to market to buy provisions and in a little while the servant came back, white and trembling, and said, «Master, just now when I was in the market-place I was jostled by a woman in the crowd and when I turned I saw it was Death that jostled me. She looked at me and made a threatening gesture; now lend me your horse, and I will ride away from this city and avoid may fate. I will go to Samarra and there Death will not find me.» The merchant lent him his horse, and the servant mounted it, and he dug his spurs it its flanks and as fast as the horse could gallop he went. Then the merchant went down to the market-place and he saw me standing in the crowd, and he came to me and said, «why did you make a threatening gesture to my servant when you saw him this morning?» «That was not a threatening gesture,» I said, «it was only a start of surprise. I was astonished to see him in Baghdad, for I had an appointment with him tonight in Samarra.»'"

He looked at me intently.

"I think I can also help you with that sort of perplexities."

"I cannot just imagine how."

"Be patient. We will start by remembering what a concept is in the human world."

"A concept."

"Yes. Among other things, without concepts the mental life of human beings would be chaotic, given that we would perceive each thing as unique. Every morning upon opening our eyes, we would be born into a new world from which we would have to learn everything. The alarm clock would not be an 'alarm clock,' but would be a new object that we would have to analyze, just as we would have to do with each thing that we found."

"It would not be such a bad idea to forget that an alarm clock is an alarm clock. I do not like alarm clocks."

"I do not either. In any case, without concepts, we would be overcome by the fantastic diversity of what we experience and we would be incapable of remembering even a fraction of what we see. Consequently, concepts function, in the first place, to categorize. When as human beings, for example, we go into a room, we experience each particular object as an example of a class, category, or concept that we already know and that we have recorded some place in our brain. If we come across a wooden object that is made up of an 80 by 140 centimeter board resting on four legs 75 centimeter high, our cognitive system probably activates the entry of the concept 'table.'"

"Not always!"

"Say that it normally happens like that."

"As you wish."

"Let us suppose then that if we come across a wooden object that is made up of a board resting on four legs, our cognitive system probably activates the entry of the concept 'table.' And that is because our concept of 'table' allows us to identify the wooden object made up of a board and four legs as a 'table.'

Therefore, among other things, the concept of 'table' assumes the knowledge of something about the properties of the entities that belong to the class of table, and whose properties can be used to categorize any new object that we see and that has a board and four legs as a 'table.' In addition, if we do not recognize a new object that we see as a table because, for example, it is made of plastic and is transparent, but we are told that it is a type of table, we can prove that the object has all or many of the properties of a table; that is, we can use those conditions that underlie our concept of table."

He stopped for a moment.

"Okay?"

"More or less."

"Secondly, concepts have the property of being able to be combined with each other. This allows expanding the catalogue of objects that can be categorized through the combination of existing concepts to provide for new concepts, such as the case of the concept of 'table' and that of 'chair' being able to be combined to give the concept of 'furniture,' because we identify the table as one of the objects that are found in any house."

He stopped again.

"Do you follow me?"

"I think so."

"Thirdly, concepts effectively relate to language, which makes possible communication among human beings. Thus, the sentences that we hear and say can be easily interpreted, given that the words correspond to concepts. Finally, concepts allow the cognitive system to reason about the world without the need to always have the world in front of it."

"Okay, but where is this going?"

"I cannot find in Arkadia anything that corresponds to concepts. Although it may appear impossible to you, not only do Arkadians not know what a concept corresponds to, they have not even reached the point of defining any human concept, not even that of 'table.'"

"How is that possible?"

"The distinguishing characteristic of the Arkadian kognitive structure as compared to that of human beings is that all their conceptual competence is slife-dependent. Sometimes the effects of this peculiarity are seen in situations that are not conceptual but that show how the kognitive system works. An example would be what happened to Katherine the other day, when she ran into someone she knew on the street, and even though she was aware that she knew this person, and that she saw him on a daily basis, she could not figure out who it was until he told her he was the local butcher. Seeing him somewhere other than in his usual place, dressed in a different way, had dispossessed him of the slife context necessary for her to recognize him."

"But that is a problem of recognition, right?"

"Yes, but I only wanted to make the point that Arkadians do not have concepts as something separated from slifes. And recognition may be the easiest way for you to understand."

"If you say so."

"The rest of Katherine's conceptual knowledge is just as slife-dependent. If she knows something, that something has a full name, first and last; that is, it is inscribed in a specific slife context."

"Okay, but do Arkadians have conceptual capabilities or not?"

"In a way, they do. Arkadians seem to demonstrate a capability to think abstractly, to create a general idea from the occurrence of particular cases. So, Arkadians understand and can correctly apply the idea of cause and effect that they appear to have abstracted from the occurrence of specific events, like billiard balls hitting each other."

"Can that capability be compared to what human beings show?"

"I would say that I consider Arkadians capable of attaining the same things that human beings have achieved, like understanding the basic forces of nature, discovering and manipulating their genetic code, and even visiting the moon."

"Can Arkadians simulate human conceptual capabilities to that degree?"

"Let us say that if we were to examine the kognitive system of an adult Arkadian, and put it to the test, we would be surprised because we would see effects of categorization and conceptualization that are quite similar to those of human beings. Although the kognitive system is based on slifes, when an Arkadian has to show a degree of conceptual capability, the kognitive system is capable of making conceptual abilities emerge that are like human ones. Arkadians also tend to group elements together the way human beings do, like in natural classes —dog, elm tree— or elements classified by human beings as artifacts —hammer, computer. K has even observed connections between elements that human beings call *ad hoc* categories."

"What?"

"*Ad hoc* categories."

"I have heard you perfectly well, but I do not understand what you mean by *ad hoc* categories."

"By *ad hoc* categories I mean categories that we create when the situation makes it necessary or desirable."

"Like what?"

"Like things to take out of a burning house."

"I see."

"Additionally, Arkadians also group elements that have no easy theoretical description, like the ones that allow Katherine to say that a painting by some artist —Klee— has been influenced by another painter —Cézanne. When Katherine is told to differentiate between animals that give milk and those that do not, she is capable of activating her memories of cows, and when she is told to activate animals that graze in the pastures of the island of Gor, she can activate memories that include cows and horses. If someone asks Katherine what the most typical bird is, her answer will be possibly similar to the human one. If she is asked to describe the characteristics of a car, her answer may also be similar to what human beings would say. Likewise, all Arkadians can, for example, identify conceptual properties in the specific memories of their slife background. They can tell you if a house has the property of having windows, and they can tell you that the Tyrolese house is the most typical."

"How do you know that they do not have concepts?"

"Note that the burden of proof is on you. That is, it is you who would have to show that they have concepts, and that is something that nobody has been able to do, up to the present. Arkadian conceptual organization corresponds to slifes, and conceptual phenomena can be explained from the point of view of the slifes. The only thing that the kognitive system shows is that it is capable of conceptually organizing the world, that is, it can organize past slifes, or at least the ones that are presented to the subject in the psychology department laboratory, and it is done in such a way that these slifes can be extracted, divided, or sectioned as if they were being divided into categories. We could say that this conceptualization is only a mechanism used for the exploration of their slifes. Thanks to this mechanism, our average Arkadian can adapt to lab tests and respond effectively and according to any human conceptual theory. The most typical birds are the ones that appear the most frequently in the individual's memograms and the ones that are associated most often with the word 'bird.' If at school Arkadians were shown representations of penguins instead of goldfinches, I can assure you that penguins would become the most typical bird. Similarly, the required characteristic of cars is that they have a motor, because all the cars that Arkadians have panceived have motors. Slife background allows Arkadians to fulfill, as I will explain later, the kognitive requirements that concepts are so useful for, without them having a conceptual structure like the human one. I would say, therefore, that Arkadian conceptual competence is one of conceptual effectiveness more than a conceptual structure."

"What?"

"In Arkadia, the assessment of an individual's conceptual competence would be based on whether the person can adequately discern an object, an apple, for example, or an attribute, its red color, and that the person knows, implicitly or explicitly, the conditions that make that concept what it is. With given circumstances, the Arkadian would show that the person does not confuse the object, and can make himself or herself understood, all of it without the concept. In other words, if the concept of 'apple' helps human beings to discriminate between apples and pears, it would be reasonable to expect that the slife background of Arkadians will allow them to discriminate between apples and pears. If the concept is also useful to the human in talking about the attributes of apples, comparing them with pears, then it would also be reasonable to expect that an Arkadian can carry out the same activity. And so forth and so on."

"Cannot you give me any proof of the absence of concepts?"

"Let us see. If instead of asking Katherine to distinguish between horses and cows, you ask her to distinguish qualities of cows from qualities of horses that have not appeared in her slifes, even though they are qualities of cows and horses, then Katherine would not be able to do it. Another way to reveal the slife structure would be to ask Katherine to describe different kontents of her past. If this could be done with enough time and systematization, we would see that Katherine can describe many more and varied kontents than concepts she can apply. However, you can ask Katherine to try to establish categorical divisions among different human concepts, and you will see that, with some exceptions, she will never be able to do so. So, for example, the different nuances that Katherine can find in the analysis of the human concept of 'love' correspond to a great many slifes. However, if we do an experiment in which we ask an Arkadian to define the five most important feelings, love will be one of them, and it will incorporate the characteristics belonging to what underlies the human concept of 'love.'"

"I am not sure if I understand."

"Look, when we ask a talented human tennis player how to serve the ball, two things may happen. If that player learned without receiving theoretical lessons on the game's movement, the tennis player will probably respond, 'I cannot explain the movement; I just do it.' However, if we ask a tennis coach, we will probably hear the description of the movement divided into parts and times: 'The first movement is throwing the ball up in the air, while we bend our legs, bring the arm and the racket back, and lean backwards. The second movement is leaning forward and moving the racket toward the ball, and finally the contact phase, when we use all our strength to send the arm forward....' In short, when human beings want to, we are capable of breaking down the movement into parts and times, although the movement is not the articulation of parts and times but a coordinated and continuous action. The Arkadian kognitive system displays the same ability for conceptual segmentation 'when necessary,' even though it does not have a structure based on segments."

I heard some barks in the distance, and a laughter, and then a ship siren. The town appeared to be living the same life as the day before. The light had the same degree of intensity, and the clouds were still battling against the wind. The church bells broke that sensation.

"How can the conceptual similarity between Arkadians and human beings be explained, then?"

"It will not be easy to explain it to you, but I will try. Remember, the kognitive system of Arkadians has two basic large capabilities. One of them corresponds to their competence in discerning a huge amount of kontents, which allows them to analyze a slife at a very subtle level. The other corresponds to their capability to find similarities and likenesses and establish connections between current slifes and past memograms, and among the elements of these slifes with elements of other memograms. Yesterday, we dealt with their capability to discern, and today we will talk about the other one. I will try to explain how I believe that the absence of concepts in Arkadia is overcome."

"Go right ahead."

"Now you know that slifes are comprised of kontents, of all the elements that the kognitive system of an individual notes, that these kontents have an activity within the time limits of a slife, and that they are modeled by the same system. I have also explained to you that the slifes leave imprints, dynamic imprints that can associate with one another, and that are not representations or copies of reality. Arkadians need no representations or copies. Their brains are powerful enough to discriminate, without representations, cows from horses: what they see as a cow is so particular that nothing, or very few things, could be confounded with it."

"That is what you say, at least."

"Trust me. We have also seen that every slife, as insignificant as it may be, is a particular slife, at least at the moment that it is recorded in the nervous system. We said that in the first few years of life an extremely rich and varied group of slifes is formed. During this critical period, an individual may have thousands of slifes, and these are the ones that, in the long term, will support the kognition and the life of that individual. From the moment of birth, and probably even before, each Arkadian has had hundreds of thousands of new slifes that are recorded individually. At the beginning, this is due to the circumstances, since new slifes are constantly occurring: the baby hears its mother's voice for the first time, then it hears another voice and differentiates it, then a third voice is distinguished, more voices that start to be associated to each other, and the association of similar things represents a slife in itself, and so forth and so on."

"I still think that is too many slifes."

"I understand that the magnitude of slifes that this implies would appear impossible for one brain to take. Let us suppose, for example, that each slife lasts five minutes, which is a lot. This would mean that in the first four years of life, Katherine could have around two hundred fifty thousand slifes. However, considering the design of the Arkadian brain, this phenomenon presents no problem whatsoever. According to current research, the capability of the Arkadian central nervous system to record memograms is extremely high, and we have no difficulty in thinking that they may have hundreds of thousands of different memograms for each specific situation."

"Can you prove that?"

"No, but indications exist. The capability to individualize slifes and to remember them is extraordinary. Arkadians can remember instantly a particular slife that took place sixty years ago, for example, their first sip of alcohol, without having to have remembered it ever before."

"Do all slifes have the same importance?"

"No. As I earlier said, for some slifes is probably true that the Arkadian brain will need more activity than for others. However, all situations have the status of slife, regardless of how much cognitive, perceptual, or emotional effort is devoted to it, what time of life it takes place in, that day's situation, or the degree of awareness involved."

"So that brings us back to the problem that the Arkadian brain is packed with particular slifes, right?"

"No. As I pointed out yesterday, once the memograms are established, something strange happens. Upon having a new slife, the brain superimposes the kontents that shape that slife on those past kontents that have a degree of similarity, which we will talk more about later, and it disregards the differences in detail that are maintained in the original memogram. You could say that a kind of 'confusion' between current and past kontents takes place. Thanks to this confusion the life of an Arkadian is not an endless series of unique events, of particular slifes."

"Confusion indicates poor functioning, doesn't it?"

"Not exactly. I call it confusion so that we can understand each other, but it is more like a 'superimposition.' Moreover, the poor functioning of this capability for confusion, that is, the inability to find similarities among kontents, has serious consequences, because it means that the Arkadian has to live in a different world every day. In fact, some Arkadians suffer from this inability to 'confuse,' and are thus able to tell about their kontents practically from slife to slife. This may appear like an advantage but it is not. These Arkadians show limited kognitive capabilities, because they are incapable of what we human beings call 'generalizing.'"

"Very interesting."

"But let us continue with the subject of 'superimposition.' Yesterday, I gave you the example of Katherine going up a flight of stairs. We said that when Katherine went up the stairs for the first time, the slife of climbing the first step was constituted as an original slife, just as the second step, and then the third, the fifth, until she got to the top of the stairs. But starting with step number 50, the kognitive system may begin to confuse the 'going up steps' kontents and that after a while Katherine will no longer differentiate between the twelfth time she climbed a step and the two hundred and twenty-fifth time, although she might between the first and the twelfth. As a result, a time comes when the kognitive system begins to superimpose the different kontents for going up steps, and will begin fusing them together to finally have only the 'going up steps' kontent or 'steps.' This process can be extended to all other slifes in the life of an individual."

"And then?"

"When two slifes are comprised of similar elements, and we will have to clarify this concept more fully, the kognitive system tends to group them, to confuse them, to let the differences disappear. In other words, panception discerns, and memory confuses. The Arkadian brain is sharp when it comes to discerning kontents, but not sharp when it comes to remembering the distinction between two kontents that play a similar role in similar slifes. Two things can happen now. Similar kontents, although they are not the same, tend to be confused and therefore to superimpose one another. Slifes with similar kontents and associations also tend to superimpose each other. Looking at herself in the mirror after getting up in the morning is a slife for Katherine; however, it is so similar to the ones she has had every day that her brain confuses them. Once the kognitive system connects the slife to another one, the two are superimposed, they fuse, and thus become a single memogram."

"Sounds fine to me."

"From now on we will use the term *konceptual connections* for the network of connections that are established between the occurrences of particular kontents, and that are carried out based on panceptual similarities; that is, they include elements that in human terms are perceptual, emotional, and cognitive."

"Examples, please."

"Suppose that Katherine has a slife, let us say she sees a cow for the second time. As soon as Katherine sees the cow, her kognitive system establishes a connection with the kontent that shaped the slife of a few days before when she was walking through the countryside and saw a cow for the first time, including in that kontent all kinds of panceptual elements, from the color, the shape, the movements, even the emotional impact that the vision of this animal produced in her."

"What does it explain the connections between 'cows' and not between 'cows and horses?'"

"The truth is that no differences occur among the connections of the memories of many kontents that we human beings categorize as different. But more intense connections occur between the memories of particular kontents, and based only on this differential intensity it would be possible to speak of categories. All of Katherine's memories of 'cows' will present more intense connections among each other than those memories of 'horses' and 'cows.' However, until some particular figure/ground configuration appears, which I will explain later, only a continuum of magnitude will occur among connections, and not a critical change. In fact, a common tendency among Arkadian children is to extend associations to memories of kontents that do not belong to the category that we as human beings would assign them. This is what happens when Arkadian children say that the moon is a ball, or that horses are dogs. The ambiguities, the mistakes, the excessive generalizations are natural phenomena derived from the very nature of konceptual connections."

"Then it must be very difficult for an Arkadian to find out what makes something similar, right?"

"Right. For Arkadians themselves, appreciating the incredible amount of konceptual connections that a given kontent has is not an easy task. But just because this network is not apparent and cannot be seen does not mean it is not there. Curiously enough, it is this inability to appreciate the amazing capability of the kognitive system to sustain, manipulate, and organize the large number of memograms and konceptual connections among them that makes Arkadians think they have the same conceptual structure as human beings do. But the great wealth of konceptual connections makes it impossible for Arkadians to analyze the ease with which, for example, a child creates connections between the kontents that appear in memograms. These connections go beyond what can be analyzed by looking only at what an Arkadian child does, and this is especially so if the analysis takes place in the confined world of lab experiments."

"How many types of connections can be established?"

"No limit exists. In each slife, we can discern a multitude of different kontents, and the memory of each one of them can establish associations with many other elements of other memograms. The number of these konceptual structures is enormous; it is much higher than the number of human concepts. For each Arkadian, hundreds of thousands of slifes and of particular memories of kontents, and of konceptual connections occur. For each memogram numerous connections with other memograms can exist, so if we expand that to all possible memograms, the number can reach astronomical heights. The slife of being, for example, 'in danger,' like being intimidated by a threatening dog, can connect with other slifes experienced by that Arkadian that have the same kontent of 'danger,' like being intimidated by a threatening professor, but in addition, the kontent 'dog' that appears in the slife can connect to other memories of dogs that appear in other situations. Also, as I said yesterday, a great deal of kontents, and therefore of connections, are established between unconscious kontents, of which we still have only a small catalogue."

"What would you say is the main difference as compared to human beings?"

"That the kognitive system can use any type of kontent to establish connections, not just what 'appears' to be the same, in the human sense, that is, taking into account only perceptual aspects. Arkadians do not just say that a specific cow looks like another cow because it has 'four legs' and it is 'white with black spots.' Something more exists in the connection between cows than the simple perceptual kontent understood from the human perspective. Emotional elements are involved, like the kontent that K would characterize as 'completely-inoffensive-animal' and even cognitive elements, like the one K would say corresponds to 'apparently-stupid-animal.' The connection is based on the integration of several panceptual kontents."

"Then what are the criteria used to determine that 'the next day's cow' is similar to 'the preceding day's cow?'"

"I wish I could answer you. Proving what I am saying would require having a clear idea of what 'the same as' means; that is, I should have an Arkadian theory of similarity. But I do not. However, keep in mind that even we human beings lack a robust theory on what similarity means. We can say few things though, such as we will never discover the way the kognitive system establishes connections if we base our approach only on the perceptual analysis of the world's objects or properties. We need the other kontents as well."

"You cannot say any more than that?"

"Knowing what Arkadian similarity consists of is difficult, since the kognitive system fuses the panceptual elements, as it compares them. I will give you an example. On some occasions, Arkadians may find a likeness between two family members, so they may say that Erik is 'the spitting image of his father,' although Erik cannot see the likeness anywhere, and we have a hard time finding 'objective' data for two faces that establishes the likeness. Furthermore, to drive the point home, sometimes Arkadians will say things like 'Churchill looks like a bulldog.' The analysis of how these likenesses are established goes beyond what we human beings would call the perceptual characteristics of both elements. Something in the slife of a father and son makes them similar to Arkadians which goes beyond the simple perceptual analysis of the kontents of each individual. The emotional sensations produced, for example, also have to be kept in mind, as well as their relationship with the surrounding, and lots of other potentially relevant characteristics, because these are discerned by the kognitive system in each slife of a father and son, or of Churchill and a bulldog. A detailed analysis of them would take a long time. The same thing happens when an Arkadian says, 'Nikole has a thread of a voice,' and the friends who are listening understand instantly. The sensation provoked in an Arkadian by a quiet voice with a high pitch is spontaneously connected with a thread, which is fine and delicate. However, the connection is not made only because of an analysis of the perceptual characteristics; a lot of other kontents have to be added as well, and many of these, remember, are unconscious. Among other things, the complexity of similarity based on panception has the result of it being difficult for Arkadians to say how two objects are different, even when they are convinced that they are different, such as in the case of 'a threatening look' and 'a friendly look.' In the same way, for them is easy to say if they are similar when many kontents are combined at the same time —deciding if Churchill looks like a bulldog— but saying if two objects are the same as regards one particular kontent is quite difficult —saying if Churchill and a bulldog have the same eyes. In short, the similarity connection is made by the kognitive system based on general panceptual characteristics, including perceptual, emotional, and cognitive kontents. So it is the fusion of these kontents, and in order to characterize them, we need the kognitive system and its architecture, as well as the object or property."

"To say that what makes Erik look like his father depends on the kognitive system, on the slife, and on the context in which it is inscribed, is not saying a lot."

"You are right. I hope that I will be able to answer you more fully before too long. In the meantime, the only definition that I have available is that what is similar is what Arkadians find similar. Even though this seems circular, I believe that for now we can work with this hypothesis. Human beings also have to trust other people to know some things, like knowing which particular people are considered beautiful, since we still do not have objective and absolute criteria for beauty, although we have worked out a few. Remember the example of the panception of color. The color that an Arkadian panceives is not a property of the object to which the color is attributed; objects do not have the colors that Arkadians, or human beings, attribute to them. Color, as kontent, comes from the relationship between the kognitive system and the object. As a result, the solution as to why an Arkadian finds an orange and the sun at dawn to be similar cannot come from an analysis of only the objects or the individuals, but of the relationship of these objects with the kognitive system. The making of connections of similarity between a father and son is 'the' consequence of the whole kognitive system being activated and of the contrast between the current slife and the past slifes. A perceptual analysis of the kontent will not give us the answer. At any event, I am convinced that when the basic operations of kognitive architecture are discovered, the problem of similarity will be resolved. So, until that moment comes, let us leave aside the analysis of what it is that makes today's cow similar to yesterday's cow, while taking into account that K has observed an astonishing regularity in the way in which the kognitive system establishes connections: all Arkadians find the same similarities between fathers and sons, and all Arkadians agree that today's cow is similar to yesterday's cow."

"You are letting me down."

"If you press me, I could say that the Arkadian capability for finding similarity is characterized by being dynamic, exhaustive, and contextual. It is dynamic because the type of similarity applied changes from one stage of kognitive development to another. In other words, it is influenced by age, slife, the surroundings, the method of presentation and even the emotional state of the individual. It is exhaustive, because the panception of similarity tends to use multiple sources of information. And it is contextual because the way in which associations are established between two objects can be based on different elements, depending on what the purpose is."

Non-Professor O stopped talking for a minute. I took the opportunity to stand up and stretch my legs. The smell of orange blossom was slightly stronger than it had been the day before.

"I do not understand how to differentiate between the slife in which Katherine sees an apple without knowing that it is an apple, another one in which Katherine sees the apple as an apple, and a third in which she sees the apple and sees it as a kind of fruit."

"In the first slife you describe, Katherine has not yet established a konceptual connection among the memories of apple, which is what she experiences in the second, while in the third, she has established a figure/ground in which the figure is the konceptual connection of 'apple' and the ground is the konceptual connection of 'fruit.'"

"I do not know. It appears strange to me that all the conceptual capabilities take place in slifes. Do not they think abstractly about any element, outside of the slife?"

"No. The connections exist only between kontents, which are prisoners of the slifes, are completely absorbed in them, and cannot be separated from their participation in those slifes. When Erik sees his mother pour water into a glass, the memogram derived from this slife establishes 'pouring water' as the figure, and 'kitchen' as the ground. Later, Erik may see his mother ladling soup into a bowl, and still later putting silverware into a drawer. After these situations, the kognitive system establishes a connection among the figures of these three memograms, in such a way that Erik can panceive something similar among the actions, although he is not in a position to say what it is. Then K can say that the system has established a konceptual connection for the relationship contents/container."

"Is not that an element extracted from the slife?"

"No. The konceptual connection does not exist independently of the kontents anchored in the slife, in that it is not a new type of entity. In the connections among memories of cows there is no more than the traces left in the kognitive system of the cows Katherine has experienced in the past. It is not a representation of the 'cow' that is connected, nor is it a mental scheme, nor an image; it is the panceptual residue that, if it is repeated, establishes a connection with the original."

"Not even in the case of more abstract concepts like 'freedom?'"

"No. These human concepts in Arkadia are anchored in slifes that have transferred a particular signifikance from ordinary slifes, acquired during spontaneous interaction with the world, constrained by the kognitive system, and by the social and physical environment."

"Could you explain that a little better?"

"Let us suppose that Katherine is crazy about a television program that is on at seven in the evening. But her mother only lets her watch the program once in a while because, according to her, that time of day should be homework time. Katherine does not agree with this rule, and jumps at the chance to watch the program whenever she can. One day her parents have to go away on a trip for a week and they leave Katherine under her grandmother's care, who is a lot more easy-going than her mother. When Katherine gets home from school the first day she has the slife of 'turning on the television without being told not to.' So this is her first slife of 'freedom.' From then on Katherine will have many other slifes of freedom that will be characterized thanks to that first slife in which the figure/ground was 'being able to do something without being stopped by anybody.' So, the day that Katherine hears on the television that the people of Pulanda are demanding 'freedom' for the island, her kognitive system will transfer that first personal slife in order to understand what is happening in Pulanda, and this transfer will be characterized with the signifikance 'Pulanda wants to be able to do something without being stopped by anybody.' In short, Katherine understands how the people of Pulanda 'feel' and 'what they want' and this is because she transferred her slife in the matter. Without that transfer, Katherine will not understand what is happening in Pulanda."

"Are these transfers frequent?"

"Yes, and they work for all kinds of what we human beings consider to be abstract concepts, like the hierarchical relationships between concepts, such as those that allow human beings to know that a poodle is a dog, that a dog is a mammal, and that a mammal is an animal. Again, Arkadians manage this by taking into account that konceptual connections can become a figure/ground of a slife. For this to happen, first we need the Arkadian to have experienced slifes whose figure/ground is one of 'relatedness' or 'part/whole' and which are in turn specific figures/grounds. This figure/ground can then help in understanding that a 'dog' is an 'animal' as it is transferred to a slife in which the figure 'dog' is located next to a ground with the konceptual connection of 'animal.' The fact that they are necessary obviously has disadvantages."

"Like what?"

"Establishing this type of hierarchical relationship between konceptual connections in specific slifes means that the relationships do not have to preserve all the properties of relatedness, as the one established by human beings does. For this reason, a lot of incongruous situations can occur, that do not respect the logical structures of hierarchical relationships. So, an Arkadian child can say that a 'dog' is not an 'animal,' even though the same child is capable of spontaneously grouping dogs with cats, horses, and other animals. Another consequence is that, even though no limit exists to an Arkadian's ability to establish the relationship of parts/whole between konceptual connections, they do display difficulty in detecting the relationships of inclusion in classes that we human beings would call theoretical, such as that dogs are animals. This is not a limitation in their logic; it just means that this type of relationship is poorly represented in slifes. Arkadians have no problem discerning the connection that links a poodle to a German shepherd and not to a cat, because they have seen plenty of poodles and German shepherds, and because these two kontents share some crucial panceptual elements, such as that they bark, they are expressive, loyal, affectionate, etc. However, the concept 'animal' corresponds to a weak konceptual connection: Katherine does not have many memories of that kontent, and therefore putting it into the context of a slife is not an easy task. The associations imposed from the human perspective, like 'Arkadians and horses are animals,' can reorganize the slifes, but their slife strength is much less than the usual kontents."

"Let us take a break."

"Fine. I will take the opportunity to show you another Arkadian specialty."

Non-Professor O disappeared from the terrace, returning shortly with an unlabeled bottle. He opened it, splashed some liquid on his hand, spread it around and then gave me his hand.

"Smell it."

It appeared ordinary enough.

"Arkadian perfume. What is special about it?"

"You will see later."

"If you say so."

"Shall we continue?"

"Yes. I am still not quite sure that what you have told me is enough to explain how Katherine can think about tables, horses, love, or freedom. When I talk about tables, I am talking about tables, and when I talk about horses, I am talking about horses, and when I talk about numbers, I am talking about numbers. Concepts are things that are fixed, stable, coherent...."

"True, we cannot say that thinking 'with' a concept is the same thing than thinking 'about' a concept. To say so would be confounding a tool for thought —the specific memories of the concept— with an object of thought —the meaning of the concept. One thing is to have formed, thanks to slife, a fluid set of similar objects, such as feeling that all spherical leather objects have some likeness to one another, and quite another thing is the concept of ball. The concept has to correspond to units of thought, stable generalities that have the potential to become real through language."

"That is what I say."

"But in Arkadia things do not necessarily happen like that. The Arkadians have a brain that structures their past in such a way that it allows them to adequately fulfill the conceptual requirements of their environment."

"Wait a minute. The human concept of cause and effect is pretty abstract."

"You are partly right. The concept of cause and effect cannot be understood in human beings as something concrete because the concept is an abstraction, and not the summary of a great variety of situations. However, in Arkadia, the wealth of the cause and effect relationship can be established in the different figures/grounds of the slifes of an individual. The way in which konceptual connections allow for a generalization, in human terms, is possible thanks to the occurrence of a specific figure/ground, like the cause and effect in a game of pool. It can connect with other memories, like the slife in which a ball broke a window pane, or the slife of eating and not feeling hungry any more. In the long run, the great wealth of all these slifes allows the connection to be emphasized around what they share, the 'panceptual weight' of cause and effect that we are talking about, and therefore it will always carry with it those properties that appear to distinguish the human concept of cause and effect, namely, contiguity and temporal sequence."

"But try as I might, I cannot imagine what kind of 'panceptual weight' would explain that a chair and a table are considered 'furniture.'"

"Again, you are partly right. For human beings, in order to categorize a chair and a table as 'furniture,' we have to have more information than what comes from the similarity between a chair and a table. Categorizing and finding things to be similar are two separate processes. Categorization appears to depend more on theory, to be more motivated by the purposes of the individual as regards the objects, and it involves properties that are not obtained from the similarities among individualities. However, it is not that way in Arkadia. What makes an Arkadian believe that non-slife information is in the category of 'furniture' is that the connection between a chair and a table goes beyond what is perceptually similar, in the human sense, but not beyond what is panceively similar. The relationship between the types of furniture is not a visual similarity, but a functional similarity, and this is also included in the panception of a kontent."

"How can everything that defines a concept be included in a slife? The concept of 'apple' includes, for example, the characteristic that the apple is 'round' and that it 'satisfies hunger,' but it would be hard to incorporate that into a slife, wouldn't it?"

"Two ways exist to guarantee that the occurrence of kontents in slifes fulfills what we could call the properties of a human concept. The first, and the most common, is that the memories carry with them these properties, whatever the nature of the properties may be."

"How is that possible?"

"I will explain. Let us suppose that Erik has an intense konceptual connection among his memories of apples, and he has konceptual connections among all round objects. The konceptual connection between the different round objects is present in all the memories of apples. This is the reason behind the idea that the konceptual connection of apple carries with it, and preserves the property of 'roundness' without having it as specific data. Among the consequences of this is that if Erik is asked to separate round objects from non-round objects, he will always put apples in the category of round objects. We would say that a human 'has the implicit information that apples are round.' Extending the case, we can say that more or less the same thing happens with all the other conceptual properties."

"And the second?"

"The second way in which conceptual properties are preserved in the structures of the memograms is if the property, the attribute, has been converted into a signifikance, that is, if it has become the focus in a figure/ground. If, for example, the konceptual connection that joins all round objects is focused on as a figure, with the konceptual connection of apple as ground, then the property, the attribute will become the signifikance. We would say that a human 'has explicitly conceived that apples are round.'"

"So no difference exists between the category of, to give a wild example, 'all cows that I have seen on Saturday and that are more than two years old' and 'all the cows that I have seen?'"

"No, that is not it either. You are right to point out that even in Arkadia not all konceptual connections have the same 'value.' Some konceptual connections, like the network of associations between the memories of 'cow' can work like an element, like a unit, an atom, at least potentially. Their preeminence, caused by repetition of the connection, allows the structure to present special conceptual properties. The connection joining all the occurrences of a kontent make it possible that when one of them is activated, all of them are activated and act in coordination, as if they were a context, a ground upon which a new slife can be based. The robust and intense connection among the particular memories of 'cow' means that, among other things, the kognitive system can discriminate cows from other animals as if it were a fixed element, and guide its activity in the world and its perception according to, approximately, the basic rules of human conceptualization and categorization. This type of connection underlies what we have called the *kontent* of a slife."

"You are telling me this now!"

"Patience, because this is what allows us to indicate that every Arkadian contains a type of structure that can function as a nuclear element. When we say that the kontent 'house,' or 'red' or 'relatedness' appears in a slife, we suppose that the Arkadian kognitive system has established a connection among the individual memories of slifes that stays active. And this connection has properties that are superimposed, at least partially, on the properties of the human concepts of 'house,' 'red,' or 'relatedness.'"

"Is not that a concept?"

"No, because they are konceptual connections like any other, except that they can function as units in a dispositional way."

"Dispositional?"

"By dispositional I mean that property that is manifested only under certain circumstances. You see, sugar has the dispositional ability to dissolve in water, it being dispositional because it is an ability manifested only under circumstances, when it is added to a glass of water and shaken. Similarly, the kontent 'cow' is a dispositional entity, since its reality is not different from that of other connections that also exist between elements of a memogram, such as the connection between 'tables' and 'cows.' Both tables and cows can be seen as having four legs and a body, although the connection between instances of cows works partially like a conceptual structure of the human type because it facilitates discrimination between cows and horses. This dispositional entity has, therefore, kognitive power, because each time that a memory of kontent is activated, all the other memories connected to it are also activated. This way it can guide the perception and the action of the system with a categorical knowledge. However, this knowledge will always be anchored in the slifes that gave rise to these konceptual connections."

"Do not they have any rules that help them define the borders of a concept when they make it emerge, as you say?"

"Let us see what happens with the concept of 'gift.' Just like a human, an Arkadian can discern what objects can be considered appropriate birthday gifts. Choosing an appropriate gift depends on several variables, such as:

(1) The age, sex, interests, and socioeconomic status of the recipient.
(2) The relationship between the giver and the recipient (parent-child, employee-boss, student-professor, friends, lovers, ex-lovers, acquaintances, etc.).
(3) The reason for the gift (birthday, graduation, reconciliation, Christmas, gratitude, etc.).
(4) The appropriate amount of money to spend.

So, when Katherine has to choose a gift for her ten-year-old neighbor, she must keep these variables in mind, and more. That is how Katherine knows that a machine gun, a car, a cheese sandwich, a potato, a copy of the Yellow Pages, and lingerie would be inappropriate gifts. But the Arkadian community has never made explicit rules about these variables, and children are not taught more or less general rules about it either, but Arkadians do learn to give appropriate gifts. No specific rules exist; instead, the konceptual connections of 'gift,' of all the gifts Katherine has seen being given and accepted, work as a unit to allow her to discern the right objects and times."

"So what criteria does the kognitive system follow to consider something to be a kontent?"

"They are many and varied."

"Are they similar to the human ones?"

"Sometimes they are and sometimes they are not. In general, we can extract criteria with which panception appears to adapt itself to a concept. Allow me to cite a case, the concept that we human beings call 'object.'"

"Go right ahead."

"In Arkadia, people have studied what all the 'things' that we human beings call 'object' have in common with each other, and they have reached the conclusion that, in general, the objects correspond to the 'things' that are panceived according to three conditions. One of them is the 'condition of contact,' by which the surfaces of an object move together. A car can be panceived as an object by an Arkadian, in that all its surfaces move at the same time. But a pack of wolves is not panceived as an object because the surfaces of each wolf do not always move jointly with those of its fellow wolves. The second condition is 'cohesion,' by which all objects are connected because their surfaces are always connected. A ball is connected with everything that we human beings call 'object' because when it is hit, all of its particles follow the same trajectory. But a stream of water is not connected with other objects because it can be broken down into thousands of drops that each follow their path, and the surfaces of the droplets are only connected temporarily in the stream. Lastly we have the 'condition of continuity,' by which an Arkadian konceptually connects everything that describes only one trajectory in space and time. This means that the trajectory of an object, for example, a moving train, cannot be occupied by another object, such as a car going through the moving train."

"So?"

"Adding up these principles allows us to define the basis of the connection established by Arkadians among those things that human beings call 'objects.' These principles do not define what a human philosopher would consider the sufficient and necessary conditions to characterize an object as 'object.' Because of this, not everything that the Arkadian notes as 'object' will be an object, but at least these principles allow for the identification, the isolation of objects as 'objects' in a large percentage of the cases, without having to carry out complicated operations of conceptual analysis. These conditions depend on the characteristics of the kontent, of the kognitive architecture of the Arkadian brain, and the slifes accumulated by the individual over time."

"Are not these like the conditions of a human concept?"

"They do not appear so. In human beings some conditions would allow us to say whether an individual has or does not have a concept. This is true, among other reasons, because a concept can be said to be defined independently of a specific individual and that person's slife. A concept is something that human beings can share regardless of the life that each one has lived, of the objects seen. Quite few people have shared the same slifes with tables, nor have they seen the same tables, yet in spite of that, they all have the same concept of 'table,' whatever that concept may be. This is why people can understand each other. Also, they have those concepts that seem completely independent of slife, such as the concept of cause and effect."

"Does not language play a role in Arkadian conceptual capabilities?"

"The appearance of language is crucial in the evolution of the kognitive system, in that it allows most children to manipulate the konceptual connections. After the first six months of life, the Arkadian child incorporates linguistic forms that anchor slifes and konceptual connections. Thanks to words, the child can fix connections more intensely than others, which will end up making them special. Many kontents are established thanks to the social environment reinforcing the connections among the memories of a category through language. Thus, the connections of the 'cow' kontents were reinforced in Katherine by the community, her mother, her friends, so that in the long run they became much stronger than the connections that link 'cows' with 'horses.' Each time that Katherine's mother says 'cow' when she sees or says something about a cow and not a horse, Katherine is incited to look for something among the connections of 'cows' that fix those connections and not others. This does not mean that Katherine will stop confounding 'cows' and 'horses,' since the connections of similarity do not depend on language but on the connection between the kontents 'cow' and those of 'horse.' Moreover, this process does not guarantee that all the konceptual connections are connected with words, because many connections correspond to kontents of which the Arkadian is unaware, like the connection that exists among objects that are at floor level, that are paid a lot of attention, and those that are above their heads, and are barely noticed. This is why the best place to hide in Arkadia is in the branches of a tree and not behind a bush. In any case, as I told you, the kontents that an Arkadian has experienced may be identified, or named, or they may not be, but the number of unnamed connections is fantastically higher than the ones that do become named, and therefore recognized as what human beings call 'concepts.' Konceptual connections are much more numerous than the names that the Arkadians have to name them. As a result, the number of konceptual connections derived from panceptual similarities among elements of the slifes is much higher than the words that an Arkadian will learn."

A cat appeared on the balustrade out of nowhere. It looked in our direction, and then just ignored us while wrapping its tail around itself.

"I cannot understand something. If each child depends on personal experiences to make connections, then every Arkadian child will likely have konceptual connections that are completely different from those of his or her classmates, right?"

"Two independent factors combine and guarantee that konceptual connections are shared among Arkadians. First, we have the brain's architecture. The kognitive system restricts, by way of its structure, the establishment of types of konceptual connections. Thus, Arkadians tend to unify the 'continuity' type, the 'cohesion' type, and the 'contact' type. Second, the Arkadians have a great slife wealth; they have a lot of slifes that are rich and varied, which brings about a good degree of homogenization among the different Arkadians. Because Arkadians interact with the same objects, with other people from Arkadia, and that they do more or less the same things, after being in Arkadia awhile, a child ends up having about the same number of slifes with equivalent signifikance. As figure 2 illustrates, all children end up seeing the same number of chairs, which they have looked at from all possible angles, and which they have used for many

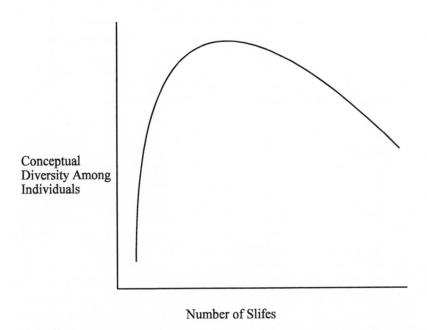

Conceptual
Diversity Among
Individuals

Number of Slifes

Figure 2. The Conceptual Homogeneity of a Given Community Is Guaranteed by the Richness and Variety of Slifes

different purposes. Similarly, it does not matter that at the beginning Katherine has fixed a cause and effect relationship in the form of one billiard ball hitting another, because Katherine will have experienced several situations to which she has transferred this type of relationship that will be superimposed on many that Erik has had, who started by fixing the relationship of cause and effect in his backyard, when he broke a window with a rock. Even if only these two slifes determined the transferable signifikance, all the particularities of that konceptual connection, its consequences, its formal implications, will be the same as, or else quite similar to, the ones that may have been formed by another Arkadian in a past slife. Therefore, when both of them light up the slifes in which the figure/ground is the relationship that K characterizes as cause and effect, the conceptual properties that are derived from them will be the same, as will be the capability to transfer this figure/ground to new situations. Thanks to these two factors, the architecture of the kognitive system, and the great slife wealth that the Arkadians possess, we can understand how Arkadians share the same conceptual understanding."

"Can this be proven in children?"

"It is difficult. To start with, the Arkadian kognitive system does not develop in stages, as has been postulated for the human cognitive system, in such a way that we can check to see if the child has already gone through this or that stage. No specific milestones exist at which point the system begins to work in a completely different way and which deserves special attention. As the slifes do not follow a specific outline, they are liable to have an infinite number of contextualities, and the kognitive evolution of the child is quite variable; stages of general learning are not observed. Nobody directs the life of Arkadians to the point that they are forced to have or not have slifes. The real konceptual milestones that the child reaches are always in reference to specific slifes, in which types of kontents are discerned that become a figure/ground, and that later can be transferred to other slifes or can modify past memograms. No rules decide which konceptual connections will be established first, and which ones will come later, although sequences do respect the laws of logic, such as hierarchy: to experience the konceptual connection of 'cardinal point' the Arkadians have to have first experienced 'east-west.' Another interesting aspect is that, although no fundamental difference occurs between what is specific and what is abstract, from the human point of view can be said that an evolution occurs, and that Arkadian children seem to begin with knowledge of the physical world, and only then do they move on to understand terms like 'justice,' 'nation,' or 'peace.' However, a lot of evidence exists that a sense of the abstract is being applied to many kontents that appear early, such as the particle 'because' that Arkadian two-year-olds use quite easily. True, after the age of two, children emphasize, reinforce, thanks to the appearance of language, those konceptual connections that are superimposed on human concepts, that is, those that refer to objects, properties, and specific actions. However, reinforcing these connections does not mean that the earlier ones no longer exist, that they play no role, or that new ones are not created."

I heard the shrieks of children, as if they were all leaving some place at the same time. But I could not see them.

"Okay, then how and when can we say that an Arkadian has something equivalent to the human concept of 'cause and effect?'"

"I am still not sure about how it can be determined that an Arkadian is competent in a given concept, that is, I do not know what would indicate that a person carries out kognitive activities as if he or she had the concept. No clear criteria exist concerning this point. Some depend on what an Arkadian can do and on other occasions on how the situation is apprehended, or how it is reasoned. My characterization of concept in Arkadia is of the pragmatic type. In this sense, we could say that an Arkadian is conceptually, in the human sense, competent if the structures of the slifes and the associations among them allow the Arkadian to sufficiently fulfill the requirements that a conceptual structure fulfills in human beings."

"At least a moment must exist when we could say that Katherine knows what a table is?"

"More or less."

"What do you mean by that?"

"You will agree that in human beings intuitively assessing whether someone is competent in a given concept or not is certainly possible."

"I do not know what to tell you."

"Let us say that we will not be satisfied until the konceptual connections fulfill what we could call the 'conceptual conditions' of a concept. And we will say that the conceptual conditions are the conditions that, when they are described by human beings, correspond to the properties of one concept, and only that concept. For the time being, it will be enough to suppose that the conceptual conditions are the sufficient and necessary conditions that K has about that concept, and therefore we will call them:

K Conditions: The sufficient and necessary conditions of a human concept.

In this sense, what allows us to say with certainty that the Arkadian displays conceptual competence is if that person fulfills what I am going to call:

Conceptual Competence: A konceptual connection is conceptually competent when it 'satisficingly' fulfills the K Conditions of a concept.

"Oh, good heavens."

"Let us look at what all this means, starting with the term 'satisficing.' Consider the example of a soccer player. When a forward shoots the ball toward the goal, the goalkeeper needs to predict the movement of the ball in order to stop it. To correctly calculate this trajectory, the Arkadian kognitive system would need to apply a branch of physics called dynamics. Dynamic information describes the forces that cause the movement or that act on objects with mass, taking into account variables, like the mass of the object, in our case the ball, its force, velocity, etc. However, the kognitive system of the Arkadians apparently does not calculate the trajectory of objects according to dynamics, since it does not take magnitudes such as mass or force into account. Research carried out up to the present indicates that the kognitive system is only sensitive to magnitudes described by another area of physics: kinetics. Kinetic information describes the pure movement of the bodies without taking into account their mass, only the position, velocity, and the acceleration of the object."

"And?"

"The problem is that kinetics is less effective than dynamics for predicting the trajectory of objects with mass. Experiments show that Arkadians make a lot of mistakes when predicting the trajectory of objects with mass. However, in daily life, in soccer games, they manage to get by quite well in spite of the mistakes. Not only do they stop goals, they also are capable of moving around without running into each other, and of anticipating the trajectories of players or balls in order to intercept, follow, or avoid them, which is useful for soccer players, or for anybody who wants to avoid being run over by a car."

"Why does the kognitive system use such an imperfect system?"

"Kinetic computation is much simpler than dynamic computation. By adopting kinetics, the kognitive system saves itself from having to use a much more complicated system. And the mistakes made are usually small and solvable with the constant update of information provided by the senses. What I mean is, the kognitive system may make a small mistake in predicting the trajectory of a ball as it leaves the forward's foot, but the sense of sight allows for the almost immediate update of the real trajectory. Therefore, we can say that when we look at the capability of Arkadians to deal with objects in real situations, like a football match, they adapt themselves effectively, although not completely, to the real movement of the object. This incomplete but satisfactory effectiveness is what I mean by 'satisficing.' In other words, the kognitive system fulfills the K conditions of the trajectory of objects satisficingly, predicting the object's trajectory pretty well, and avoiding, for example, that the other team scores against them. If we generalize this point, we can say that conceptual competence of Arkadians does not strictly correspond to knowing the K conditions that make the concept of 'object with mass' the human concept of, 'object with mass.' No Arkadian has the sufficient and necessary conditions of, 'object with mass,' but as long as the condition of competence is fulfilled, 'stopping goals and not being run over,' they can probably get by in the world without too much difficulty."

"When is something satisficing?"

"A given konceptual connection is satisficing when it effectively contributes to the survival, reproduction, or communication of the Arkadian. The konceptual connection among 'stairs' is satisficing if it is not confounded with that of 'cliff,' when that of 'apple' is not confounded with 'spider,' and if two lovers understand each other when they say, 'Let us make love.'"

"Is anything ever satisficing enough?"

"The concept of satisficing is a continuous and dynamic one. For one thing, an Arkadian fulfills the condition of competence in a partial way; that is, not a point at which it is fulfilled exists, while it was not fulfilled previously. Instead, normally, as the person grows, he or she fulfills it a little bit more each day. In other words, Arkadians do not acquire conceptual competence for 'apple,' 'freedom,' or 'love' all of a sudden. If that were the case, they would have to be based on some kind of rules that are acquired, but, as we have seen, konceptual connections are entities that connect memories immersed in a magma of slifes. What helps a konceptual connection get closer to conceptual competence is what we could call competitiveness among konceptual connections:

Satisficing Condition: A konceptual connection is optimized, it gets closer to K conditions, if and only if it has konceptual competitiveness.

In other words, a konceptual connection only needs to do a better job at fulfilling a conceptual competence when conceptual interference occurs, such as when Katherine eats a pear because she confounded it with an apple, and she realizes that she hates pears. At that moment, her kognitive system becomes activated, and it looks for new kontents that will allow her to distinguish better between apples and pears."

"What advantages does this satisficing have?"

"A satisficing fulfillment provides many advantages. I will give you an analogy from the human world: chess. In a game of chess, no player, no matter how good, can examine all the possible moves, because it would take forever to decide on one. Keep in mind that in a game, choosing the ideal move would involve evaluating something like 10^{120} combinations, which is beyond the capability of any human being, or any Arkadian. Players can only generate and examine a small number of possible moves, deciding on one as soon as they find one that is satisfactory, which is the move that appears the best out of the subset that has been evaluated. Since the player cannot examine every single outcome, a chess move is not ideal, but satisficing."

Non-Professor O stopped talking. I got up. The cat had disappeared. Swallows were above me, having a bite to eat.

"Is everything you have mentioned so far enough to explain the conceptual competence of the Arkadians?"

"No. We have only explained a part of their conceptual competence."

"I am not surprised. What is supposedly left to be explained?"

"The conceptual capability of Arkadians in those human concepts that cannot be conceived by the kognitive system."

"What are you referring to?"

"I am referring to concepts like 'atom,' 'multiplication,' or 'Big Bang.' Even though these concepts cannot be conceived by the kognitive system, Arkadians can use these concepts just like human beings do."

"So how do you explain this ability?"

"Through a type of slife that I will call *surrogate* slifes."

"Here we go again...."

"I will explain. Some human concepts cannot be anchored in slifes, and therefore Arkadians cannot understand them. No way exists for an Arkadian to understand the concept of 'infinite,' or the amount, the numerosity, represented by the number 125, and this is because no slifes that anchor these kontents. Learning the concept of the amount of '125' for an Arkadian is different from learning 'red,' 'love,' 'contents/container,' or 'shoe.' The slifes involving the kontents and konceptual connections of 'red,' 'love,' and 'shoe' have, let us say, a direct slife dimension of the kontents, while 'infinite' does not. However, thanks to the amazing plasticity of kognition, not every kontent has to be anchored in direct slifes. In these cases, the network of konceptual connections does not contain the impact of the kontent; instead, it evokes a set of slifes that guarantee the K conditions for the kontent. The concept understood from the human point of view is delegated in these slifes."

"If you cannot explain this a little better...."

"I will give you an example that will help you understand the idea. I am sure you have measured an object, say, a table, using the length of your hand, right?"

"Yes."

"When we measure an object with our hands and say that it is '50 by 30 inches' we have delegated to our hands the function of measuring, even though they are not a measuring stick, nor is measuring one of their uses. However, since 'we know that a hand measures more or less 6 inches' we can use our hands as a surrogate measuring stick. Arkadians are competent in many non-slife concepts because they have a set of hand-slifes in which non-slife concepts have been delegated, making them surrogate slifes."

"How is that possible?"

"Say we are talking about the concept 'atom.' Many Arkadians know that an atom is made up of electrons, neutrons, and other particles, and that hydrogen and oxygen are atoms. Since panceiving an atom directly is not possible, the Arkadian requires another type of slife to be able to conceive 'atom.' Let us suppose, just to make things simple, that in secondary school the teacher has shown Erik a plastic mechanics model that has colored balls representing the protons, and other balls representing the neutrons, and little ones going around the nucleus that represent the electrons. Fine, this model in the class slife is panceived as a plastic model, and I will not go into why and how Erik panceives it as a plastic model, because I would have to talk about a million previous slifes. Let us just say therefore that Erik panceives it as a plastic model and that is what becomes the figure of this figure/ground. Now, the plastic model is incorporated into the class slife as figure, and the word 'atom' as ground. Starting at that moment, Erik's kognitive system has available to it a slife that will be connected to all the other slifes of 'atom.' That slife will serve, for example, as another part of the kontent 'molecule.' So, for example, perhaps in the future more connections will be added with slifes in which 'valences,' 'chemical notations,' and 'H_2O' are mentioned. However, Erik will not derive mental outlines or abstractions from these specific slifes; instead, the kognitive system will use the model-slife as a surrogate slife of the concept 'atom.' True, the surrogate slife will not always be able to possess some kind of 'similarity,' such as may exist, however distantly, between a model and a real atom."

"I do not know if I understand the stuff about the surrogate slifes. Could you give me another example?"

"Let us take the case of arithmetic. The slifes that allow an Arkadian to be competent in arithmetic are not truly arithmetic slifes, but they are slifes whose kontents have been delegated arithmetical concepts."

"How?"

"Remember, the numbers 1, 2, 3, 4, 5, 6 correspond in the human realm to 'numerosity of sets.' When we say that 25 students are in a class, the '25' refers to a property of that class, what we could call 'numerosity 25,' which is the same property that a drawer with 25 pieces of silverware in it or a solar system with 25 planets, or any other set of 25 things. Just as we can say that all the students in the world have the property of having sometime gone to class, we can say that all the sets of 25 elements in the universe have the property of having a numerosity of 25. For each number, obviously, we have a different numerosity. If Arkadians did not know how to count, they could not differentiate a group of 25 things from one of 26 things, and that is why they cannot conceive the kontent 'set of 25 things.'"

"But they do know how to count."

"Yes, but what I want you to understand is that counting is 'the' resource that the Arkadians have to make up for their inability to conceive the numerosity of sets of more than five or six things. Arkadians share this inability with ordinary animals. A dog, a bird, or even a primate does not differentiate between a set of 25 things and another one of 26. Groups of 25 things do not have anything special that groups of 26 do not have. Similarly, Arkadians do not have the concept of 'sets of 25 things.' When they have a set of 25 things in front of them, they do not feel the 'twenty-fiveness' of the set, while if they have a bunch of apples before them, they can conceive that they are in the presence of apples and not of pears. Because they can count, they can identify that this group has 25 things, but they cannot conceive that it has 25 things. They need an instrument, counting, to be able to identify this fact, but they do not need an instrument to conceive that it is a group of 'apples' or 'horses.' When an Arkadian says, 'in this class are 25 students,' that individual does not have the concept of 25, because he or she has no slifes that allow for that kontent to be conceived."

"You said that they can conceive groups of a few things, right?"

"Yes. The kognitive system is only capable of experiencing kontents of low numerosities. An Arkadian can distinguish between sets of 1, 2, 3, and even 4 things. That is, Arkadians can attribute the numerosity of '1,' '2,' and '3' to any group of one, two, or three objects. If you offer an Arkadian child three pieces of candy in one hand, and two in the other hand, and you say to choose a hand, the child will go straight to the hand with three pieces of candy, without counting. If you offer five candies in one hand and six in the other, the child will have to count. Therefore, Arkadians can be said to have slifes characterized as slifes of the numerosity '1,' '2,' or '3' in the sense that the figure/ground is the act of focusing on the property of numerosity '1,' '2,' and '3.' With groups of four or more objects, the Arkadian can only roughly distinguish the difference between two sets, and can say things like 'more than ten objects,' or 'around 20 objects,' or 'many objects.' These slifes are, however, considerably less rich in examples and much more contextualized."

"So where is the problem?"

"The problem is that in order to carry out arithmetical operations, Arkadians need to operate with amounts, with numerosity. Therefore, since they do not conceive of amounts higher than four or five, when an Arkadian child does the following math problem:

256+345+456= 1,057

the child is not carrying out an arithmetical operation in the true sense. In order to have the concept of addition, the Arkadians should be capable of understanding the numerosity '256' and add it to the others. But, as I just told you, Arkadians are incapable of having the concept of '256.' In the same way, when Arkadians say, 'We have 12 classes with 25 students, therefore we have 300 students,' they do not have the concept of multiplication, nor do they have the concept of division."

"How do they manage to carry out and understand arithmetic problems?"

"Thanks to surrogate slifes. In the specific case of arithmetic, we have several types of surrogate slifes that make use of different abilities and instruments. First is the ability to count. Thanks to the ability to count, establishing any numerosity is possible. The higher it is, the longer it will take. Also, adding or subtracting on your fingers ends up being complicated, and multiplying and dividing is not possible. For that reason, the following instruments are the most important for competence in arithmetic: language and Arabic notation. These instruments allow for the delegation to numerals of amounts that cannot be conceived slifely. Thus, when '125' is written, said, or heard, an Arkadian does not have to understand the concept of, '125.' The concept is delegated to the numeral. Finally, another type of surrogate arithmetical slife exists, the operation-slifes, which are the slifes that record, among other things, the multiplication tables, or special algorithms, such as that of addition. Remembering, without having to conceive, that 'three times four equals twelve' or that while adding up the first column:

$$\begin{array}{r} 24 \\ +37 \\ \hline 61 \end{array}$$

'we carry the one' is a great advantage when it comes to doing mathematical operations. Language, algorithms, paper, pencil, and other structures, allow for the creation of slifes that delegate real operations. In short, the slifes that enable Katherine to say something correct about '125' or 'atom' are slifes that do not contain or result from the impact of these kontents, but are complex slifes structured around slifes that incorporate or satisfy the slifes that guarantee the K conditions for that concept."

"Do not Arkadians distinguish between the two types of slife?"

"No, because the surrogate slifes end up being transparent; the Arkadian is so unaware of their use that it appears they are not different from the genuine slifes. Just like when someone learns to play chess by learning the rules of movement for the different pieces and then forgets the rules, even though they are still being applied, the use of words like '125' or 'atom' has taken the same path."

"If these surrogate slifes work so well, why are not all concepts delegated?"

"Because Arkadians would not understand anything about the world. Also, disadvantages exist with the kontents '125' or 'atom' being anchored in slifes that guarantee the K conditions, and not the direct impact of these kontents. The most important of these disadvantages is that often errors in the application of the kontents occur; sometimes the Arkadians will take one of the slifes that corresponds to another term. The slifes for the term '125' are quite similar to those for '126' and even for '156,' as are the slifes for 4x7 and 5x7, and confounding them is easy. Arkadians can easily confound 'atom' and 'molecule,' especially if they have not enriched their original memograms with lots of additional memograms, which is what physicists and chemists do. They can also confound 'X is 166,000 light years away from Earth' with 'X is 166,000,000 light years away from Earth' since the panception of 166,000 light years is quite similar to that of 166,000,000 light years, even though it is a colossal difference as a property of the universe. Kontents that are delegated tend to suffer a lot more application errors."

"Do not these errors occur with the genuine slifes?"

"No, these problems do not arise in the case of genuine slifes, since an Arkadian will unlikely confound the kontent 'love' with that of 'fear' by mixing up the discrimination of some slife having the property 'love' with another containing 'fear.' That would be the situation in which Katherine is being held up by a robber, and she does not know whether to 'declare her love to the robbers' or 'run away from them.' In these cases, the konceptual connections used by Arkadians do have a basic and fundamental occurrence in the slife background."

"Do not surrogate slifes have any advantages?"

"Yes. Surrogate slifes are much more flexible; their uses can be varied in a much simpler way than for original slifes. This has happened in the history of Arkadian culture, since some of these slifes have changed their guaranteeing the K conditions for some kontents when something new has been learned about the original kontents. This occurred in Arkadian science when it was discovered that a person with epilepsy is not possessed by the devil, or when it was discovered that atoms are composed of elements more fundamental than protons and neutrons. In all of these cases, the slife can vary its conditions of application, since the memogram in which the kontent is inscribed can vary its structure without any problems."

He stopped talking.

"Are we doing okay?"

"I do not know what to tell you. Before that darn sun goes down and puts an end to the afternoon, and keeping in mind how different the Arkadians appear to be from human beings, I would like you to tell me how the conceptual capability of Arkadians should be studied."

"In my opinion, since the elegance of the conceptual structure does not correspond to the true nature of Arkadian kognition, what we should do is beginning an area of research that dissects the slifes to the most minute detail, examines what, of those slifes, the Arkadian identifies, selects, how it is organized, what kind of associations are established with other slifes, when and how transfers are carried out. No doubt about it, this is an arduous task, and what lies ahead is the detailed study of kontents, of the structure of slifes, which will take us a long time."

At that instant, as if it had been listening to me, the last golden rays of the sun disappeared from the terrace. I looked at the horizon, and saw the lingering glow of the sun.

"Time to go to bed!"

"But I have a lot of things to ask you."

"As I told you yesterday, we will have time to talk about whatever you want. You have been able to ask a lot of things today, haven't you?"

"Yes, I have, but I have other questions to ask you."

"Tomorrow."

"Tomorrow, tomorrow. Always tomorrow!"

"You have to be patient."

"Give me one reason to be patient."

"Have you ever been to an art gallery?"

"Yes, I have."

"Do you think that you were able to appreciate the last paintings of your visit in the same way that you appreciated the first ones?"

"You have a point there."

We stood up. I got to my room just slightly more alert than the day before. I went to the window. From there I could see the same part of town as from the terrace. As if by magic, it appeared that even the dogs had gone to sleep. I sat on the bed and tried to think about everything that Non-Professor O had told me.

Five

WEDNESDAY
On How to Live in a Virtual World

Much to my dismay, the rabbit was, once again, my alarm clock. I turned toward the wall, while the rabbit continued insisting that we hurry.

"Leave me alone."

Suddenly, I felt a strong desire of taking a bath.

"Go ahead. I will get there soon enough."

"You will be late for tea."

The rabbit disappeared behind the door. I got up and cheered myself up with a nice bath, which had the effect of stimulating my appetite, both in my stomach and in my head.

"Good morning!"

"Good morning. I thought you were not coming."

"How could you think such a thing?"

"You are late for tea."

"Oh, come on. Do not tell me now that you pretend to believe that silly rabbit...."

"You never know. Have you remembered another perplexity?"

"I will just have something to eat first."

"Fine."

I ate my breakfast. Silence reigned, and for a few minutes I enjoyed what was perhaps the most relaxing time since I had arrived in Arkadia, although it did not last long.

"So?"

"I do not know if I have told you, but I am fascinated by proverbs, and I believe that the fascination stemmed from what happened with the following one: 'The fish is the only one who is not aware of water.' I remember the moment I first heard it, and all the useless efforts I made to understand it. Until I recalled what happened to me one day I met a brilliant friend of mine in the street. He was quite peculiar. He stopped me and asked: 'Why is it that people believed that the sun goes around the Earth?' I answered, 'because it just looks that way.' Then he asked again, 'I wonder what it would have looked like, if the sun had been moving around the Earth?' Then I felt the stupidest Alice in the universe, because the point is it would have looked exactly the same! Such an anecdote helped me to understand the proverb because I saw myself as a fish that cannot be aware that it will always look that the sun moves around the Earth. I would like you to explain to me what happened there."

"I will try. Let me begin by summing up what we have been talking about.

From everything we have said up to this moment, it should be clear to you that the slife is the axis of Arkadian cognitive abilities. Starting at the moment of birth, the kognitive system fixes the moments in that individual's life, and it records them in the form of memograms, which along with the associations that are made between the elements of the slifes, will allow the Arkadian to deal effectively with the world. Likewise, we have seen that the memograms acquired by Arkadians in the first few years of life constitute their basic body of knowledge. At the beginning stages of development in an Arkadian's life, the foundations are laid for almost all the memograms. These will become the kognitive structures to which the future slifes will be incorporated, or with which they will be associated. Thus, in order for an individual to be able to behave like a conceptually competent adult, the baby Arkadian must have tens of thousands of slifes in the first months of life. I would not be at all surprised if the weight of these first memograms represents the great majority of the slifes that will be acquired in life. As I said, each situation creates a different slife, which would appear to support the opposite version, that life provides new memograms every day and that, until the quite end of life, the Arkadian does nothing but experience new slifes. However, adult slifes are usually based on episodes that have already been experienced. Although later slifes are the ones that will occupy or determine the life of the adult, childhood slifes are essential. In other words, even though an adult lives mainly on the slifes of childhood, and the slifes that fill up daily life are proportionally fewer, because they are the ones that are most decisive, they become the most important."

"Examples, if you do not mind."

"A doctor, during work hours, lives in a world that has been shaped by many crucial slifes, but they are insignificant compared to those he or she had during childhood. However, the childhood slifes create an invisible floor that the person walks upon, while those slifes related to medicine are more visible."

"All this is fine and dandy, but I would like you to explain how memograms participate in the life of Arkadians, and how they help in the comprehension of the world during each situation faced by the individual."

"Let us see. As we have said up to now, memograms are self-containing structures that record the panceptual characteristics of a personal experience. The idea is that all memograms that are relevant in a situation are activated in the current slife. Basically, their function is to establish a context and to transfer its signifikance whenever necessary. This way, the Arkadian can understand the situation, and decide the course of action to be taken. Therefore, we have an individual who goes through a familiar situation, in well-known surroundings and with a course of action that by this time is automatic. Then, those past slifes, now activated, guide the person, leading the individual through the situation with no need to analyze anything in particular."

"What do you mean by saying that the kognitive system activates the relevant slifes?"

"To make the story short, I could say that the Arkadian brain apprehends every new moment in the life of an individual with one question in mind: Which part of the past does this moment belongs to?"

"Clarify that, please."

"When Katherine gets up in the morning and walks toward the bathroom, her brain activates all the slifes related to bathroom-upon-getting-up-in-the-morning activities. More generally, the mechanism by which the slifes become activated is similar to what happens to us human beings when our brain activates a sphere of knowledge that we believe to be appropriate for dealing with a situation. To put it another way, it is the activation of cognitive processes based on an informative stimulus that 'notifies' the pertinent system. This occurs, for example, when an individual is told, 'Now I am going to ask you questions about animals,' and the individual then responds to the first question about animals more quickly than another person who had not been given the initial information. When Katherine is walking to the bathroom, her kognitive system activates all the memograms pertaining to 'bathroom,' which functions as if it were a context. Everything that Katherine sees, and touches, and all the activities she carries out are connected to the superimposed memograms of slifes that Katherine has had in her bathroom, and all other bathrooms in which she has been in, and everything that Katherine looks at, touches, or smells is done through these memograms."

"How can all the slifes be activated at the same time? According to what you have told me, the kognitive system can record tens of thousands of different slifes, in tens of thousands of distinct memograms, with hundreds of elements in each one, is not that right?"

"Yes, but the kognitive system is good at finding similarities, so that when a slife is like another, it is superimposed on the other one, and they end up fusing together. For this reason, perhaps it would be possible to identify in Katherine's brain the first day she went into her bathroom, but it would be impossible to recover her original slifes when she was already familiar with the bathroom, if we wanted to compare the bathroom slife of the 13 February six years ago and that of the 25 March four years ago. Thanks to this fusion or superimposing the slifes do not become too weighty, in the sense that when Erik is shaving, for example, he does not have the feeling that it is the 2,500[th] time that he is doing it, but one of many times that he has shaved. Furthermore, the fact that a slife is activated does not mean that it has to be conscious, or that the information is then 'subjectively experienced' the way a memory is. The activation of all the memograms relevant to that situation works like an invisible floor, like what is activated in your brain when you wake up at night and go to the bathroom without having to turn on the light. That ability to get oriented and calculate distances exists even though you have never counted the number of steps from your bedroom to your bathroom. That is something like what the activation of all the relevant memograms represents."

"What happens if the slifes relevant to that situation are not activated?"

"Something similar to what happens to us when unforeseen situations crop up. When an Arkadian has an unexpected slife, that individual has no idea what is going on until the relevant memograms are activated, which may take a few thousandths of a second, several minutes, or an entire lifetime. This 'not understanding what is going on' includes not understanding what we human beings would characterize as sensorial, perceptual, cognitive, and emotional stimuli. For a few moments, the Arkadian receives a flood of chaotic signals that do not fit with any past slife. Once the situation is associated by the kognitive system with some slife or group of slifes, then the situation fills out and begins to make sense. This can occur in any situation, and even in contexts that are familiar to the individual. One case that occurs frequently is when an Arkadian falls asleep for a little while in a place that is not familiar, say, in an airport while waiting for an airplane, and then wakes up all of a sudden. Right after opening his or her eyes, a moment of unease happens when what just seconds ago was a string of check-in counters is now seen as a group of meaningless shapes and colors."

"How can we relate this slife background to what human beings experience?"

"A possible relationship can be found, especially with what we understand to be knowledge, although how to associate the two is complicated. The main difference is that the concept of kontent does not have an easy equivalent in the human world. Kontents, like we saw, are not given to the Arkadians by the world, nor are they provided innately by the kognitive system; instead, they appear through interaction between the kognitive system and the world. Without the world, no concept of 'object' exists, since it is a type of connection among specific memories of objects that have been experienced, but without the kognitive system no objects exist either, since the connection is established through criteria that are peculiar to the kognitive system. Only through living life and interaction with the world kontents emerge in the slifes. Also, the differences between human beings and Arkadians extend to the concept of 'sense data' and 'thought processes.' As we saw, in Arkadia we cannot draw a line between the two, since the sense data is contaminated by the kognitive processes. The sense data do not exist independently of the kognitive data. The 'redness' of an apple is not sensorial data prior to the perception of the apple; instead, as we said, it shares in the panceptual party. Distinguishing between the sense data (what emerges from the nerve running from the eye or from the ear) and what we human beings would call a judgment of that data is not relevant. The Arkadian senses are useful for associating, or connecting the kognitive system and all its previous slife background to the world. The metaphor that we used to characterize this aspect of Arkadians was an orchestra. When an orchestra begins to play, the listener cannot separate the note of an instrument from its contribution to the melody. They are linked in time. No 'sound of the clarinet' occurs and then 'role of the note in the melody'; they are one and the same. We cannot separate the soundwave from the role of the instrument contributing to the melody. Similarly, each slife is composed of cognitive, perceptual, and sensorial elements, and the processing of the information that is noted through the senses is a complex group of different processes that includes sensorial ones and those called cognitive, in the case of human beings. The moral of the story is that, in the context of a slife, we cannot differentiate between the information of the senses and what modulates the kognitive system through its architecture. What we see in a slife does not correspond to sense data in a pure state. There is not perception and then judgment; instead, both are prior to the final stage, the slife. The opposition between perceptual processes and cognitive processes does not have much basis, since the perceptual processes cannot be divided by sense nor do the cognitive processes correspond to a general processor."

"Do you mean that every part of the brain does the same thing?"

"No. The kognitive system is extremely specialized when it comes to modeling the different kontents from the world, but at the same time it plays an extremely interactive and integrating role because no analysis is done without taking into account the other aspects of a slife. Each kontent is included in a general slife, and its shape, contents, and meaning are dependent on other aspects of the slife."

I realized that the air was agitated. The wind seemed syncopated. The dogs were barking more, and the seagulls were dipping and diving above our heads.

"Let us get to the point. What does Arkadian knowledge consist of?"

"To better understand what knowledge is in Arkadia, I will use a metaphor. The knowledge of an Arkadian is the *virtual world* in which he or she lives."

"Just what I needed, a virtual world."

"Let me explain. Each episode in an Arkadian's life creates something we call a slife that is recorded in the form of a memogram, which preserves the panceptual traces of the original episode. The set of objects, properties, and associations that would complement the memogram of a particular Arkadian creates a kind of world. A virtual world should be seen as a fictitious world that only K could conceive after analyzing the set of slifes that the individual in question has experienced. Note that not all the virtual world will be knowledge, but let us leave that for the moment."

"As you wish, but where is this virtual world represented?"

"Nowhere. The virtual world does not correspond to a representation of the world, nor does it correspond to the world that could be observed 'in' the kognitive system. The brain does not contain representations of the world. That world is nothing more than what complements the traces, imprints, that the original slifes left in the kognitive system. It does not consist of copies but of what gave rise to, or what theoretically gave rise to, the memograms of that Arkadian: the impacts of the slifes. Therefore, this virtual word that the Arkadians have should be understood as the world that would exist if we were to build a world based on the slifes of the Arkadian in question."

"I do not follow you."

"Remember the analogy of phantom limbs. As I told you, following the amputation of an extremity, nearly all patients have the illusion that the missing limb is still present. This illusion can persist throughout the amputee's life and can often be reactivated by injury. Then, we could hypothesize that a virtual world is some sort of phantom world; it is the world that was one panceived, but it is no longer there, even if Arkadians have a complete 'sensation' of it."

"Can you be more precise?"

"To be more precise we have to begin by defining the following:

Kognitive Homeostasis: The state of equilibrium between a kognitive system and its environment.

And with that we can define the virtual world of an Arkadian as:

Virtual World: The world that maintains the homeostasis of the kognitive system.

In other words, the virtual world would be that world that maintains the stability of the kognitive traces, the world that would not surprise the Arkadian, if that Arkadian were to give it a thorough examination. It can only be imagined by K, who is the only one who can read the kognitive imprints of the Arkadians and extract from them the kontents that correspond to the traces of the memograms. In the case of the phantom limb it would correspond to the limb that would fit the body image for that Arkadian."

"What makes up a virtual world?"

"In principle, the virtual world is made up of all those elements that complement the Arkadian's slifes. Therefore, this virtual world contains the kontents that the kognitive system has shaped, just as slifes are made up of the kontents that are discerned in a specific moment. That is, the virtual world consists of a set of virtual objects and virtual scenes."

"Examples, please."

"Suppose that in Erik's slifes the circumstances were such that:

'It only rains when there are clouds.'

The consequence of this is that in Erik's virtual world a kind of law exists that could be described as 'for it to rain there must be clouds.' This is a virtual law, in that Erik's kognitive system does not have it written down anywhere in his brain. It is as if this virtual world derived from Erik's memograms *satisficed*, from satisficing, this law implicitly, like the real world satisfices it explicitly. In the same way, if in all of Katherine's slifes horses cannot talk, nor do they have wings, we can say that in Katherine's virtual world 'horses cannot talk.' It is not that she has a file in her head containing that information, it is that if Katherine comes across a horse that talks one day she will be surprised."

"When we talk about slifes we will always have to refer to the whole virtual world?"

"No. For each slife a chunk of virtual world exists from which it is derived. This chunk of world can be defined as:

Virtual Perspektive: The part of the virtual world that maintains the homeostasis of a slife.

When Katherine has a slife in which the figure/ground consists of relating different past slifes under what human beings would describe as 'Katherine believes that unicorns live on the slopes of Kuo,' a chunk of virtual world exists derived from this slife in which unicorns are living on the slopes of Kuo. Therefore, to analyze this belief, in the human sense, deriving all of Katherine's virtual world is not necessary, just that part of it that maintains the homeostasis of that slife, or in other words, that part of the virtual world that is derived from that slife. In short, having a slife implies adopting a point of view in the virtual world, seeing this world in one way, noting aspects of all the slife background. Furthermore, the definition of perspektive allows us to define equivalence among slifes:

Principle of Equivalence: Two slifes are equivalent if and only if they share the same perspektive.

"Why do you say that this world is virtual? Is not it the 'real' world? If memograms are recorded through the slifes of an individual, then this world that complements the slifes is the world that participated in the slifes, and therefore it is the real world, isn't it?"

"True, but you must not forget that the kognitive system records the relationship of the kognitive system with the world, and that it is not exhaustive in its shaping of kontents. An Arkadian's kognitive system does not discriminate all the possible kontents of each slife, nor has it recorded all the kontents that another Arkadian may have detected, or that K would have detected. As a consequence, the world that complements, say, Katherine's memograms is not the real world, but the world discerned by Katherine, the world according to Katherine. Moreover, while discrimination is normally consistent and comparable among all Arkadians, it is not perfect, and what can happen is that something, such as a horse with a cone-shaped hat on its head, is seen not how it is, but as if the hat were attached to the head, as if it were a unicorn. However, you and I know that unicorns do not exist, even in Arkadia, and so the world that complements those memograms does not correspond to the real world. Thus, we would have to refer to a fictitious or virtual world. If Katherine were human, we would not be able to say that Katherine 'knows that unicorns exist,' only that Katherine 'believes that unicorns exist.' The virtual world is virtual because it does not coincide with what we call the real world. Also, it is not the real one because no virtual world maintains the homeostasis; instead, a set of possible virtual worlds maintains the homeostasis."

"Possible virtual worlds?"

"I will explain what I am getting at. If Erik visited the Leaning Tower of Pisa, he may experience slifes in which the Tower was leaning 5 degrees, thirty minutes. However, the world in which the Tower of Pisa is leaning 5 degrees thirty-three minutes can also maintain the homeostasis of these slifes, as could the world of 5 degrees and twenty-six minutes, and so on. Therefore, we can say that not a sole virtual world can maintain the homeostasis; instead, a set of possible worlds. Like on so many other occasions in Arkadia, we do not have measuring sticks that can indicate to us when a virtual world enters this set of possible worlds; instead, we would have to look at each specific Arkadian in each particular situation."

"Is that all?"

"No. The virtual world is not the real world also because it does not contain all the properties of that world. Thus, although all the apples that Katherine has eaten have weighed between 150 and 250 grams, it may be that Katherine was not aware of this kontent, even though it is a property of the 'apples eaten by Katherine.' Since the kognitive system has not established a connection among the weights of the apples, this kontent does not exist in her virtual world. In other words, the virtual worlds do not contain all the kontents that could have been panceived. However, because it is a virtual world, we can conceive it with holes. Finally, it is virtual because it can be a false or incongruous world. Katherine's virtual world is exactly complementary to her slife imprints, and this world does not have to contain all the logical consequences of its kontents, nor the natural consequences of these kontents. The virtual worlds can contain kontents that would not be possible in any physical world."

"How can that be?"

"I know, at first sight it does not appear possible that the virtual world of each Arkadian does not contain all the logical or natural consequences that could be derived from it, especially if this virtual world has kontents that behave logically or in accordance with natural laws. However, an Arkadian does not believe all the logical and natural consequences that are derived from the virtual world where he or she lives. So, for example, even though in the real world in which Erik lives an exact correlation exists between deficiency in vitamin C and the appearance of an illness known as scurvy, it does not necessarily follow that in Erik's virtual world a vitamin C deficiency causes scurvy. Only when that kontent is panceived by Erik will it become part of his virtual world. Thus, although the real world behaves in agreement with laws that may be inferred from its phenomena, the virtual worlds of the Arkadians do not have to be sensitive to, or have conceived, such regularity. Arkadians are not competent scientists; as a result, their worlds may not be quite 'real.' Only K's virtual world contains all the natural consequences of this real world. The virtual world does not contain all logical consequences either."

"Could you clarify this?"

"Let us suppose that Erik tries to convince Katherine about the truth of something by showing her that what he says is a logical consequence of his virtual world, like saying that 'Rain is made of water, rain comes from clouds, and therefore clouds are made of water.' However, Katherine does not immediately see this consequence; she has to reflect and assess the arguments. But if the virtual world of the Arkadians contained all the logical or natural consequences of this world, and Katherine knew that rain is made of water and comes from the clouds, then she would not have to reflect about whether clouds are made of water. She would only have to look at her virtual world. For this reason the Arkadian virtual world cannot be compared to the possible worlds of human beings."

"To what does the real world correspond then?"

"Intuitively, we could say that the real world is the world that exists independently of the Arkadians. This real world is inhabited by things, properties, relations, and even by events, like 'Brazil won the World Football Championship in 1994.'"

"So, what is the problem for Arkadians to think about such a real world?"

"You must not forget that the real world is hard to describe or characterize or conceive without recurring to the kognitive system. For example, as we said on Monday, to explain what a color corresponds to, we need to call upon the kognitive system."

"How is that possible? Do not things have their color? Is not the sky blue, roses red, and oranges orange?"

"No. Color does not exist as an intrinsic attribute of objects. Instead, it is a property of a special relationship between things and the kognitive system. To define a color, a combination of factors is required, such as the type of wavelength of the light reflected by the object, the texture of the object is surface, and other elements. In the same way, we believe that the solidity of a rock is a property of the matter, but empty space is the most abundant component of a rock, or of a reinforced door."

"Then, how are we supposed to describe these properties? Is the real world solid, does it have colors? Cannot we describe the 'real' world from an objective point of view?"

"If we opt for the most objective and basic description, the physical one, then we will run up against a problem upon creating the intersection between the real world and the virtual one, because Katherine may not sleep well anymore if

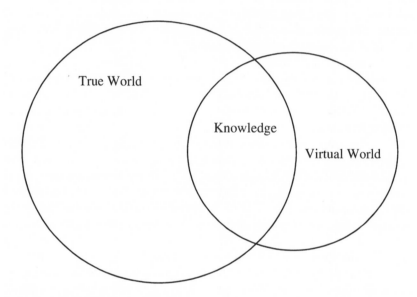

Figure 3. The Arkadian Knowledge.

she thinks that the most crucial component of the reinforced door of her house is empty space. Therefore, the idea of the real world that we want to address here has to be established at the same level as the one that an Arkadian has, in order to effectively evaluate if that person has or does not have knowledge about something. We have to be capable, for example, of saying if Katherine knows or does not know that 'snow is white,' independently of being able to say, in the terms of a physicist, that snow is neither white nor red, but that it is seen as white by the kognitive system. The real world exists, but it can only be characterized through the filter of the kognitive system and its properties. Consequently, I think the best thing would be to recur to a kind of 'true' world, the virtual world in which an omniscient being like K would live."

"Great, another world, to make things simpler."

"I am sorry, Alice, but we need this true world because it is the reference world. Basically, the true world corresponds to the world that contains all the kontents that could be discerned, and shaped in the real world from the perspektive of the Arkadian kognitive system:

True World: The omniscient world (or the world conceived by K).

Among other things, this true world gives us a lot of advantages. If we were capable in each situation, in each slife, of determining the true world and the virtual world of a particular Arkadian, we would see that areas exist in which the virtual world and the true world would be superimposed, and other areas where they would diverge. And in those areas where they overlap the virtual world would correspond to the true world. This allows us to define a quite crucial concept:

Arkadian Knowledge: The intersection between the virtual world and the true world.

Logically enough, in those areas with no intersection, no knowledge exists. Also, the part of the virtual world that does intersect with the true world can be of different magnitudes, ranging from zero to complete correspondence with the true world. The possibility of zero intersection is only theoretical, because in that case Arkadians would not be able to get by in the world. That the 'solidity' of the floor in the virtual world overlaps with that of the true world is enough for the intersection not to be zero."

"Then the true world is a kind of place of which the Arkadian will only have a shadowy idea, a world that can never be known?"

"No. The true world can potentially be experienced by Arkadians. In fact, everything that counts as knowledge overlaps with the true world of K. So, the problem for the Arkadian is not that this world is beyond his or her cognitive capability, but that there is not enough time to attain a complete overlapping."

"Suppose that all Arkadians were Katherine for that day in which she saw a horse with a cone-shaped hat as a unicorn, and no way existed to see a horse with a cone-shaped hat as a horse with a cone-shaped hat; it could only be seen as a unicorn."

"You are right that it may happen that the panception of a given kontent is incompatible, for all Arkadians, with the real world. The way that some memograms are created means the world that would be complemented with these memograms does not correspond with the true world. In the situation in which Katherine saw something that she interpreted as a 'unicorn,' we would have to say that Katherine's perspektive contains unicorns. Let us suppose that the bad lighting prevents all Arkadians, no matter how good their vision, from seeing that it is a horse wearing a hat; they all see it 'as a unicorn' instead of as a horse on which Erik had put a hat. In other words, under those conditions a unicorn is always what is seen, and that would even include K. So, in a sense, we would say that the true world also has unicorns, at least one, since in these lighting conditions always an overlap of the real-world-of horses-with-hats-in-bad-lighting and the virtual world that has unicorns will exist."

"And?"

"It would be wrong to infer from this that the true world, the world of K, must contain unicorns, and this is because the true world contains a lot of other elements that not only exclude the possibility of the existence of unicorns, but that also explain why something may be seen 'as a unicorn.' K knows other facts with which the unicorn can be undone; K has all the time in the world, and the capability to know that in those lighting conditions the thing is not a unicorn but a horse wearing a hat."

"What does it mean to say that he sees it as a unicorn? How can we describe this virtual world that does not coincide with the real world, if we can only see it from Arkadian eyes."

"Saying that Katherine 'saw the horse wearing a hat as a unicorn' means that under those circumstances, for that kognitive system, with that slife background, what she sees overlaps the kontent 'unicorn.' It is not that 'something' that looks like a unicorn is seen. It is seen the same as if looking at those drawings of unicorns that can be found in medieval books. Consider the Ames room. This room is a specially constructed structure designed by Adelbert Ames that provides the optical illusion that two objects of the same size appear to be of different sizes depending on the position they occupy in the room. To attain such an illusion the room is of distorted construction: three of the walls are actually trapezoidal and the ceiling slants markedly. However, because of the use of the cues of shading, linear perspective and interposition, the room appears normal to an outside observer. Looking into the room produces many illusions: objects and persons appear distorted especially in their apparent size, round objects appear to roll uphill. Another case is Müller-Lyer (figure 4) illusion in which two lines appear to have different lengths when they are the same."

"Right. What about it?"

"In circumstances the world looks as if it were a certain way."

"All Arkadians would see the room or these lines in the same way? Including K?"

"The truth is that I do not know how K would see those two lines. To begin with, the way in which the world is shaped depends on the slife background of that individual. Perhaps K's background would change the way of seeing that room, just like an Arkadian would have a different way of seeing that room if he or she had lived in a world in which the buildings were made like the Ames room."

"What are you referring to?"

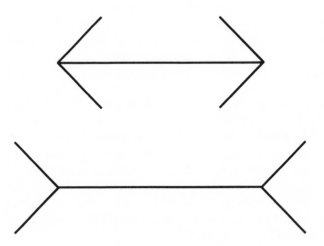

Figure 4. Müller-Lyer Illusion.

"The optical illusion of the Ames room arises from the fact that in Arkadia the walls and ceilings always have right angles, while the lines of Müller-Lyer are seen like that because in Arkadia the lines that end in open angles normally correspond with lines that are further away. Therefore, any difference in size relative to the same distance is taken as a difference in the size of the objects. If Arkadians had lived in a world of Ames then they would have become accustomed to estimating sizes in a different way. Arkadia has conditions allowing Arkadians not to believe these illusions, such as, in the case of the Ames room, when a ball bounces through the room, the illusion is broken. This may happen because the trajectory of objects is more fundamental in the Arkadian world than the right angles of buildings. In any case, K would know that it is an optical illusion."

"How is an invention, the product of an Arkadian's imagination, distinguished from an original slife? How is the 'real' virtual world differentiated from the 'imagined' one?"

"No difference exists. The imagination is made up of original slifes, and so it has the same quality as the real slifes."

"What about projects, or wishes? What, for example, do future plans correspond to, or dream houses, or the ideal vacation? Are these things part of the virtual world?"

"In a way they are, because 'the dream house' probably evokes in Erik, for example, a slife that he had on occasions when he saw a house that he liked, or another time when he saw the perfect location for a house. This way, the dream house is also a combination of parts of this world, although, as we will discuss later, the kognitive system has the capability to modify the remnants of a slife in such a way that its perspektive in the virtual world changes and can be considered as a new vision."

"Does the fact that each Arkadian lives in a virtual world mean that each Arkadian lives in a different reality?"

"No. You should not understand this as implying that individual Arkadians build their personal world through their abilities and slifes, and that each world is different and has different knowledge. Arkadians live in virtual worlds, but their kontents are, in large part, shared with K, because they overlap the true world. Therefore, Arkadians do not live in different realities, with different knowledge. They do not build their reality; instead, they discover the true world with their slifes as the starting point."

The first bolt of lightning left us quiet. The thunder came four seconds later. The air was heavy and damp. The swallows were there too, but I could feel they were anxious.

"A good storm is on the way."

We looked at the storm for awhile. I stretched my legs. The cat was hidden behind the balustrade, spying on us. It jumped over the railing, and sat down feigning indifference, until something made it run off.

"Now that I am thinking about it, what kind of relationship exists between truth and knowledge?"

"Once again, you have hit upon a sensitive problem. The truth is crucial to human beings. In Arkadia is also crucial, but no complete and direct correspondence exists between the two. For example, to be able to say of Catherine, the human, that 'Catherine knows that unicorns do not exist,' we need to fulfill three criteria. First, that what is being stated as known, in our case 'Unicorns do not exist,' has to be true. This is what differentiates the human sense of 'knowledge' from other states of the mind like beliefs, opinions, etc. 'Knowing' is a word with no middle ground; either you know or you do not know. This alone is not enough. Many statements are true, but not everybody knows them. Before Galileo, the Earth was round but nobody knew it. Consequently, in the case of human beings, the individual need be aware of the fact. In short, Catherine has to believe that 'Unicorns do not exist' for it to be counted as part of her knowledge. These two criteria are still not enough, since Catherine may say something like, 'I am convinced that the next lottery drawing will award first prize to number 11,250' and it may be true that first prize goes to number 11,250, with

Catherine believing firmly that she knew. However, this is not enough, because 'guessing' does not count as an act of knowledge. Consequently, the third requirement is that the individual must have good reasons, or proof, to believe what he or she believes."

"What kind of proof?"

"In the case of human beings, the reasons or proof come from direct observation (seeing something allows us to say that it exists), from reasoning (we can know that 'dead' is the opposite of 'alive' by simple use of reason), or from authority (if a scientist tells us that unicorns do not exist, we believe it)."

"So?"

"In Arkadia things are a little more complicated. First, establishing the criteria regarding the truth of a belief is not possible. Right now I cannot tell you why not, because we need ideas that I have not explained yet, although I will do so tomorrow. Just to whet your appetite, I will tell you that in order to establish the 'truth' of this virtual world in which the Arkadian lives, we should be able to transform her or his slifes in elements that can be true or false, that can be compared with something from the world that either confirms them or denies them. In the human world, this is achieved through language and its expressions, which is not possible in Arkadia. Arkadian language is not reliable in its ability to fix, relate, or characterize kontents; therefore, we must do without it. Since we do not have any other way of describing these true or false 'things,' we cannot say if they are or not."

"Hence?"

"In the case of Arkadians, the requirement can be made up for by the overlap of the virtual world and the true world. Since the true world is a world conceived by an omniscient being, it can be supposed that it is 'true' in a general sense, not in opposition to anything false, because we cannot characterize each one of its parts as elements that can be described as true or false. As a result, wherever it overlaps we can say that part of the world is 'true.'"

"Is that enough?"

"No. The problem for an Arkadian is how and when to decide if the worlds overlap. For the time being, considering that the overlap can take place and that we can refer to that circumstance as a possibility, and as such, it can be used as an argument is enough."

"But what you are saying is not possible. According to you, if an Arkadian says, 'Brazil won the World Soccer Championship in 1990,' another individual cannot respond, 'You are lying, because Brazil did not win the championship in 1990.' What has to happen so that someone can say, 'That is not true?' Or do Arkadians not say that kind of thing?"

"Okay, in Arkadia they do often use expressions that refer to the truthfulness or the falsity of something. What happens is that the map of what is true or false is not that easy to determine. As I said, the Arkadian language is not reliable in its ability to fix, relate, and characterize kontents; therefore, we must determine the truthfulness or falsity of things without it. We do not have another way to characterize these 'things,' since neither the virtual world, nor even the true world, can be said to be true or false. Arkadians can reach an agreement with one another, and in fact they do, to use the qualifier true or false in a subtle but simple and intuitive way to refer not to a sentence like 'Brazil won the World Soccer Championship in 1990,' but instead to confirm or reject the perspektive that a speaker adopts and that the sentence does not describe but indicates. This 'indicating' activity, as we will see tomorrow, is not guaranteed by the sentence, so they cannot merely trust the sentence. It is in the perspektive, which cannot be characterized with a sentence, where Arkadians fix truthfulness or falsity. True, the sentence is another aspect, a necessary one, of the act of agreement between the speakers regarding the perspektive to which they are referring. However, the Arkadians know, or sense by intuition, what the perspektive is with the help of the sentence in question, but also thanks to a lot of additional aspects. Consequently, if two speakers cannot adopt the same perspektive, then the sentence in not useful as a medium in which to establish truth or lies. For all of these reasons, when Katherine says, 'Brazil won the World Soccer Championship in 1990,' and Erik responds, 'That is not true,' what Erik is referring to with 'that' is not the 'human sense' of the sentence, 'Brazil won the World Soccer Championship in 1990,' but the perspektive adopted by Katherine regarding her virtual world, which is not comparable to Erik's perspektive, nor to the true world. That is something we will talk more about starting tomorrow."

"Tomorrow, always tomorrow...."

"Be patient. Let us go on to the second criterion. Here things are not compatible with human beings either. Just by referring to the virtual world of an Arkadian, it is already implicit that the Arkadian individual believes in that world, since it is the world that is derived from the memograms of the individual. If these memograms are formed with a world in which unicorns exist, then Katherine believes, in the human sense of the word, that unicorns exist."

"Does Katherine know anything true about the world, or not?"

"We have to address two questions to understand this aspect of the Arkadians. The first is, how do we assume that the memograms are reliable, that is, how is it possible for them to get by in a real world if they live in a virtual world? The second is, how can the Arkadians themselves know if they are close to or far from correspondence with the true world?"

"What are the answers?"

"The response to the first question is that, thanks to the conceptual competence that we talked about yesterday, Arkadians manage to get by in the real world. Conceptual competence allows us to say something quite vague and even changeable about the conceptual competence of an Arkadian, namely, that the individual can apprehend and deal with the world under normal conditions as if the individual had the concept, which allows the Arkadian to carry out cognitive activities in a satisficing way, as if he were competent in that concept. As we saw, Arkadians need not panceive the kontents of 'mass' and 'force' in order to interact with the physical world safely and effectively, since they only have to be sensitive to principles of kinetics and to kontents like 'velocity' and 'acceleration' in order to fulfill satisficingly the kognitive functions that the concepts of 'mass' and 'force' fulfill in the human world. The kognitive system constantly adjusts between the trajectory of a real object that moves in accordance to the principles of dynamics, and the trajectory of an object that moves in accordance to the principles of kinetics. This adjustment is made thanks, above all, to the sense of sight. Also, even if the adjustment is not made, the differences between the two trajectories are usually small and irrelevant to the interaction of the Arkadians with the world."

"And the second aspect?"

"The second one refers to how Arkadians can know if they are close to or far from correspondence between the true world and the virtual world. It might appear that in principle only K could determine it, since K is the only being that knows the entire true world. However, Arkadians can have indications that their virtual world coincides with the true world. And these indications are quite similar to what we said before was the third criterion for truthfulness to be granted in the human world. Such a criterion is what will allow Arkadians to conceive the degree of correspondence between the virtual world and the true world, and therefore determine what is knowledge and what is not."

"How can they do that?"

"Arkadians cannot have a complete verifying ability to establish if they 'know something' or not. They cannot know beyond a shadow of a doubt that the virtual world corresponds to the true world, because they do not have the absolute mechanisms that would guarantee it."

"So?"

"To guarantee the correspondence between their true world and the virtual world, Arkadians can use as a basis what we will call omniscient guaranties, or K guaranties, which mark the degree of verisimilitude of the perspektive, which is never absolute but greater or lesser:

K (omniscient) Guaranties: The conditions that guarantee the correspondence of the virtual world with the true world.

"Oh, dear heavens. Is it necessary to come up with this now?"

"Yes, but do not worry. These guaranties are quite similar to human conditions."

"Talk about 'quite similar' makes me a little nervous."

"Let us see. Some of these guaranties refer to common sense, like the guaranty of direct observation, social authority, or experience, and others that have been provided by science. Thus, the guaranty of seeing-with-your-own-eyes is a good omniscient guaranty. For example, Erik may say, 'Rik went to the movies because I saw him go in the cinema,' the omniscient guaranty being having-seen-it-with-his-own-eyes. But Katherine may say, 'Rik did not go to the cinema yesterday because he said that he did not,' the omniscient guaranty being what is called *the charity principle*, which consists of assuming, at least initially, that the perspektives evoked by some sentence are equivalent for any two Arkadian speakers and their true worlds. Another type of guaranty exists that human beings would say is more objective, as if Erik says, 'Rik kissed Nikole,' based on the K guaranty of a video in which Rik appears kissing Nikole."

"And in the case of Katherine saying the false statement, 'Brazil won the World Soccer Championship in 1990?'"

"In that case, the problem is that in Katherine's virtual world we have to say, 'Brazil won the World Soccer Championship in 1990.' However, Erik can say, 'that is not true,' because he has K guaranties that the event, whatever it may be, is closer to what is evoked by 'Brazil did not win the World Soccer Championship in 1990.' These guaranties can be quite diverse, such as that the event coincided with something personal that cannot be argued like, 'I turned 20 the day Germany won the 1990 World Championship.' Or they can be of a different type, like 'A book on the history of football championships says so.'"

"What or who decides what counts as a K guaranty?"

"The question of what counts as a K guaranty and what does not cannot be decided in advance, and it will not be resolved until somebody reaches the state of knowledge of K, whereby that person can know what does and does not sustain the correspondence between a virtual world and the true world."

"Surely something can be said, like that some K guaranties are worth more than others, or not?"

"Who or what decides on the strength of a guaranty is a hotly-debated point among Arkadians, but in general they have agreed that properties of the guaranties determine their greater or lesser verisimilitude. Direct observation is more verisimilar than observation by a third person. Variations exist for each guaranty, such as night observation being less verisimilar than daytime observation. Even contextual variations exist in which the hierarchies may be modified; if someone, for example, says that he or she is going to show an optical illusion, then the telling in the third person is more verisimilar than direct observation. We could compare the K guaranties with an analogue gauge. Sometimes, verisimilitude goes down because the conditions of omniscience go down, and at other times it goes up, for the opposite reason. In this sense, we can say that some guaranties are more reliable than others. In general, however, the K guaranties are evaluated for their verisimilitude according to two basic properties. One is the *intersubjectivity*, which means that everything that is accepted by more than one

Arkadian is considered more credible than what is accepted by only one individual. In the second place, we have the *groundability*, which means that everything rooted in the most primitive structures, in the sense of the slife development of the Arkadian's virtual world, will be more verisimilar."

"What do you mean by that?"

"'Seeing' a cow that flies is more verisimilar than reading about a cow that flies, because 'seeing' is more integrated in the foundations of the virtual world. Although we can also interpret groundability as having a larger base. Thus, if a doctor tells Erik that to get better he will have to take a medication, the doctor's recommendation will have more groundability than advice given by a non-doctor because it is based on knowledge that is based in turn on the history of medicine and on tests involving the medication. Aware of these aspects, Arkadians have established a methodology to guarantee knowledge according to the degree that it fulfills K guaranties. This methodology, you will not be surprised to find out, is science. Arkadian science, just like human science, is usually based on determining knowledge with the most K guaranties possible."

"Then Arkadian science is K?"

"No. Science must not be interpreted as the ultimate source of K guaranties. Science provides, beyond any doubt, the highest number and the highest of quality K guaranties, but science is not K. It is a little closer to K than the rest of the Arkadians. The access by science, or by the scientist, to the real world is also torturous. One scientist saying, 'The law of gravity exists,' and another one saying, 'The law of gravity does not exist,' does not allow us to directly access this fact, no matter how fervently Arkadians believe that this is so. 'The law of gravity' may correspond to nothing because, as I told you a while ago, Arkadian language does not describe facts, but indicates perspektives. The K guaranties sometimes follow a long and winding path before reaching the fact itself. When Arkadian scientists talk about the Big Bang, the fact itself is not observable, but one they obtain guaranties that it happened or did not happen in such and such way. A scientist saying, 'I have undeniable proof that the universe was created in a Big Bang,' should not be interpreted as if that scientist had the definitive K guaranties, because that would be hard to achieve. The only thing that can be derived from this statement is that any other K guaranty against this perspektive is much less verisimilar than these are. To sum up, the crucial thing is the K guaranties that each scientific assertion relies upon."

"Then how do we differentiate between Katherine saying, 'I think today is Tuesday,' and her saying, 'I know today is Tuesday?'"

"Yes, we must clarify the distinction between Arkadian knowledge and Arkadian belief because among human beings a great difference exists between what is knowledge and what is belief. A human being can believe something like, 'Paris is the capital of Angola,' and not be right, so it could not be said that this person 'knows' what the capital of Angola is. However, in Arkadia, we can only distinguish between knowledge and belief if we manage to superimpose the virtual worlds and the true worlds. We know that this cannot be done completely. Arkadians cannot distinguish by themselves between belief and knowledge until they have all the K guaranties, but since that is not possible, they cannot determine by themselves what is knowledge and what is belief. In other words, no kognitive state for Katherine exists in which her perspektive contains all the K guaranties for this perspektive, and another state that corresponds to what human beings call an opinion."

"So?"

"Arkadians adopt a pragmatic approach to expressions like 'I believe' and 'I know.' Since we have not yet talked about language, I do not want to go into details, but I will tell you that the use of 'know' versus 'believe' is just a matter of the degree of K guaranties. In some cases, Arkadians feel they have justification to state that the world is so and so, and they use, 'I know that...,' while at other times they are not so sure and they use, 'I believe that....' The sensation of justification is personal, to the point that in the same situation one Arkadian may use 'believe' and the other 'know,' and even at two different times, the same Arkadian may use both versions for two equivalent situations, but no kognitive difference exists between states of knowledge and belief."

"Examples, please."

"Erik may say, 'I know that Rik went to the movies because I saw him go into a cinema, even though he says that he did not, because I trust my sight more than I trust his honesty,' while Katherine, who was in the same place and saw everything with the same clarity, says, 'I believe that Rik went to the movies because I saw him go in, although I am not sure because he says he did not, and I trust him more than I trust my sight.' Or, one day Erik may say, 'I know that Rik has cheated in this poker game, because I feel it, and I am sure about what I feel,' but another time he may say, 'I believe that Rik has cheated in this poker game, because I feel it, although I am not sure of what I feel.' In short, the use of the terms 'believe' or 'know' only points to the degree of verisimilitude with which they indicate their perspektives. And from a third-person point of view, we could say that an Arkadian knows something when the K guaranties that sustain that Arkadian's perspektive overlap those of K."

"What about those situations in which Arkadians 'believe' that they know something, like how to ride a bike, but actually do not know? Or when they think they know where their car is parked, but they actually do not know? O when they think they know the answer in an exam, but they do not know it? What is a virtual world of Arkadians like when they believe something that they do not know?"

"It is as dictated by their memograms. Let us suppose that we are talking about playing chess. Erik believes that he knows how to move, for example, the knight. But it turns out that when he starts a game with Katherine he does not know where to put the knight. Suppose that nobody taught him how to play chess, and that Erik thought he had learned by watching other players. After watching a game for awhile, Erik experiences a slife that focuses on the movement as the figure/ground of his point of view as regards the moves of the knight. This figure/ground is superimposed, say, on a movement of a piece on the board that has a spatial relationship with the other pieces and the board. Erik has never experienced this particular movement, but he has had sensations of relationships between the pieces and the move. With this, Erik projects his future moves. But now, when he executes the move, Erik discovers that these past sensations are not finely-tuned enough to know if the move is correct or not. We could say that the problem is that he had not explored his virtual world well enough."

The church bells rang. I got up and was surprised to see that the storm had completely disappeared. The sky was almost clear, and the sun was shining again. Lots of different odors pervaded the air. The orange blossom was still predominant, but I could also detect others, including a hint of musk.

"Tell me something, does the virtual world include all types of knowledge? It is not the same thing to know that Paris is the capital of France, how to ride a bike, and that my mother will always love me, right?"

"Human beings, just as you have pointed out, distinguish between the knowledge that underlies abilities like riding a bike, driving, or playing the piano, and the knowledge that we could call knowledge of 'data' or of explicit information. For example, Catherine knows *that*:

(1) Paris is the capital of France.
(2) Fire is hot.
(3) Christmas is the 25th of December.

but at the same time she knows *how*:

(4) To swim.
(5) To play chess.
(6) To tie her shoelaces.

In the case of knowledge-*that*, knowledge of data, the object of the knowledge is assumed to be, in the case of human beings, a type of information represented explicitly in a code in the cognitive system that the brain accesses when necessary. While a big controversy exists about what kind of code represents that data, a general agreement pervades that a code exists. This code is comprised of basic elements, which, by way of rules of combination, create complex and articulated constructions. To put it briefly, it is a form of language of thought. Among the properties of this language is that when an individual accesses this kind of data, it becomes conscious. When we ask Catherine what the capital of France is, and she answers correctly, then we can be sure that the piece of data, 'Paris is the capital of France,' has become conscious in Catherine's mind, special cases excepted. Because of all of this, human knowledge-*that* is conceived as a data system recorded in an enormous database. On the other hand, knowledge-*how*, like skills such as riding a bike or playing the piano, does not appear to be based on explicit data that program or direct the behavior. A piano virtuoso plays without having a theory about his or her skill, and carries out the work to be done without a lot of deliberation, without being conscious of each movement. True, at the beginning, when these skills are being learned, human beings use a set of instructions that are given in any teaching process, like when someone who is learning to drive is told, 'to turn right you must turn the steering wheel to the right,' even though these instructions are normally forgotten in the long run."

"How is this applicable to Arkadians?"

"As for knowledge-*that*, in Arkadia nothing can be compared with mental symbols, phrases, or data that describe explicit data."

"I do not follow you."

"To help you understand this, I will give you the example of understanding a joke:

Definition of a Hippie: Someone who dresses like Tarzan, walks like Jane, and smells like Chita.

"That is a good one."

"Some of today Arkadians may find this definition funny, but some others, probably the youngsters, may not. Those who may find it to be funny share a lot of Western cultural background, which allows us to explain why we are not amused by the following:

Definition of a Hippie: Someone who dresses in rags, has an effeminate walk, and smells bad.

In order to explain the different effect of the joke we would need to adduce as proof an enormous body of cultural and psychological data, like:

• 'The main characters in the Tarzan movies are Tarzan, Jane and a chimpanzee called Chita.'
• 'Chimpanzees usually emit an odor unpleasant to human beings.'
• 'Hippies do not follow conventions regarding clothes and personal hygiene.'
• 'One of the conventions that hippies break is that of masculine and feminine roles in any daily activity.'

- 'The Tarzan movies are completely unrelated to hippies.'
- 'A type of person can be defined with reference to a combination of features belonging to another type of person, thing, or animal.'
- 'The Tarzan movies are light-hearted, and they do not try to make socio-political statements.'
- 'Hippies take their lifestyle quite seriously.'
- 'To make fun of someone is ideas the best thing is to compare them with something that is light-hearted and not quite serious.'
- Etc.

In human beings, this data is supposedly recorded in a database, while in the kognitive system of Erik this data is implicit in a set of slifes. So, simplifying things, one zone of Erik's virtual world, what we could call Fiktioland, contains the characters, scenes, and storylines of Tarzan. In another part of his virtual world, we would have the hippies and their socio-political context, including a series of characteristics regarding their appearance and way of life. The joke occurs because of the overlap between the two geographic areas of his virtual world, assimilating serious characters and details about them, with amusing characters and their details. Therefore, when we talk about knowledge in the knowledge-*that* sense, we have to translate the statements, the sentences behind 'knowing that...' to the virtual world of the Arkadian in question."

"To what does this translation correspond?"

"Translating a given piece of human information, of human knowledge to Arkadian knowledge is not easy."

"Can you give me some examples?"

"'Cats have four paws' could correspond to different slifes, one of them with a figure/ground in which the numerosity 'four' is placed as the figure, while the kontent 'cat' is the ground. The specific nature of this slife depends on the slife background of each Arkadian. We can generally suppose that it will always be different. However, we can also suppose that most will fulfill conceptual competence for what we could call the human conceptual structure that can be derived from 'Cats have four paws.' The crucial thing is that the format of knowledge is not based on a special code, but in slifes that are organized and connected."

"Can knowledge of 'how to build bridges' or 'how to play the piano' be explained in the same way?"

"We can say that knowledge-*how* is another element of memograms that are especially concerned with actions having a sequential dimension. And these actions are also kontents."

"Is that possible?"

"Yes. When I explained the slife with the bicycle, I told you that the sensations of riding a bike also count as kontent. The actions of the individual also remain in the memograms as remnants of kontents, and these remnants contribute to knowledge. The skills of an Arkadian, like adding, riding a bike, diagnosing diseases, etc., are kontents that have been repeated and related to each other and are preserved in the memograms. When Katherine rides a bike, the kognitive system activates the memograms that contain those kontents. Again, the relevant thing is that Katherine does not know how to ride a bike because she has a kind of instruction booklet in her kognitive system that she reads every time she gets on a bike. To exaggerate the idea, let us say that we could describe the instructions for tying shoelaces as follows:

(7) Hold a lace in each hand.
(8) Cross the laces so that they form an X.
(9) Put the end of lace A under lace B.
(10) Pull both laces strongly.
(11) Fold lace A in half so that it forms a loop.
(12) Wrap lace B around the folded end of lace A and the finger that is holding it.
(13) Put the middle part of lace B in the space occupied by the finger.
(14) Hold the middle part of lace B and pull both laces firmly.

When Erik ties his shoes, his kognitive system does not act as if it were reading the manual. The data is implicitly incorporated in the slifes that anchor the ability to tie our shoes. If we broaden the example we can say that any complex ability of an Arkadian corresponds to the effective articulation of the memograms that anchor a specific function. That is, the nuclei, the atoms of a kognitive ability are to be found in the slifes, and the more general abilities in the articulation of these slifes. In this sense, knowing how to play chess corresponds to a set of self-containing but related memograms."

"So no distinction exists between the two types of knowledge?"

"Only in that the knowledge-*that* corresponds to the knowledge in which language is the mode of access or of manifestation. To access, or manifest, the perspektive of Katherine that corresponds to human knowledge-*that* Paris is the capital of France we only have the phrase 'Paris is the capital of France'; we cannot explain it, for example, by pointing to the city of Paris on a map."

A ship is siren broke the silence. The dogs responded obediently. I stood up. The sun, low in the sky, bathed the slopes of the volcano with soft light, making it appear an intense green that appeared even more so because of the clean, clear air.

"What about learning? How do Arkadians increase their knowledge?"

"As we said, an individual's knowledge constitutes the virtual world that derives from its memograms. Therefore, in Arkadia learning is a process by which the virtual world is enriched. But, as we know, not all increases in the virtual world correspond to knowledge, since we also need to be superimposition or overlap between the virtual world and the true world. That is, we cannot count Katherine's unicorns as learning, nor can we count as learning her belief that she knows how to ride a bike when she has not learned yet. These modifications of the virtual world are not effective; they do not overlap with the true world. Only when Katherine's virtual world overlaps the true world of K will it be possible to speak of learning. Consequently, we will define learning as follows:

Learning: Any modification of a virtual world that increases the intersection with the true world.

This excludes any change, any new slife, from learning if it is not followed by an effective adjustment. Thus, in addition to not counting Katherine's modification of her virtual world with unicorns as learning, this definition excludes modifications in the virtual world of simple magnitude, like the fact that going up the same stairway every day reinforces konceptual connections but does not increase knowledge. The moment in which Katherine establishes a konceptual connection between the occurrences of the liquid that her mother pours in the glass and that comes out of the faucet, Katherine is reinforcing original knowledge. The same is true for the moment in which the slifes of going up different steps fuse together, or seeing herself in the mirror every morning after getting up. But if one morning she discovers a new wrinkle that she had not noticed before, then this episode will become a new, particular slife, and Katherine will learn a new kontent. Finally, the definition allows for the differentiation between the moment in which Katherine already knows how to ride a bike, or how to add, and the moment in which she still did not know."

"What are the mechanisms of learning?"

"With the definition of learning that I have set forth, by now you should see that an original slife must occur, in that a new unit of kontents is established in the virtual world. This element is the base of Arkadian knowledge; therefore, any effective incorporation that satisfies conceptual competence results in an increase of knowledge. So the description of Arkadian learning should be explained through the basic mechanisms for the forming of slifes that we have been talking about all along: discrimination and similarity."

"To what are you referring?"

"Among other things, the systematic repetition of a type of slife that has, as a consequence, more intense learning. Let us say that Erik has become an expert in distinguishing between male and female ducklings. The more slifes that Erik has had involving the sex distinction of ducklings, the more developed his ability to find differences between males and females will be, although at the same time, because of the contrary influence, he will be less able to detect similar elements between male and female ducklings."

"Is not that how we human beings learn?"

"Yes, some of the human regularities, like that of repetition and association, can be applied to Arkadians. However, these regularities are just the tip of the iceberg of Arkadian learning."

"Why is that?"

"I will explain. Let us suppose that when Katherine is a baby we perform the following experiment. Before each feeding, Katherine hears the sound of a doorbell. Suppose we repeat this slife many times. The systematic repetition of a doorbell followed by a feeding may lead to the appearance of a kontent of the 'doorbell-food' type, so that each time Katherine hears a doorbell, she starts to salivate, awaiting the arrival of the milk."

"Would not the same thing happen in human beings?"

"Yes. However, the Arkadian 'doorbell-food' association does not take place between two stimuli in a pure state. Instead, it is the association between complex slifes: the doorbell-slife and the milk-slife, the temporal-sequence-slife and a lot of other ones. The doorbell is only the tip of the iceberg of what occurs in that slife. We human beings can simplify these situations and say that Katherine associates a 'doorbell' with 'feeding.' However, if we wanted to apply this simplification in a predictive way to other situations, we would find a lot of failures. Some doorbells would work, but others would not; some temporal sequences would work, yet others would not; some rooms in which we repeat the slife would work, and others would not; at some times of day it would work and at others it would not; some stimuli that are similar to a doorbell might work, while others would not. In other words, each one of these slifes has its history that cannot be simplified. For this reason, it is not a simple association between stimuli that describes the experiment, but the understanding of a regularity in the part of Katherine's virtual world pertaining to feeding in a room at a time and tons of other characteristics. The explanation requires the characterization of the slife in all of its complexity, and the connections established between these slifes and their elements and many other slifes and elements, the nature of the particular figure/ground, and how it is transferred to other situations. So the slifes must always be analyzed in great detail. The problem in Arkadia is describing a slife, which is what will explain to us how Arkadians learn."

"What about learning 'by memory?'"

"In Arkadia, everything is learned by memory, although that expression is used only in this sense: the learning of surrogate kontents, like learning the multiplication tables, math formulas, or even verbal elements that correspond to data in the human world, 'Paris is the capital of France' or 'World War II lasted from 1939 to 1945,' etc."

"You have said that learning can also be the re-organization of already possessed kontents, right?"

"Exactly. We know that kontents consist of objects, properties, and the relations that are shaped by the kognitive system. We know that the only way to discern these kontents is through slifes. However, the kognitive system can also manipulate the virtual world. To put it briefly, a kognitive system can adopt a perspektive as regards its virtual world and modify the arrangement or the relations of these kontents. It cannot create new kontents, but it can manipulate them. If Erik says that 'Rik turned 20 yesterday' Katherine can learn something by relating the kontents 'Rik' and that of '20 years old.' Another way of re-organizing kontents is by transferring certain figure/grounds. If Katherine burns herself one day with the fire on the gas stove, and another day she sees fire in another place, Katherine can transfer the original figure/ground of 'pain' to this new fire without having to burn herself. In the same way, it can be her mother that manipulates the kontents, saying, when Katherine experiences her first burn, that 'All fires can burn you.'"

"Of what exactly does this thing that you call transfer consist?"

"To help you understand it, I would say that it is similar to what we human beings call metaphor. Metaphor is a phenomenon that can aid in understanding Arkadians, and especially in understanding how the mechanisms of Arkadian transfer work."

"In what way?"

"In human beings, metaphor has been explained in two ways: as an alter-ation of the literal meaning of a sentence or as a way of thinking. The first perspective contemplates metaphor as something outside of normal language that requires a special interpretation by listeners or readers. Some see in this a break with the literal meaning of the sentence, which is detected as an anomaly by the listener, who has to use strategies to construct the intended meaning. That is why metaphor is understood as a defect of the message to be transmitted. The sen-tence, 'time is money,' is interpreted as a metaphor in that the deviation must be completed with considerations like 'time is money inasmuch as it can be quanti-fied, saved, wasted, etc.' The capability to process the metaphor comes from our capability to see that the object or property that is being compared, time, shares properties and associations with the other one, money. Understanding the meta-phor implies transferring these properties from money to time. The second approach understands the metaphor as an integral part of thought and language, representing a way of experiencing the world. Those who defend this position consider that human conceptualization and reason are based on metaphoric mechanisms to which language gives expression. So, for example, there would be no distinction between the literal meaning of 'Time is measured with instru-ments' and the figurative meaning of 'Time is money.' This second approach is better suited to explaining how the kognitive system manipulates slifes, there being only one difference: it is a good characterization of how it manipulates slifes, but not of how it uses language."

"How is that possible?"

"We will talk about that tomorrow. For now, saying that the transfer process between figure/grounds is carried out by connecting two different slifes that are panceived as similar is enough. So, the phrase 'Time is money' may correspond in Katherine to an association that she established between a slife in which the figure/ground was her becoming aware that 'to carry out an activity requires time' and another slife whose figure/ground confirmed that 'to obtain objects requires money.' The crucial thing is that the mechanism is the same mechanism that the kognitive system uses to connect all kontents."

"Even a golf ball may be conceived as a metaphor for a soccer ball?"

"Yes."

"How can that be possible?"

"In Arkadia, the konceptual connections between a golf ball and a soccer ball originated in mechanisms that function in the same way as more sophisticated metaphors. Golf balls were connected to soccer balls because, to get the idea across, golf balls remind of soccer balls. And I say this process is metaphoric because it obeys the same transfer mechanism used by the kognitive system."

"I do not quite see it."

"It seems strange to you because you are not aware, nor are the Arkadians, of all the slife background of soccer balls and golf balls that is behind this comparison. The mechanisms that underlie the konceptual connections between occurrences of soccer balls and golf balls are no different from what occurs between hands and starfish, or between a chess game and war."

"But objective properties can be established as common between the two, and not between time and money."

"No. From the Arkadian point of view, the similarity of money and time is also objective. Time can be understood with respect to an organism that is living and finite, and that can be attributed 'quantifiability' and 'spendability' and other types of objective properties, which can also be attributed to money. Therefore, the metaphor reveals new kontents, which in some cases may have not been noticed by an Arkadian before adulthood, or perhaps they were not detected by anybody in the entire Arkadian community. That is why poets exist in Arkadia, so that they can detect the transfers that nobody has detected before."

"Only poets can detect these transfers?"

"Of course not. I was just simplifying things. Any Arkadian can invent new transfers. Moreover, some of them may become embedded as popular metaphors. An example of this would be proverbs, which correspond to a metaphoric transfer of folk wisdom."

"Does Arkadian science also produce metaphors when it comes across a new finding?"

"If the finding is completely new, then it will doubtless have the rank of metaphor. If Newton had been Arkadian, saying that bodies 'attract' other bodies would have to be considered a metaphor, since it uses a mechanism that can only be understood as a transfer of a previous kontent."

"Is not comparing gravity to attraction abstract? Does not it have something that the comparison between a starfish and a hand does not have?"

"The comparison of gravity to attraction has no more abstraction than a comparison between a starfish and a hand. The mechanisms are always experiential and based on panceptual similarities."

"Examples, please."

"Let us suppose that Katherine says that Rik is the 'rotten apple' of her class. Here Katherine is performing a transfer of the figure/ground of the konceptual connection 'rotten apple' in the context of 'not rotten apples' to the konceptual connection 'Rik' in the context of 'class.' As she says this sentence, Katherine literally superimposes the association between rotten apple and apples and that of Rik and the class. In this transfer we could imagine an amount of abstraction of the transferred element, that what the Arkadian transfers is a mental structure extracted from the specific memogram. However, we cannot get away with it, because the application takes place in the context of the slife. So, when Katherine transfers the figure/ground of 'rotten apple/not rotten apples' to the 'individual/class,' she transfers many of the characteristics of the original association and context, as little as this appears to be the case. Thus, it may be transferred that asfadfasd adfafasd addfasdfas:

(15) The most direct contact with a rotten apple/individual is what most affects a healthy apple/individual.

(16) If the apple/individual is removed from the class the process stops, unless the rest of the class has already begun to spoil.

Moreover, it may be because Katherine detects similarities that the connection between the two situations is established. However, the transfer will never be free of the original slife. When Katherine uses the sentence 'He is a rotten apple,' she is evoking that connection between the slife of seeing 'what a rotten apple can do' and the slifes of groups of people in which 'someone may have a spoiling effect because of their spoiled condition.' The fact that the connection is anchored in specific slifes excludes the need for an abstract property that has been extracted from somewhere, whether it be a slife or a mental state. When Katherine uses the sentence it carries with it the slifes in which it appeared, and it cannot be removed from them. If she wants to reflect, for example, on the characteristics of the contents of the sentence, Katherine finds herself trapped by the slifes she has experienced. The properties of the signifikance of a slife, which is what can be transferred, depend on the characteristics of the slife."

"What transfer mechanisms does the kognitive system have?"

"Transfer mechanisms are many and diverse, applied according to the relevance accorded by the kognitive system. Slifes that evoke in Arkadians statements like, 'Your attitude is indefensible,' or 'Their arguments were devastating,' or 'She was attacking throughout the entire debate,' reflect connections among different areas (for example, between combat and rhetoric areas). Such connections occur because some type of slifes remind of others. We can even establish areas of types of slifes that work more easily as sources of transfers. In general, these areas are the most primitive, in the kognitive development sense. Thus, one group of transfers is characterized through associations that have to do with bodily interactions among Arkadians. Among them are the slifes evoked by sentences like, 'Their spirits lifted,' 'He fell asleep,' 'She is in tip-top shape,' 'They have control over the country,' 'He is reaching for the stars,' and 'It is highly considered.' These transfers are based on the bodily slifes of lying down and getting up and their associations with consciousness, health, and power. In Arkadia, this type of corporeal transfer is quite popular, due to their slife importance and their having been in existence such a long time. But it is not the only area from which connections are established. The fact of the matter is that the majority of the original slifes had by an Arkadian baby start with bodily sensations, and their extension and importance appear to have become undervalued, since these slifes turn out to be extremely crucial for the rest of an Arkadian's life, and through them part of the Arkadian's later understanding of the world can be explained. The body is established as a central axis of many slifes, and therefore we must make use of it in order to understand the structure of the slifes, because these initial slifes comprise and structure later slifes. Bodily slifes are only one of many types of slife structure that can be significant for the transfer capabilities of an Arkadian. While corporeal slifes are frequent, many others are also present. Think about the Arkadian expression, 'To have a thread of a voice.' To compare a sewing thread with a fine and delicate voice shows that the metaphorical capability is an autonomous transfer capability, applied to any source that may be relevant. The understanding of the world by an Arkadian is based on the slow and subtle metaphorical capability applied episode by episode starting at birth, with the goal of understanding things."

"A problem arises here. If the past slife of an Arkadian is what counts, one situation to which the connection is transferred could be interpreted differently by different Arkadians, right?"

"Yes, in effect, but that is not a problem. Let us suppose that the origin of, or an important part of, the 'rotten apple' slife is what occurred to Katherine once when she left a basket of apples in the pantry, knowing that one of them had started to rot but thinking, 'Oh, well, most likely nothing will happen.' However, a few days later, when she went to get the basket, she found that the apples that were near the rotten one had in turn rotted. Suppose that this has never happened to Erik, and the rotten apples have never spoiled the healthy ones. Then, if they analyze Rik's situation, and they agree that Rik is rotten, it would be interesting to see that the transfer of the original slife involves a radical distinction in the way Katherine and Erik characterize the situation."

"How are individual differences in these aspects recognized?"

"That is a key point because it directly connects the capability to sustain many relations with another capability, that of transferring or looking for connections. The differences among individual Arkadians in what we human beings call intelligence has to do exactly with this ability to transfer more and to sustain more kontents in a slife. The intelligence of a given Arkadian is measured by the quantity of kontents that the individual can discern and by his or her ability to manipulate these kontents, to make transfers."

Right at that moment the sun disappeared below the horizon. And the ritual of disappointment, resignation, and good-byes was repeated almost exactly as it had occurred in the preceding days.

Six

THURSDAY
On How Words Lost Their Meaning

I do not know how I managed to do it, but I opened my eyes a few seconds before the alarm clock-rabbit filled my ears. I wanted to play a joke on the rabbit by getting out of bed, but I felt incredibly tired. I struggled against my laziness and got up. The sun appeared to be a little higher than it had been the first day. Other than that, everything was the same. I let the rabbit spew out his stream of little sentences without answering, for the first time, I think. As usual, he left after a few minutes, and that was fine with me. I took my time getting ready, and when I left I was in much better spirits than when I woke up. I went onto the terrace, and good Non-Professor O was still there. We looked at each other, smiled, and I served myself some tea while he prepared his pipe.

"Tell me something, do Arkadians speak a language? And if they do, is it like any of the human languages?"

"Why do you ask? Another perplexity?"

"Yes. It happened during holidays. I was on a trip with Cristina. We were lost out in the country. We ran into a peasant woman. We asked her for the road that would take us to our hotel. 'You are on the right road. Keep going straight and you will reach the town. At every intersection, go straight. And you will get there. Always straight, do not forget.' I do not think I have ever seen a road that went 'straight' and did not take you straight toward a wall, off a cliff, or into an argument. But I am sure that the peasant woman would die believing how 'straight' the itinerary is."

"I get your point. Arkadians speak and write a language that is quite similar in its formal aspects to the language of human beings. However, little of what explains how human beings use language will be useful to us in explaining the language of Arkadians. That is why I believe that to grasp Arkadian language you will have to put your imagination to work, because it cannot be understood through the basics of human language."

"I will try."

"Let us take it by parts. We will begin by remembering a bit about our language. In human beings, linguistic signs are a case of signs in general, for which we can determine the following relationship:

$$\text{sign} \rightarrow \text{object}$$

The sentence that defines this relationship was formulated hundreds of years ago: *Aliquid stat pro aliquo*. This is the scholastic definition of signs: something that 'stands for' something else. The sign ☎ stands for the objects we call 'tele-phone,' a red traffic light stands for 'obligation to stop,' the word 'table' stands for the object table. Representing is what makes a sign a sign, its being used in the place of the object, like an ambassador acts in place of her or his country. In general, three types of signs are said to exist: the *symptom*, which is something that indicates to us the presence of something else, like pus indicating infection; the *icon*, which is something that has similarity with the thing it stands for, like the picture ☎ stands for a telephone; and the *symbol*, which is something that stands for something else by convention, like a flag representing a country. The relationship established between each type of sign and what it indicates has a

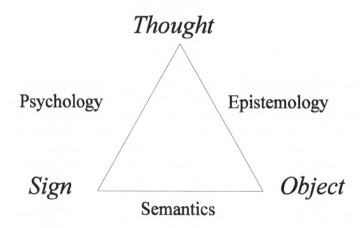

Figure 5. The Triangle that Represents the Relationship Between Minds, Words, and Objects.

special nature according to the type of sign. Thus, the relationship between a symptom and its object is one of naturalness, because nature relates pus to infections. The relationship between an icon and its object is one of similarity, since a picture of a telephone looks like the silhouette of a telephone. Finally, the relationship of a symbol with its object is arbitrary, since the community estab-lishes the relationship between a symbol and its object; authority, not nature or a perceptual likeness, establishes the relationship between the two objects. This relationship between object and sign, the representation, is not an aspect derived from objective aspects of the object and the sign, but it must consider the presence of a thought or an interpreter. Only a mind can decipher the operation of representation, because no matter how similar the sign is, or natural the relationship, it cannot be explained without awareness of the relationship. Therefore, the relationship does not involve two elements, but three: the *object*, the *sign*, and the *interpreter*.

"And?"

"The meaning of the relationship 'to stand for,' to represent, has not yet been fully explained. Since the first theorists came up with this definition, many people have addressed the issue of what the relationship 'to stand for' means, and they have searched for suitable possibilities for explaining it. Some say that signs stand for an object, while others say that the sign stands for a concept, or that any expression whatsoever stands for a meaning, or that any expression stands for a concept, or that the expression stands for an idea, and even that an association exists in which the expression stands for an object, that in turn is mediated by a concept. And so forth and so on. What does appear clear is that for the time being 'to stand for' is an expression still awaiting an interpretation."

"What about it?"

"The relationship between object, sign, and interpreter has been explained with the help of the triangle that appears in Figure 5. The triangle indicates the existence of different relationships. First, we have the relationship between language and the individual, or between the word and the concept. Then, the relationship between language and the world, which encompasses in a general way language as a code of signs, and its symbolic capacity, and the disciplines that study meaning. Finally, a relationship exists between the individual and the world, which is the area of study known as epistemology, or, the science of knowledge."

"Is it not the same for Arkadians?"

"No. In Arkadia we have to dispense with the basic triangle of concept, sign, and object in order to understand the way language works: no triangle exists. The main difference could be said to be that the sign does not acquire a nature that is different from that of other kontents; it appears instead as just another element 'within' the scope of the slifes. Linguistic signs do not appear in Arkadian kognition as an act of symbolization between a sign and an object, but as just another panceptual element that enriches slifes, and therefore, memograms, just as a sound or a color does."

"What do you mean by that?"

"Let us suppose that a word, 'water,' is discerned as a 'sound' kontent by Katherine as a little girl while her mother pours water in a glass. This kontent, the sound of the word 'water,' is incorporated into the slife with the same status as a lot of other things that are incorporated, such as the sound of the water being poured into the glass. From then on, the word becomes a part of her memogram of pouring water in a glass, of drinking it and quenching her thirst. The sound 'water,' discerned phonetically, is nothing more than another kontent of the memogram."

"I do not know what you are trying to get at."

"Let us follow Katherine a little more. Suppose that a few hours or a few days later, she wants to drink some water. Thirst has stimulated in her mind the activation of the memograms in which her thirst was quenched, and in them the word 'water' appears. Katherine wants to point out that she is thirsty, and it occurs to her to indicate her wish to drink by uttering the word 'water' since she cannot reproduce the sound of the water, make a glass appear, or show her thirst. Well, this action of imitating a kontent, the sound of the word 'water,' which evokes the memogram that the Arkadian wants to reproduce, is probably the first successful verbal action performed by all Arkadian children. With this new type of slife, the Arkadian learns to use utterances aimed at obtaining an objective, since the person associates the use of a kontent, the utterance of a string of sounds, with the reaching of his or her goals. Obviously, Katherine learns to use the word in kommunicative situations other than those having to do with 'drinking.' Thus, Katherine starts to use the word to 'say something' such as when she says to her father 'water' when she leaves the kitchen, meaning 'I just drank some water.' On other occasions, Katherine uses 'water' to evoke other types of slifes that she wishes for, always referring to the slife in a general way."

"I repeat, what about it?"

"Let us say that from then on out the word 'water' is said by Katherine's mother in other situations, and in these other situations, the liquid that we characterize as 'water' appears, even though Katherine does not know it yet. Sometimes, the water comes out of the faucet in the kitchen, at other times, it comes from the bathroom, sometimes, it is from a bottle, at other times, it is in a fountain, etc. Thanks to the functioning of the kognitive system, the occurrences of water in all these situations begin to associate with one another, konceptual connections are established among the kontents and the complete memograms. The slifes in which the word 'water' appears are enriched by these connections, each one individually. So, she says 'water' for something to quench her thirst, and also when she is looking at the sea, or when she hears people talking about 'water.' With time and continued repetition of the word in a variety of situations, the konceptual connections become richer and more robust. Katherine touches sea water, and the sensations are similar to the panceptions of water in her glass, or of the garden hose, or of the shower. Little by little, the utterance 'water' evokes all of these different situations. This causes confusion in Katherine because she still uses 'water' for only one of these situations. Eventually, therefore, she will need other elements to evoke the original situations, that of asking for a drink of water; that is, she will need other linguistic or kommunicative elements, while the word 'water' will start to evoke what all of these memograms have in common, the kontent 'water.' Thus, starting with the enrichment of the konceptual connections among slifes with water, and with the conditioning and strengthening of the connections among these properties of water that are panceived in several contexts, some of which are completely different, the use of that panceptual structure will evoke only those structures that are normally associated with the meaning, in human terms, of the word 'water.' The word does not stop being an element integrated in the past slifes, and the existence of the word cannot be considered to be a separate structure: the sound 'water,' like any other panceptual structure, cannot be understood independently from the memograms in which it is anchored."

"Is not that what happens in human beings?"

"At least it does not appear so. From what I have said so far, the most crucial thing is that the word enters a slife just like any other kontent. However, this particularity has a tremendously significant difference as compared to the other kontents, and this is because Katherine can manipulate this kontent, which she cannot do with any other panceptual element. She cannot manipulate the colors, the shapes, the emotions, as a word can be manipulated. This operationality of words allows Katherine to go much further than she could before that point. When Katherine learns to use and manipulate this kontent, she can return to the memogram whenever she says the word. And upon returning, she returns to everything that is connected to the memogram. Moreover, she can access the virtual worlds of her mother, her father, or whoever that happens to be listening to her. This is the crucial point in Arkadian learning, and a parallel can be found with human beings. In effect, the human step from pre-symbolic language to symbolic language is comparable in Arkadians to the step in their awareness that words evoke things that are not present and that they can evoke these things in other people as well."

"I still do not get it."

"Think about onomatopoeic words. Arkadian onomatopoeias are similar to those of human beings, and they also have the same characteristics of an Arkadian word; that is, they can substitute for it without causing any alteration in the kommunication. If Katherine's mother says, 'I do not know where the rrrmmm rrrmmm is,' while she is cleaning the house, Katherine will possibly know that she is talking about the vacuum cleaner. If the mother says it in the parking lot, she's probably referring to the car. Katherine learns to use the word in this way, by accessing the memogram or memograms in which it is inscribed. This slife, accessing a perspektive by way of a tool, the word, corresponds with the beginning of Arkadians showing linguistic capabilities."

"If you say so."

"Notice that the relevant characteristic is the deliberate access to memograms. This is the key moment in linguistic acquisition by Arkadian children. Right at that moment the Arkadian enters a new dimension, the linguistic dimension. Almost all of what we need to understand about the function of Arkadian language involves understanding this phenomenon, the moment in which the Arkadian understands that expelling air in a way can take him or her to a different moment in life, either past or future, if, for example, the idea is to get a drink of water, and it can take those Arkadians who are around the person to that moment as well."

"Is not that how human beings learn to talk?"

"Again, it does not appear so. Just like what happens in konceptual competence, Arkadian children do not develop their linguistic capabilities in precise stages, in a way that we can say that an Arkadian is in such and such stage. An Arkadian can even manifest characteristics of one stage and the next stage at the same time. Up to approximately a year and a half, the kognitive system records and organizes the slife base upon which the adult kognitive life will be developed. In this stage, comprehension appears to come before any type of linguistic production; the child understands words but often will not know how to use them. At the beginning of language use, Katherine does not recognize that this panceptual structure, one of many, can be linked to some element of the memograms. Instead, she takes it as a new element, like the first time she sees a snake or listens to a flute. That is, it begins by being incorporated as just another kontent, but after a while, when Katherine discovers that it can evoke a type of perspektive, she only has to discover which perspektive it is. What often happens is that the word is easily incorporated into an active konceptual connection in the slife background. Thus, when Katherine incorporates the word 'water,' the konceptual connections upon which the word is incorporated are already established. The relations among the occurrences of the liquid water in bottles, faucets, kitchens, bathrooms, swimming pools, the sea, and fountains already exist, so the word is easily anchored."

"Is that enough?"

"No. We must not think that the anchoring is perfect, or better, that it adapts to the conventional uses of the word. The mistakes observed in language acquisition have to do with the incorrect activation of pertinent kontents. Words tend to evoke slifes or types of slifes in a general way, like a child saying 'ball' to refer to all play activities. Later, starting with the first part of the third year of life, the Arkadian child starts to fix konceptual connections with increased intensity. At that moment the child learns to anchor words in kontents, although the anchors are provisional. For example, the word 'ball' will evoke those memograms in which the child is playing ball, but also those in which the child points to the moon or to a spherical fish bowl. The child uses the words to evoke kontents having what human beings call perceptual similarity, from 'ball' to 'moon,' or functional similarity, like how to use the word 'water' for any slife in which thirst is quenched. Children become accustomed to what we say generalizing, but they always do it within panceptual criteria. They do not anchor the word 'woof' only in the dog kontents, but may also include cats and horses, while they do not evoke 'tables.' At this age they are still not sensitive enough to the manipulation of the konceptual connections to be able to include them in other slifes in such a way that allows for hierarchical relationships to be established. Children will not acknowledge that a dog is an animal and will state instead that it is only a dog. This probably responds to the idea that the child can use the word to evoke previous kontents, but wherever no konceptual connection exists, the anchoring will not fulfill the usage conventions of the word. In many cases, especially at the beginning of a child's linguistic life, the words evoke konceptual connections that are partial or incorrect. However, these mistakes are not a serious problem, and many Arkadians even use words with unstable evokations, but this does not prevent them from leading perfectly normal and effective lives. Soon after, because the basic kontents of the virtual world have already been settled, children enter a stage in which they quickly anchor the words to the kontents that are relevant to satisfy their kommunicative needs. Between the ages of two and a half and six years, they can learn from 4 to 15 words per day."

"From 4 to 15 words per day? That is tremendous!"

"Not really. Almost the same thing happens to human beings. The word being incorporated into previous konceptual structures also explains the speed of the incorporation of the lexicon in quite a short time. Since the konceptual structures are already established, the only thing left to do is to incorporate the words. From then on, when the words have been anchored in kontents equivalent to those of the community, syntactic competence begins to be developed. The child enters a situation in which the virtual world is shared, above all, with his or her parents and classmates, and the child has also acquired the ability to manipulate, to evoke, and to kommunicate effectively with fellow Arkadians. So, kommunication between parents and children, between students and teachers becomes smoother and more effective."

"Are parents and teachers crucial in language acquisition?"

"Yes and no. In all learning processes determining factors on the part of the community exist, including the family, teachers and classmates, which will permit the conventional use of words. In any case, Arkadian individuals are autonomous enough to anchor words spontaneously and to come up with the rules for coordination among them. For this reason, the child and the community live for a time in different virtual worlds, which does not make kommunication easy. A father explaining to a child, 'Daddy puts a seed in Mommy' is at a pointless activity until the child has had the relevant slifes. The interaction with the community stimulates linguistic development and conditions the anchoring of words."

I got up and walked around the terrace. I looked at Kuo. Something strange was happening at the top. It had become a river of clouds that were flowing down the slope, and then thinned out and disappeared. It had changed into a waterfall of clouds. I pointed at the volcano.

"Is that normal?"

"Yes. It happens once in a while, especially when a difference between the humidity of the coast and mountain occurs. It is impressive, isn't it?"

"It sure is."

I watched the show for awhile.

"Is that enough for today?"

"No, no. I could spent hours watching it, though."

"I understand."

"Maybe it would be good if you could clarify for me how everything you have explained so far is different from human language, because I do not see it."

"Differences exist, and not small. But for you to understand them we will have to make a little incursion into human language."

"I do not like incursions."

"Traditionally in human beings is said that language, words, refer to the objects of the world. Let us take the sentence, 'Einstein smoked.' The name 'Einstein' serves to refer to a person that existed and won a Nobel Prize, while 'smoked' refers to an activity, smoking, engaged in by some people that also exist and can be described in the world. These theories receive the name *referential* theories, because they are based on the idea that words refer to, indicate, something in the world. 'Einstein' refers to a person, and 'smoked' to a property of that person. In principle, the simplest case of reference is that of proper nouns. Human beings understand that proper nouns are like labels for people, places, etc. It makes no sense, for example, to ask what *Arthur Miller* means apart from enabling us to talk about an individual. Human beings recognize that just using the name is not enough; something of context also has to be added. If someone says 'He looks like Albert Einstein,' we can suppose that the speaker and the listener know to whom the expression is referring, although maybe one of them does not and therefore the name alone is not enough."

"So?"

"The simplest meaning theory sustains that the meaning of a word is its reference. In its most common form, this theory defends the position that the reference points out elements of the world:

Proper nouns	*refer to*	individuals
Common nouns	*refer to*	groups of individuals
Verbs	*refer to*	actions
Adjectives	*refer to*	properties of individuals
Adverbs	*refer to*	properties of actions

These referential theories allow for the identification of the meaning of a sentence based on the analysis of its components. So, to know the meaning of the sentence, 'Einstein smoked,' we have to break it down in parts: the expression 'Einstein' on the one hand, and 'smoked' on the other. The meaning of the sentence, 'Einstein smoked,' depends, therefore, on the name 'Einstein' referring adequately to a specific individual, the person who discovered the formula $E=mc^2$, and also on the property of 'smoking' applying to Einstein. Similarly, the difference in meaning between the sentences, 'The Eiffel Tower is in Paris,' and 'The Eiffel Tower is not in Paris,' comes from the fact that the sentences describe two different situations. If we consider that the sentences were said at the same time about the same city, we could say that they are incompatible, that one of them does not describe the situation truthfully. This situation can be described by many different sentences and in many different languages. The sentence, 'Paris is the capital of France,' has the same meaning as, 'The capital of France is Paris,' 'France's capital city is Paris,' or 'París es la capital de Francia.' All of these sentences are said to have the same meaning. All of this cannot be applied to Arkadians, because when we say that the sentence 'Paris is the capital of France' means that Paris is the capital of France, we are using language, and as I said, Arkadian language is not useful for referring to the objects or properties of reality. However, for the time being, let us accept the idea that we understand each other when we say that Paris is the capital of France."

"Accepted!"

"Let us continue. Referential theories are *compositional*, that is, the meaning of a sentence is a function of the meaning of its components. Each component of a sentence has a reference, and the combination of the elements of a sentence combines the references of its elements. The rules for combining the elements, the syntactic rules, establish the relationships between the references to the elements in such a way that the final meaning can be established automatically. This means that if we know the references of the nuclear elements of a sentence, such as 'Einstein smoked,' that is, if we know the references of 'Einstein' and the application of 'smoked,' then we can know the meaning of the whole sentence. Thanks to the compositional property, human language is *productive*, that is, if we understand the sentence 'Einstein smoked' we can understand many other things in which one of the elements appears, such as 'Erik smoked' or 'Einstein drives.' Yet, not all of it is that simple."

"I suspected as much."

"The meaning of a sentence does not depend only on the words that form it; the kommunicative context in which the sentence is uttered also influences it. A sentence used to express a thought can be used to present the thought as something true, or at other times as something false, or at still others is hinting at irony. So, when Catherine says to Eric, 'You are really smart,' because he has solved a problem that she could not do, the meaning of the sentence can be derived from her words. However, if she says the same thing to him when he wants to trick her, the sentence is not uttered in a true sense, but in an ironic sense. Utterances are used not only to transmit thought, but also to reveal the attitude of the speaker as regards a thought. But we can leave that for another day."

"Whatever you say."

I looked at the volcano again. The spectacle continued, and the contrast against a clear sky made it even more impressive. Swallows had shown up too, fluttering in circles in front of the terrace, and demanding my attention.

"How are we to understand the meaning of Arkadian words then?"

"We just said that words are anchored in slifes just like any other kontent, like color or shape, although unlike these elements, words can be manipulated. So if the word is a panceptual trait that allows us to manipulate its memograms, then it is not symbolic. The word is not used as representation of something; instead, the word acts more like a switch."

"A switch?"

"That is just a way of putting it. What I mean is that Arkadian language is not based on a symbolic relationship between sign and meaning but on a relationship that I will call *evokative*, because its function is to activate the memograms and kontents in which the word is anchored."

"Examples, please."

"Let us take the word 'north.'"

"North?"

"'North' according to the Arkadian dictionary is 'the cardinal point located in front of an observer to the right of whom is east.'"

"That is ridiculous."

"No, it is not. The dictionary is not trying to define the term, only to evoke in the reader the slife that will allow for the application of the kontent 'north.' This may be fulfilled if Erik has experienced a set of slifes in which he has learned to use a compass to locate the cardinal points and apply this knowledge for navigation, with the use of maps. In other words, I am saying that in Arkadia no separation exists between 'north' and all the other kontents that occur in the slife in which the word is used, and I also say that this set of kontents, activities, and not the object itself, allows the Arkadian to get oriented and to know what 'north' means."

"Although it may be complicated, it must be possible to find an explanation for the relationship between Arkadian words and the objects of the world. Does not Katherine end up understanding that the word 'water' refers to something that is water?"

"In the original slife, the word 'water' is anchored as a panceptual element. However, Katherine experiences new slifes in which the word 'water' is associated with the liquid that her mother pours for her, and then that her father pours, that comes out of a faucet, or out of a blue bottle, then out of a white bottle, then

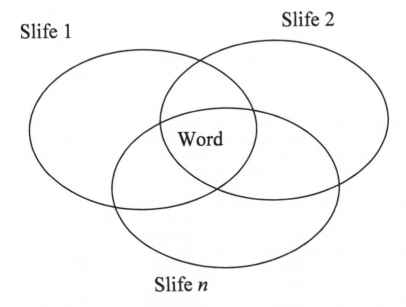

Figure 6. The Meaning of a Word Is the Perspektive Derived from All the Past Slifes that Evokes.

the refrigerator, then the cupboard. As a result, the same word appears in a larger number of slifes, and using it does not evoke just one memogram anymore. Instead, it has become more sophisticated and evokes a set of memograms that gets bigger and bigger. So, with time, Katherine enriches the connection structures among the occurrences of the word 'water,' in such a way that its uses are conditioned. These uses could, after a long time and great effort, be described by a human being, by using the set of characteristics that would correspond to the conventional sense held by the human community, as illustrated in Figure 6."

"So the word stands for the kontent 'water,' right?"

"No. In human beings, if we say that the word evokes kontents recorded in the memograms, then we could say that 'it stands for' the kontents of that perspektive. It would also appear that the Arkadian could use the word in a symbolic way, in the sense that the word takes the place of the kontent. However, the word must not be taken for the kontent or the slife, but for what evokes these things."

"Can we discover the meaning of a word, then?"

"By analyzing the virtual world of whoever is using it. In Arkadia, semantiks does not concern itself with words, but with the virtual world. Semantiks is not the characterization of the meaning of words, but the characterization of the virtual world of each Arkadian, and the way that a person's memograms and konceptual connections satisfice the conceptual competence of kontents."

"I am not quite following you."

"Let me give you a culinary analogy. Suppose that Eric says that the wine he is drinking is 'a full-bodied wine.' If we attempt to understand the sentence through the words that comprise it, we will find that no term corresponds strictly with a kontent. The word 'body' is a short cut to understanding different peculiarities of a series of wines that do not have much in common with each other except that they could gather under the description 'wine that goes well with stews,' which only complicates matters further because the word 'stew' corresponds not only to stews but a lot of different foods that are cooked in a particular way. In other words, the use of the definitions of words is not useful for understanding the sentence; some previous learning must exist about the world of wine and gastronomy. As a result, discovering the meaning of this sentence is impossible, if we have not grasped that it corresponds to experiences that Eric has had tasting different wines, tasting the same wine in different years, making comparisons among wines and with other beverages, or with combinations of wines and food, etc. Somebody unfamiliar with the terminology of enology would not understand the sentence through explication of the concepts. Moreover, a lay person in enology might understand the meaning more easily with a sentence like, 'Dry summers make the vines thirsty to the point that the wine that is extracted gains, among other things, organoleptic properties to face dishes that are high in protein and animal fats.'"

"So?"

"What I am saying is that Arkadians understand all words the way we human beings understand 'a full-bodied wine,' by evoking the culinary and enological slifes instead of semantically dissecting the sentence. In Arkadia, a word evokes a slife, with a derived perspektive, which is specific for each Arkadian. The words do not confer the meaning, but lead to a slife with a perspektive of the virtual world. If in that world no kontents exist that a wine expert has identified in his virtual world, then knowing the dictionary meaning of the terms that appear in the sentence serves no purpose."

"How do Arkadians distinguish between the anchoring of the words in situations he is not interested in, like when they hear the word 'atom' while watching a soccer game, and situations that do interest them? Or in the case of the capital cities of the world, without having to travel to them each time that they are mentioned?"

"To begin with, the word is not permanently anchored in the first slife in which it crops up, just as a konceptual connection does not become established forever more between the first two slifes of a kontent. A child learns the word 'car' because it is rooted in a konceptual connection in which the child has understood how the community uses the word. Such a connection that already existed is associated with other slifes recorded in quite different contexts. Thus, only at the end have in common those aspects that fulfill conceptual competence for such a kontent. Furthermore, no problem is posed by the fact that the objects, the properties, or the associations that are evoked by a word are not present when it is learned or used. Again, the crucial thing is that the conceptual competence of the kontent be respected, and this is a slow process, conditioned by the community, family, classmates, teachers, etc., that indicates to the Arkadians when their use of the word is understood and when it is not, when they are applying it conventionally and when they are not."

"But some words cannot evoke the slifes that they are involved. Say, a telephone number, or a multiplication table, or a list of the Presidents, or the capitals of the world. In these cases, Arkadians appear also to have words that are comparable to those of human beings, but since they cannot be experienced I wonder how they understand those words and what they evoke. What slifes are evoked by these terms? A telephone number would have to evoke the datebook in which it is written, and the list of Presidents could evoke a rainy and boring afternoon at school."

"You are right."

"Fantastic!"

"But only in part. Up to now we have talked about words that may be involved in normal slifes, but many other words cannot be understood like the word 'love,' because the kontents that they should evoke are not panceivable by the kognitive system, such as the word 'atom.' In these cases, the slifes evoked are what we call surrogate slifes, that is, the set of slifes that guarantee the conceptual competence for the word. Therefore, the words that are anchored in these slifes end up evoking the surrogate slifes of the kontent. In some other cases of surrogate slifes, like 'The number pi is 3.14159+,' what is evoked is the sonorous or graphic memory of the sentence, as if it were data in itself, or one line from the times tables that are learned in school. So, 'The number pi is 3.14159+,' evokes a sonorous or graphic memory, like the words of a song in a foreign language."

"And?"

"Another thing we have talked about is that the words that evoke surrogate kontents are much more unstable, and their applications sometimes vary. This has occurred in the history of Arkadian culture, since some of these signs have changed their surrogate slifes when something new about the kontents has been learned, like when it was discovered that atoms do not have only neutrons, but are composed also of other elements. This property is a good way to distinguish the evokation of surrogate kontents from that of genuine kontents. So, the evokation of the word 'love' would be difficult to modify, because the slifes in which it is anchored are slifes that cannot be modified all at once. Yet, the words that are anchored in surrogate slifes can easily change their evokation if the guaranties that must be incorporated as new slifes are changed."

"What happens, for example, with signs, like

♂

and the 'male gender' or between the sign

☎

and the object called 'telephone?' How can these relations be explained?"

"The nature of these relations is like that of other relations that can be established in the framework of a slife. We have the word that evokes a kontent, but we also have a sign. When the two are associated in a single slife, and in that slife we establish a stable relationship between them, then when we see the 'symbol' the connection will be evoked. But this is an association 'within' the slife."

"So who decides the correct meaning of the words?"

"Not just one meaning for words exists, and less a correct one. However, we can say whether or not an Arkadian uses a word in a competent and conventional way."

"When does that happen?"

"An Arkadian uses a word conventionally when its evokation is equivalent to the perspektive that it evokes in the community. And an Arkadian uses a word competently when the konceptual connections in which the word is anchored fulfill the conceptual competence for that connection. An Arkadian uses the word 'north' well if the connection in which it is anchored satisfices the conceptual competence for 'north.' In the same way, 'Einstein' is understood by Katherine if the word 'Einstein' evokes in her memograms that satisfice the conceptual competence for an individual."

"What does 'Einstein' requires to satisfice its konceptual competence?"

"The conceptual competence for an individual includes many different elements, such as the ability to recognizing Einstein in a picture, knowing that he won a Nobel Prize, etc. Such a konceptual connection may correspond to a continuum that can range from an initial konceptual connection, that does not have conceptual competence of the kontent, to the connection that completely fulfills the conceptual competence. Likewise, the word 'Einstein' may activate in Katherine a memogram in which someone mentions Einstein Street in Berlin, or it may activate a konceptual association that contains all the biographical data of the physicist Albert Einstein. If, for example, 'Einstein' is anchored only in a slife in which someone said to Katherine that 'Einstein Street in Berlin is really lovely,' then she will barely understand any of the sentences that include the word 'Einstein.' Similarly, if the word 'smoking' evokes only the occurrences that involve pipe smoke, and not cigarette smoke, it may be that she has not yet reached conceptual competence for 'smoking.'"

"So can a word be used incorrectly or not?"

"The word is not what is used correctly or not correctly, but whether the perspektive that it evokes is the equivalent for that community. The incorrect use of the word should be understood therefore as being anchored in a konceptual connection that does not evoke an equivalent perspektive in fellow members of the community. At best, and if the individual manages to perceive the discordance, the word will end up anchoring itself in the konceptual connection that evokes the slife with the shared perspektive. The community of Arkadians is exercising in this case a restricting mechanism."

"Examples, please."

"Let us suppose, for example, that Erik's father likes to come off as if he knows a lot and speaks well. Let us say that he has heard many times on television the word 'languish,' and he thinks it sounds elegant. However, the word evokes in Erik's father a slife that is superimposed on that of 'being lazy' instead of 'becoming weak,' which is what it should be superimposed on. The difference that exists between the correct or incorrect use of the word is a difference between the evokation being equivalent or not."

"In any case, and even though you always respond the same way, I still think that if each kontent is different for each Arkadian, then how is it possible for two Arkadians to understand each other? If the words depend on the kontents, and these depend on the slife background of each individual, then nobody in the Arkadian community shares the same meaning for the same word, and therefore, kommunication is impossible, isn't it?"

"I already told you the answer to that yesterday. To prevent each Arkadian from living in his or her autonomous, isolated world, that has different properties, we need a guaranty that the kontents will leave traces that have the same or comparable characteristics in all Arkadians, and this is provided by conceptual competence. Erik's 'Einstein' kontent may not contain Einstein's feet, while maybe Katherine's does, but since both satisfice the conceptual competence of 'Einstein' no danger exists of non-kommunication. Crucial is that the Arkadian community shares enough slifes with equivalent perspektives for a given word, and that in the relationship among Arkadians in the world words are inscribed in memograms that can guarantee conceptual competence. But it is not just that. The life of an Arkadian ends up including such enormously varied and rich slifes that several of them seem to become superimposed in all the different Arkadians, giving shape to perspektives that are equivalent to those from the true world. The use of language that evokes these slifes fixes, in the long run, a range of shared perspektives."

"I am still not convinced. With human beings, words have a clear meaning, while in Arkadia words are not quite precise."

"More or less. A word being just another panceptual part makes it a dynamic element, so that its evokation changes as the virtual word and its connections become richer. Also, the Arkadian does not control the evokation of the words. The evokative power of a word will always be beyond the will of the Arkadian. Words are not innocent for an Arkadian. Words like 'death,' 'orgasm,' and 'fart' inevitably evoke slifes, regardless of the context in which they are used. The most common thing is that each word does not evoke one kontent, but it is anchored in many kontents and it has associations with all of them. For this reason, polysemy, understood as the evokation of different types of slifes, is much more frequent than monosemy; words are polyevokative. A single string of sounds intervenes habitually in numerous memograms in which different kontents are manifested. Just as the color red can participate in many objects, the word 'bank' can intervene in numerous memograms. The more restricted the variations, the more direct, quick, and univocal the evokation will be, and therefore it will be better. As a result, the kognitive system tends to use different words to evoke different kontents but no kognitive reason exists why it should not use the same word to evoke different kontents. The crucial thing is that the kognitive system distinguishes between the kontents, and in order to do it has quite a few indications, such as the context in which it occurs."

"Does any difference exist between a word that Katherine understands, for example 'red,' and another one that she does not understand, like 'quark,' but which she has heard many times? Do not both evoke slifes?"

"The difference is that 'quark' does not evoke a perspektive that fulfills conceptual competence for 'quark.'"

"Suppose you are right, but that does not make sense to me, for we cannot know if they are saying, or thinking, something true or false about the world. Imagine that an Arkadian travels to France and asks 'Where is the Eiffel Tower?,' and someone answers, 'The Eiffel Tower is in Chicago,' while another answers, 'The Eiffel Tower is in Paris.'"

"Okay. The case that you are presenting has two problems. In Arkadia, the sentence, 'The Eiffel Tower is in Paris,' does not describe anything about the world, but evokes a slife with a perspektive derived from a virtual world. The second problem is that even if somebody from outside, like us, can say something about the world by using the sentence, 'The Eiffel Tower is in Paris,' we cannot know, from what an Arkadian says, if he or she thinks something correct or incorrect about the world. Perhaps the person who says that it is in Chicago really wanted to say that it is in Paris, and the opposite for the person who says it is in Paris. Let us see if I can solve these problems."

"Yes, let us see."

"For each sentence, although it appears that the meaning appears in a direct way, the explanation should follow the same path taken up to now, evoking a slife with a perspektive in the virtual world of each individual. However, when someone says, 'The capital of France is Paris,' and 'Einstein smoked,' these sentences seem to take us directly to an objective fact without having to pass through the memograms of any Arkadian. But it only appears this way. As we said yesterday, it is not a matter of whether the Arkadians satisfy the sufficient and necessary conditions that can be described with the sentence, 'Katherine's dog is a terrier,' or with, 'Einstein smoked.' This is the same problem as we had with concepts. In sentences like 'Einstein smoked,' how is it decided if some one smokes or not? What substances have to be inhaled to be considered smoking? Does smoking three cigarettes per week count as smoking? And so forth. No, the question is that even if objective data (facts, states of things) described what these sentences mean in Arkadia, we would have to go through Arkadian virtual worlds to identify what these sentences mean. The words of Arkadian language are not symbolic because they do not represent anything about the world, and their combination does not say anything true or false about the world either, although the virtual world can overlap the true world. As a consequence, since in Arkadia we cannot say that the sentence, 'The capital of France is Paris,' is true, we need to transform it into a personal attributive sentence like the following:

For Katherine, the capital of France is Paris.

The guaranty that all Arkadians attribute the same meaning to the sentence, 'The capital of France is Paris,' follows from:

For Katherine, 'The capital of France is Paris,' has the same meaning as for Erik if and only if the slife evoked in Katherine by the sentence, 'The capital of France is Paris,' is equivalent to the slife evoked in Erik by the sentence, 'The capital of France is Paris.'

The guaranty that the two slifes are equivalent follows from what we called:

Principle of Equivalence: Two slifes are equivalent if and only if they share the same perspektive.

The guaranty that somebody is saying something true about the world, as compared to, 'The capital of France is Madrid,' follows from:

'The capital of France is Paris' evokes in Katherine a slife that *satisfices* the conceptual competence for 'The capital of France is Paris.'

"Is that enough?"
"No. We need a way to explain how the combination of words can maintain the conceptual competence."
"Meaning what?"

"Let us suppose that Katherine hears the sentence, 'Einstein smoked,' for the first time. In order to know what this sentence evokes, we need combination rules for the kontents that comprise the sentence, 'Einstein smoked':

For Katherine, 'Einstein smoked.'

And:

'Einstein smoked' evokes in Katherine a slife that combines the evokation of 'Einstein' and of 'smoked.'

The guaranty that all the Arkadians attribute the same meaning to the sentence, 'Einstein smoked,' follows from:

For Katherine, 'Einstein smoked' has the same meaning as for Erik if and only if they share the perspektive derived from the slife evoked by the sentence, 'Einstein smoked.'

"What happens when we refer to non-existent objects or creatures, like 'unicorn' or 'Bugs Bunny?'"

"If we understand that words do not refer but instead evoke slifes with derived perspektives, then no problem arises. If Katherine has had contact with toy figures, illustrations, or whatever, in which these words are anchored, then the evokation will take place starting with these kontents."

"What about 'World War III could start tomorrow' or 'The 1940s?'"

"In the first sentence, no reference object exists, at least for human beings, but in Arkadia no difference exists between 'World War III could start tomorrow' and 'next Friday.' In the end, it must be pointed out that the properties of these sentences can only be determined for each Arkadian at a particular moment, never like sentences that characterize an univocal meaning. As for 'The 1940s,' the evokation may be that of the konceptual connection shared by slifes that occurred in the same temporal situation. 'The 1940s' is anchored in the spatial-temporal context configured by particular events, films, biographies that have been perceived as comments about the 1940s. By itself, it evokes nothing, but it connects with all those films, biographies, etc."

"What slifes evoke words like 'here' or 'now?'"

"That is an interesting aspect. It is not possible to univocally analyze the sentence, 'Then he did that, because she did not want to go there,' through the meaning of the words, since those words only have meaning in a context. For this reason, it is said that words like 'I' and 'here' and 'now' are elements that help point out contextual individuals, things, or properties. They help the kommunicators establish a frame of reference for the discourse. Arkadians use this type of expression a lot, just as often as do human beings. However, difficulty exists in understanding how the expressions are used, because their interpretation is so easy and no calculation or sophisticated interpreting mechanisms are needed. The idea is that if the emitter and the recipient share perspektives, it will be easy to remove the ambiguity from the particles. Thus, if they say, 'He did that,' Arkadians will normally evoke a slife the perspektive of which contains one person of the male gender, and only one action performed by that individual. In other words, the condition is that the people listening must share the perspektive in their respective virtual worlds. This way, the only thing they have to do is to use these words in each perspektive."

"But, how do they learn to use expressions like 'here' or 'there?' From what you have said up to now, the words are switches. How is it possible that 'here' or 'there' always evokes the right distance?"

"These expressions are incorporated into language not to point out specific places or times, but to point out contexts that correspond with points in their spatial-temporal axis."

"Here we go again."

"I am referring to the fact that each slife is structured in a spatial-temporal environment around the individual, marking the position of that individual as regards the surroundings. So, after a few months, a baby's virtual world is articulated on an axis of which, if she or he could, the child would already say that things are 'here' or 'there.' Therefore, if the two speakers are situated in a similar way as regards their perspektive, then the memograms that guarantee the expressions conceptual competence will be used naturally. For each kommunicative situation, Arkadians establish a personal axis, that will later correspond with the spatial axis of 'here' and 'there,' and also the temporal axis of 'a while ago,' etc., upon which the discourse is processed. The expressions direct the evokation in each situation of a type of position on this axis."

"Examples, please."

"If Erik and Katherine go to a party and talk to each other, the location as regards the other people and objects will be independent from the discourse. If Katherine tells Erik, 'Caviar is served over there,' Erik will know, because the axis of the situation is already established, that she is referring to some location within the place where the party is happening beyond the reach of Katherine's arms, but closer than the next house. If Erik says, 'He told me that no more people are coming,' Katherine will probably know that even though many individuals of the masculine gender are present 'he' is the one that has a more important role in the kommunication, no doubt the host. And this is how it works for any situation."

"Are you going to explain all the problems this way?"

"Not all of them, but many of them. I will give you an example that is not strictly linguistic, but that illustrates the relationship between language and the virtual world. Let us suppose that Erik receives a bouquet of roses at his house with a hand-written card. After reading the card Erik says 'Whoever sent me the bouquet has pretty handwriting.' Let us say that Katherine sent it, but Erik does not know that because the card is not signed. We, who do know, can say, 'Erik thinks Katherine has pretty handwriting,' since the card was written by Katherine. However, if we look at it from Erik's point of view, the sentence does not represent his point of view, because he does not know that it was Katherine who wrote the card. We know that the handwriting that Erik likes is Katherine's, but he does not know it. He can only say, 'I think that whoever sent me the bouquet has quite pretty handwriting.' In other words, the sentence, 'Erik believes that Katherine has pretty handwriting,' is ambiguous, since it describes at the same time a fact of the world and Erik's possible knowledge. In Arkadia this problem is easy to explain, and this is because Arkadian sentences do not contain their meaning; instead, the rest of the slife and the derived perspektive have to be incorporated for the sentence to be analyzed. For us, the perspektive of the slife evoked by 'Erik believes that Katherine has quite pretty handwriting' has as a central element Katherine writing a card that is to be received by Erik. On the other hand, the perspektive derived from Erik's slife does not contain Katherine, but instead a person without a face who sent him flowers."

He stopped talking for a moment and stared at me.

"If you want, we can make the problem more complicated."

"Just what we need!"

"It will not take us long. Imagine that Katherine is the daughter of the town's mail carrier, although this is something that only I know and, to further confuse, I have whispered to Erik without you hearing me that the daughter of the mail carrier is the one who sent the roses. Let us suppose now that the three of us are Arkadians. So, if, when all three of us are together, I say, 'Erik thinks that the mail carrier's daughter has quite pretty handwriting,' Erik and I are going to agree that it is true, but you are not going to agree because you do not know that Katherine is the mail carrier's daughter, although you know that Katherine sent the roses. In this case, the difference is that in your virtual world Katherine does not have the konceptual connection with the mail carrier through the relation 'daughter of.' Erik does not either, but at least he has created a connection with who it was that sent him the roses."

The cat appeared on the balustrade, jumped and walked slowly toward us. It stopped, we looked at each other, and then walked elegantly away.

"Everything that you have explained to me is what Arkadian linguists study?"

"Yes, but the way they do it will appear odd to you. Books about Arkadian linguistics do not analyze sentences. The analysis of meaning in Arkadia is directly related to slifes, the elements that make up slifes, the dynamics that they have, what a perspektive is, and how it is shared. "

"A linguist without words?"

"Not exactly. As I have said, the sentence, 'John went to the movies,' does not have just one meaning in Arkadia. What Erik says to Katherine when he tells her that Rik has gone to the movies is inscribed in a virtual word that is shared by the two and in which each word, the length of the sentence, the moment of discourse, the prosody, the emphasis, and the moment in history can evoke many different slifes with equivalent perspektives, or not. One may go in the sense of 'That rascal Rik told you yesterday that he would never go to the movies,' and another may go in the sense of 'Tomorrow we can ask him what film we should go and see.' In the strict sense, the perspektive does not have one sentence that describes it. Therefore, in Arkadia collecting sentences and analyzing each one separately would be like analyzing the notes of a song to discover what emotion they evoke."

"So linguists in Arkadia have nothing to do?"

"Of course they do. For one thing, they study slifes. But another thing they do is to study the manipulation of the linguistic kontents, which would give as a result the description of a universal grammar of the linguistic kontents that an Arkadian can establish in slifes. This task is much more interdisciplinary than in the human world, but in Arkadia specialists also exist in different areas. Some, for example, deal with aspects that are merely syntactic, which are similar to those of human beings."

"How can they have a syntax similar to the human syntax?"

"Merely because the kognitive system has the capability to combine and articulate words in a way similar to how human beings do it. Syntax, like many other processes of kognition, consists of functional specialization that the kognitive system manifests and that is translated into its ability to combine words according to a series of rules that can be described by a grammar that is equivalent to that of human beings. Just like in the other functional areas that we have talked about, these rules are understood as a part of a type of slifes, and within the general context of panception. The rules that we ourselves can describe upon observing Arkadians may appear equivalent to human grammar. However, Arkadians fulfill these rules *satisficingly*. The rules represent a good generalization of the syntactic competence of the Arkadians. Yet, they are neither a series of rules implicitly represented in the kognitive system, nor are they followed, just like the rules of chess are not followed when one is a proficient player."

"To what is this functional specialization similar?"

"In the form of analogy, syntax would be a kind of activity similar to one that allows us to estimate complex relations that exist between the musical notes of a melody, or between the different pieces in a game of chess. By this I do not mean that the system that carries out linguistic processing is the same as that which explains competence in music or chess, but that the type of relations among the elements is comparable in these areas, although each field has its slife context and biological conditioning. Right now I am unfamiliar with the exact nature of this functional specialization, as I am unfamiliar with the functional specialization of the other processes. However, the kognitive processes in charge of combining and revealing syntactic structure are quite sophisticated, as those of human beings are. Through these processes Arkadians are capable of combining words, and these combinations, like any other element of kognition, are also rooted in slifes, as other kognitive activities are like balance, estimating distances, and other activities that appear simple but are actually complicated to perform."

"What do you mean by saying that the syntax is anchored in slifes?"

"That a syntactic rule is anchored in slifes means that each one of the syntactic combinations will evoke a type of relation between linguistic objects. Every one of these combinations has been established previously in a specific slife context, and therefore it has its slife reality. Some can even come from the transfer from slifes in a different, non-linguistic area."

"Is the rule learned or is it already in the kognitive system?"

"Neither one nor the other, and not both at the same time. As we said on Monday, in the appearance of kontents, we have a predisposition of the kognitive system and a property of the world. The combination of both, plus the slife background, 'create' the kontent."

"Give me some examples, please."

"Let us take a look at the case of prepositions. The basic konceptual connections to which prepositions become incorporated have to do with spatial and bodily relationships. So, the preposition 'in front of' is learned by reference to bodily slifes in which 'in front of' is used, as if the syntactic association in which 'in front of' appears were compared to the relationship with the objects that are 'in front of your body.' These relations are established as of the moment that the Arkadian child learns to situate herself or himself in space and to relate the surrounding objects with that space. This eventually gives rise to a series of slifes that could be considered like a kind of bodily schemes. Later, with the arrival of language, these konceptual connections are transferred to the slifes belonging to each preposition that modify the detail of these kontents. The interaction between these slifes of bodily schemes and the preposition slifes end up mutually evoking one other. Thus, when an Arkadian says, 'I am in a car,' 'I am in front of a car,' 'I am behind a car,' or 'I am on top of a car,' or 'I am under a car,' the person listening can easily evoke a spatial relationship. All prepositions need not be anchored in slifes that focus us spatial-bodily relationships. Some prepositions, like 'against' or 'from' may be anchored in another type of relationship. Therefore, we must not expect an easy, ordered, and stable correspondence between the syntactic functions of words and the words that we study. The rules in which language is structured, morphology, syntax, and so forth, are rules that have to be rooted in slifes, slifes that have as relevant object a word or words as well as other types of relations that are not necessarily linguistic. That is why syntactic combinations will conserve many non-linguistic aspects from the slifes in which they are anchored. Maybe for human beings the rule that governs the sentence, 'Maria is chasing John,' is the same as, 'The police are chasing John,' in the same way that the rule, 'John is being chased by Maria,' is the same as, 'John is being chased by the police.' However, in Arkadians, the words evoke in themselves a series of slifes in which the rules that govern them are anchored, so that the evokation of the sentences is also conditioned by these slifes. This is why many Arkadians will likely take awhile to figure out if 'Maria is chasing John' is the equivalent of 'John is being chased by Maria' or 'Maria is being chased by John.' However, it will not take any time at all to know that 'The police are chasing John' is the equivalent of 'John is being chased by the police' and not 'The police are being chased by John.'"

"They are quite complicated, these Arkadians."

"This is complicated to describe, but the kognitive process does not have to be any more complicated than analyzing the facial expression of another person."

"What kind of grammar do Arkadian linguists study?"

"In linguistic processing, the syntactic, semantic, and pragmatic processing cannot be distinguished. In Arkadia, the division between semantics, pragmatics, and syntax is artificial, since many of the combination rules that human beings call syntax are based on principles that have nothing to do with syntax itself, and that have more to do with matters of a pragmatic nature."

"Are all the different processes coordinated with one another?"

"Exactly. The different linguistic and non-linguistic processes that work in parallel and jointly are not watertight, or modular, but have many and constant interactions. Each Arkadian individual processes the panceptual structure of the sentence from the syntactic, semantic, and pragmatic point of view, which allows for the point of view that is being processed in the virtual world to be directed, supported, or denied."

"Does not that make things complicated?"

"Not especially. As I said on Monday, the structure of the kognitive system is plastic, and it shows a great capability for functional specialization, which does not lessen its capability for interacting, and coordinating all these functions jointly and effectively."

"Are speaking and reading different? For a human, the written word and the word you hear appear to be the same, but an Arkadian must feel a clear distinction between written and spoken words."

"The step from words as oral kontents to words as written kontents is interesting. Going from what is spoken to what is written is a big leap between objects with a completely different slife nature. This is why the process takes place slowly, in kognitive terms. The Arkadian first has to associate the verbal string formed by a set of partial sounds, and each sound with a set of visual signs. At the beginning, the Arkadian cannot associate a word that is heard with a visual word, because the slifes are so different. Associating sounds with letters is difficult for them because panception has no predisposition to find that these two entities are comparable: they are not similar from the panceptual point of view. The capability, therefore, must be learned over and over again in order to be able to convert the association between spoken words and written words in a stable, robust, and long-lasting association. It is like when they learn the multiplication tables. This association may be different for each individual, because it does not respond to an association based on kognitive architecture, as the predispositions to recognize faces or separate objects appear to be. An Arkadian can manage to establish the association spoken sign-written sign in many ways, and that is why different ways of reading exist."

"Why is it harder to read than to speak?"

"In general, achieving comprehension through reading is more difficult, because the slifes that must be manipulated through reading are more modern in kognitive development time, and they are more meager than spoken language. Oral language is more easily connected with slifes, while reading requires a subsequent process that is the translation of the oral language, the one connected to the slifes."

I looked toward Kuo. The river of clouds had almost disappeared, but the orange tinge caused by the setting sun made it that much more spectacular.

"What you are telling me is strange. According to what you have said, if the written language also depends on the slifes of each reader, then texts cannot preserve knowledge about anything, and so they are more or less empty. However, Arkadians appear to learn things from their books, or don't they?"

"You are partly right. Texts, like the ones appearing in a book, have no meaning themselves, for they are only instruments that can or cannot modify the virtual worlds of the Arkadians. The author of a text uses the words that evoke in her or him a series of slifes, which is what she or he wants to transmit. However, once they are on paper, or wherever, these words only guarantee kontents for the author, because only the author can know if these words evoke the points of view that he wants to evoke. Books only make sense if the virtual worlds of the author and the reader are equivalent."

"I do not know if I am following you, but this reminds me of one of my friends who says a text is written in a kind of code that each reader has to decipher on her or his own, and that therefore each reader makes his or her interpretation of the text read."

"It may remind you of it, but it is not the same."

"But it is similar."

"In a way. Yes, some people say, in the human world, that the text has to be applied to each reader and that the text depends on each reading, but this cannot be applied to the Arkadians. These authors believe that the text has a life of its own, a code, that the reader has to explore. And since each reader has different tools and capabilities, the world and the content extracted from the text is personal. However, in Arkadia, the text does not exist as a container of some interpretation. The text contains nothing: it is not subject to an interpretation. In Arkadia the text need not require analysis, but the virtual worlds of the author, of the reader, of the use of tools available to the author and the reader. No premises, principles, rules, explicit data allow for the interpretation of a text in accordance with each reader or group of readers. We need each reader in order to know what perspektive is derived from the text."

"So the content of a text is something that is subjective?"

"Again, no. What I just said does not imply a subjective interpretation, but that the text is only one part of the reading process. The mistake does not lie in considering that reading cannot be objective, but in considering that we need only the text. So, just as in the future sensors and computers may be developed to give us the taste of a wine, perhaps in the future we will have sensors and computers that give us the meaning of a reading for a particular reader."

"So where is the knowledge of books?"

"Knowledge, that in human beings is preserved in books, is not in books, nor is it in Arkadians, but in the complex formed by books, and the Arkadian community. An Arkadian can derive knowledge from the virtual worlds of the community with the help of books and texts. For this reason, trying to analyze a text on its own would be like trying to determine the taste of a wine by considering only its chemical composition. To find out about its taste properties, we need the kognitive system."

"Is this valid for all kinds of texts and knowledge, including science and art?"

"Yes. This is valid for all Arkadian knowledge, including what we human beings would call the sciences, the humanities, and even art. For example, the scientific knowledge held by Arkadians cannot be derived only from their texts. Science is in the slifes of the scientists, and scientific texts are useful only for evoking and organizing these slifes. Even what might appear to you an undeniable fact, that light travels at a speed of 300,000 km per second, is not a piece of information that can be interpreted without first passing through the slifes of the scientists who have reached this conclusion. In order to discover what the Arkadian scientists want to say, we would have to enter the world in which the physical kontents of time and space have a dimension that is only comprehensible in the context of that world. Among themselves, scientists can use the information about the speed of light without a problem, because the scientific community possesses implicit knowledge, and also some shared slifes and perspektives can be derived from the texts, which could be called scientific knowledge. But not because the knowledge is found in the texts."

"Even books of Arkadian literature are empty?"

"Of course."

"Wonderful!"

"This does not mean that Arkadians are not capable of creating literature, of explaining history, or of being moved by someone else's words. They can, despite the emptiness of texts, travel to faraway places, distant times, or unlikely landscapes. They say things about their past, introduce characters that they have never met, invent incredible places, monsters, fanciful notions. They have their Melvilles and their Poes, and they have no problem imagining their voyages, their heroes, and their nightmares. They can empathize and identify with the heroes of Flaubert, Balzac, Austen, and be moved by the images of Keats."

"How is that possible, if at the same time you are saying that the texts are empty?"

"You are not paying attention. Arkadians relate to literature the same way they relate to the rest of language. Just as with a normal text, the words of a work of fiction act like switches, turning on slifes. As the person reads, the words light up past slifes, and new slifes are created by the combination of memograms. In general, and since it is a work of fiction, the activation of all these memograms evokes a new slife in that person's virtual world. However, the characters, the landscapes, the situations that arise in the novel are combinations of kognitive impacts of individuals, landscapes, and situations that already exist in each virtual world, although they are arranged differently. It does not matter that they are characters from another country or another culture, people with strange personality figures or with combinations of traits that are completely foreign to the Arkadian. Depending on what their memograms contain and on the manipulating capability of their kognitive system, the new characters and landscapes will be born of the characters and landscapes experienced in the past. For each Arkadian, the recreation of this fiction will be different. The slifes that the person has had make up the virtual world in which he or she lives, and it is in this virtual world where the fiction of the author works, not in the shared world. The book acts as a 'reader of virtual worlds' that functions in different systems, each individual Arkadian, in which the elements of the program are read according to the person's particular kontents. Consequently, fiction books are recreations of the particular worlds of each reader; it is not the world of the author that is transmitted. At the most, what the author achieves is the evokation of a new look at the reader's world."

"How can we explain science fiction, for example?"

"Just like any other fiction. The fantastic objects, animals, and lands evoke previous kontents that are transferred to the current slife. For example, in the human world, books by Swift contain descriptions of places and people never seen before. However, the reader converts them into an individual slife than can be dealt with, either by correspondence with places that have been seen directly, or in drawings, or films, etc. Any fantastic object, creature, or place can easily be incorporated into the slife background if it appears in an illustration; any monster can come to life from previous images; any unknown place can be recreated from the visual background that all Arkadians have."

"I still see some strange consequences. If what you are saying is true, then in Arkadia we cannot speak of 'books.' If each Arkadian is going to evoke their private world from a given book, then as many books exist as Arkadians exist. Furthermore, if each Arkadian world evolves as the individual goes through life, then we find that not only exists a book for each Arkadian, but a different book exists for each virtual world. Reading a book at the age of fifteen is not the same as reading it at twenty, thirty, or sixty."

"That is right. With each reading, the words find a new path, because the itinerary may be integrated in new memograms and kontents. From here we can deduce a principle that is extremely crucial to Arkadians:

Textuality Thesis: A text's content is the set of its readings.

To begin with, a literary work makes no sense and cannot be analyzed if Arkadians do not exist. In Arkadia, you cannot talk about *Don Quixote*, or about '*Don Quixote* read by Katherine': only about '*Don Quixote* read by Katherine in February of 125, Arkadian Era.'"

"Whew!"

"A normal feeling among some Arkadians when they read a text again some time later is that of not recognizing the same slifes or perspektives, and not understanding it as they did originally."

"That is happened to me."

"Well, it appears to also happen to Arkadians. This is because the virtual world of the Arkadian has changed substantially, way beyond what the person can identify for herself or himself. The slife background that makes up his virtual world, as well as characteristics of a qualitative type, in the organization of the slifes, in the relations that have been established among its elements, or in the new points of view that have been acquired, is substantially different. Therefore, when the person comes across the same words that he or she came across in the past, the perspektive activated is completely different. What is more, any attempt to recover the old points of view will be in vain, because his or her world has changed irrevocably. He or she cannot even come up with a translation guide between what is now evoked by the words and what was evoked in the past. The virtual world of the past is inaccessible. All readings are new readings in the broadest sense of the term, and they are new because it is a new person, one who has a lot in common with the old one, but who is not the same person. Therefore, not only are there as many books as readers exist, but as many books as readings exist; not only differences exist among individual Arkadians, but also between readings themselves that take place at different times in the person's life."

"What about a literary work that lasts through the years?"

"Some works call upon slifes that themselves last through time, and others that have more difficulty lasting. Slifes that speak accurately about, for instance, a first love will probably survive a lot longer than the slifes that refer to the smell of a city. In any case, time is not an important problem when it comes to understanding or evaluating literary works and their ability to transmit a message down through the years."

"So they may understand authors from centuries ago much better than they understand their next-door neighbor?"

"Exactly. They enjoy the ancient poets because the subject is how sublime love is, and that is something they understand perfectly well, because the transfer between slifes is simple; we all know what love is. Let us suppose that they had a Seneca. When Seneca talks about his impressions in the hot baths, and how absurd he thinks for Romans to go to the baths to sweat and get tired out in order to stay in shape, these impressions can easily travel several millennia. Transferring them to the Arkadian gyms of today is easy, and so an Arkadian might have the same feeling. Perhaps, however, among the readers someone exists for whom staying in shape and getting tired poses no problem. Kommunication between Seneca and the first Arkadian who is receptive to the idea is successful, while if that Arkadian tries to talk about it with the next-door neighbor who is not receptive to the idea, then kommunication fails. The time might come in which, despite their universality, even the great characters of Arkadian literature, the Makbeths, will become incomprehensible. The more deeply-rooted a book is in its time, the harder it is for it to be transmitted. In general, the meaning of many kontents, and therefore of words that evoke these kontents, does not vary through history. These signs that are involved in panceptual fields are elements that evoke slifes that can preserve many of their traits through time. Likewise, it may happen that the social and cultural structures change so much that many of the slifes that make up the virtual worlds of today's Arkadians have nothing in common with those of future Arkadians. As a result, the scenes and situations in which today's Arkadians feel comfortable may be quite strange for Arkadians of the future. Some of these changes could correspond with differences in social relationships. If the families of future Arkadians cease to exist, and no real family ties exist, then the kinship relationship may no longer exist, and they may no longer be used as a transfer tool."

"So translation is also a problem?"

"Translation is the most difficult linguistic activity because the author loses the evokative power that he or she has in her or his native language to call upon words or equivalent constructions. Some translations might need sophisticated modifications, with complete sentence changes. This is why a good translator is not the one who knows the correct equivalent of the words, but the one who knows the correct equivalent of the slifes. I will illustrate this for you with one of Arkadia's interesting aspects. The fast evolution of the population already has among its consequences the development of different languages in the different islands of the Arkadian archipelago. These languages are beginning to show peculiarities. One peculiarity is the type of words that are anchored in the kontents having to do with movement. In one of these languages, known as Kastilian, the way movement is carried out appears to attract prepositional or adverbial modifiers, or adverbial and adjectival subordinate clauses, like for example, 'Juan entró apresuradamente'. Another language, Keltic, seems to fix the way a movement is carried out in the verbs, like 'John rushed in.' A similar phenomenon appears to take place in the kontents that describe the characteristics of the trajectory of the movement. In general, the trajectory of the movement is anchored by the verb in Kastilian, but it is often not quite precise. For this reason, some of the details about the trajectory have other elements that enrich the perspektives evoked by the verb, which slows the pace of the text and makes the syntactic construction more complicated. This proves that a language like Keltic may be better equipped to evoke the ways that things happen and to make more complete descriptions of trajectories of the movement. As a consequence, in the translation from Keltic to Kastilian more kontents are lost than in the translation from Kastilian to Keltic, which, on the contrary, tends to be enriched with additional details so that the text will sound natural in the target language."

"In short, can we say that human language is or is not similar to Arkadian language?"

"I think that it has both big differences and big similarities."

"Meaning?"

"I will explain. First, in almost all the circumstances that affect a human being, the description of the location of the individual does not allow us to predict what that individual will say next. A complete description of the surroundings of a person who is in a doctor's office, for instance, when the doctor asks, 'What is wrong,' will not help us know what the person is going to respond. The contrast with animals is clear, since in general, animals have a small and fixed repertoire of signs, and they are closely linked to the surroundings. Just like with human beings, predicting what an Arkadian is going to say is not possible, at least only based on what another one says to her or him, or based on the description of the surroundings. If we had a characterization of the slife that the Arkadian is having, then it would not be that difficult to imagine what he or she is going to say. Secondly, a sentence in human language appears to leave aside many details in the situation, focusing in on just one. 'John has a mustache' does not tell us any more than a detail about his facial hair. This is not the case for Arkadians. This sentence, in itself, has no semantic value if a particular slife structure is not incorporated. No meanings exist independent from the Arkadian individuals. As we have pointed out, the virtual worlds is what has semantik properties. Lastly, in human beings the correspondence between each sentence and its meaning is not something that is learned sentence by sentence. We learn the meanings of the central elements, the words, along with a recipe for how to make complete signals, sentences, from the basic elements. We understand sentences without needing to have heard them before. We can also speak of this ability in Arkadia, although it is not based on the intrinsic ability of language, or of its use, but on the creativity of kognition. Arkadian productivity is based on the fact that they can manipulate memograms through words, and not on the power of the linguistic apparatus."

Once again the sun left me with my mouth wide open. I looked at it with a threat of protest, which prompted a smile and raised eyebrows on the part of Non-Professor O.

Seven

FRIDAY
On How to Communicate Without Information

When I woke up, I did not think I was capable of getting through another endless afternoon of Arkadia. However, after a while, I got up completely recovered and ran down the stairs to the terrace.

"You sure look happy today, Alice."

"It happens sometimes."

The table was all ready, with tea and crackers.

"I hope it lasts all afternoon."

"I do, too. As I was coming down, I remembered another of my perplexities."

"Yes?"

"It was one day when I went to see Albert's orchestra rehearse. I was sitting in the orchestra pit of an empty theater. The musicians were wearing their everyday clothes, and the director appeared quite upset: 'No, no, and no. You do not see what it means, you do not get what this passage is all about. You have to approach it as if you had just found your first love, many years after having lost it. Your love is still intact, and you can see it in each other's eyes, in your expression, and you feel an explosion of jubilation in your stomachs. You are drunk with happiness, like a pirate before a treasure chest, like a child on Christmas morning. All that accumulated energy explodes like a volcano. But, and this is quite important, you must not mistreat the treasure, because it is fragile. It is like a kitten that is drowning in a river and is trying to climb onto a piece of driftwood. And you are the driftwood.' I had never thought that communication was so difficult or complicated."

"I believe that understanding Arkadian kommunication will help you to understand such sort of perplexities."

"If you say so."

"The idea is that, for an Arkadian, to kommunicate means to situate the other person in the same point of view."

"Your definition does not help me much."

"Let us go step by step. We will start by remembering the key points of human communication."

"Whatever you like."

"Human beings understand communication to be the transfer of ideas, concepts, thoughts, by one individual to another through the use of substitutes for these ideas —words, gestures, etc.— that transport the meaning. According to this general idea, communication is an activity that is established between an emitter, an agent that wants to transmit a message, and a recipient, the agent that receives it. This activity consists of the transmission of a message that is represented by a code, usually a type of language, like Morse Code, which is transmitted by way of a signal, the physical substrate in which the code is transmitted —like the electric impulses in telephone transmission by cable— through a channel, the system that transmits the signal. In short, the emitter transmits a message to the recipient when the emitter encodes the message, converts it into a signal, and when the signal reaches the recipient, and the recipient manages to decode the message."

"I insist. I did not think that communication was so complicated."

"Communicating verbally consists of putting the thoughts into words and transmitting them through oral or written discourse, so that another individual can decode the thought from the words that have been used to encode it. To use a graphic image, verbal communication consists of something like wrapping up a thought *content* in words and sending it to the recipient, who has to unwrap the message. This vision of communication is based on the property attributed to language, to words, of being representative of a thought or an idea: the meaning of a sign is the thing that the sign represents."

"Cannot we use this to explain Arkadians?"

"Unfortunately not. This model does not describe how Arkadians kommunicate. In appearance, Arkadians kommunicate the same way human beings do: they talk among one another, they show agreement or disagreement, etc. However, the idea of wrapping up contents and transmissions can only be used as a metaphor in Arkadia. Messages are not passed along like giving money to a cashier. Messages, if they exist, remain in the brain of whoever emits them. Now, if you are aware that this is a metaphor, then you can use it, bearing in mind that the person sending the message does not load the message into a code, nor does the person receiving the signal unload the message from the signal."

"Could other perspectives help us?"

"Yes and no. Another human view of communication can help us, although only partially. This approach states that communication consists of managing to reach a 'place,' which generally is a thought, through a process of inferences and analysis of the words that have reached the recipient. While the first perspective consists of the transport of ideas, in the second model communication is understood to be a process of analysis of signs. According to this approach, an individual modifies the physical surroundings of his or her interlocutor in such a way that the person can construct or infer the mental representation that the emitter wanted to transmit. Oral communication, for example, would be the modification by the speaker of the acoustic surroundings of the listener, and as a result the listener will have to analyze the signal so that, at best, thoughts similar to those of the speaker will be activated. Therefore, the idea is that an individual communicates in order to reach the objective of making the other person recognize something, instead of seeing communication as the transmission of a message from one individual to another. This means that what is relevant is the influence on others, getting them to understand, through signs, that which is being transmitted, with the hope that the influence will be enough to fulfill its purpose. Consequently, words are not containers of meanings used for the transport from one person to another, but are the medium used to make the interlocutor recognize what one wants to transmit, the keys with which the recipient will be able to reach the same place as the emitter. The function of the words in this model is to indicate, in a more or less distinctive way, the type of analysis required for the recipient to reach the desired thought. And the analysis by the recipient consists of using premises of reference to make a series of inferences based on the words uttered by the emitter, and then following the steps that logically extend from the premises."

"Can this be applied to Arkadians?"

"Again, the answer is no. For an Arkadian, understanding a message does not mean carrying out a process of inference based on symbols, using presuppositions about what the interlocutor knows or does not know. Although the second model is closer to the Arkadian model, it does not fully explain Arkadian kommunication. We cannot describe, in the context of an act of kommunication, the Arkadian recipient as performing analytical and inferential work on the words, since the action of the words is determined beforehand, and cannot be modified. When the words reach the kognitive system they spontaneously activate the konceptual connections and the memograms in which they are anchored. Furthermore, Arkadian words do not carry with them the keys for such an analysis, nor does the interpretation of an Arkadian discourse start from a set of premises of reference, since, as we have mentioned other days, Arkadians do not have data in their heads. When Katherine says to her brother, 'The best thing would be for Dad to stop working,' the two of them are not using premises such as 'Dad works too much,' or 'Dad is sick,' or 'It is not worth it for Dad to keep working,' because their kognitive systems do not record these sentences as data."

"How do we explain Arkadian kommunication?"

"Remember the nature of Arkadian language. As we have seen, it is evokative. A word does not stand for an object, individual, property, or action, but functions as something that evokes memograms involving the relevant kontent. That is, the word is a switch for the virtual world in which the kontent is located, and not its symbol. As a result, the Arkadian language cannot be conceived as a code, in the sense that each word corresponds to a specific meaning that, through rules of combination, allows for the creation of sentences in which the parts are combined and give a new meaning. Moreover, Arkadian language does not correspond with a type of instrument through which, along with a logic apparatus, an individual can infer ideas, thoughts, or more general conceptualizations. For this reason, Arkadian kommunication cannot be based on any of the models that have been presented so far."

"So now what?"

"To begin with, kommunication in Arkadia does not have to be any different from the basic structure of emitter, channel, and recipient. This basic structure is valid not only for face-to-face kommunication, but also kommunication mediated by a technological artifact, kommunication deferred through a code, or when the kommunication is initiated without the intention of reaching a recipient. Based on this outline, kommunication in Arkadia has to be defined as I said at the beginning:

> *Kommunication*: The evokation in the recipient of a slife equivalent to that which the emitter wants to evoke.

"What does the slife being equivalent consist of?"

"Let us see. Remember that an Arkadian lives in what we have called a virtual world, which is the world that complements the whole slife background of such Arkadian, or, as we also said, the world that maintains the homeostasis of such a background. A perspektive is, by contrast, the virtual world that maintains the homeostasis of a specific slife. Then, we said that two slifes are equivalent if the perspektive derived from them is the same, that is, if the virtual world that complements the slifes is the same. Therefore, a successful kommunication corresponds to the modification of another person's virtual world in such a way that a slife is evoked in the recipient that is complemented by an equivalent virtual world. For two Arkadian individuals the process of kommunication consists of the manipulation of the virtual world of the recipient in such a way that the emitter evokes in the recipient a slife the homeostasis of which is maintained by the same virtual world, or to put it a better way, by the same set of possible virtual worlds."

"Can you give me an example?"

"Imagine that the virtual world was a nativity scene, with its little figurines, its baby Jesus, its Virgin Mary, its Joseph, its angels, shepherds, wise men, and the animals. Let us suppose that Katherine and Erik are looking at this nativity scene, and that the two of them panceive the same kontents. Suppose, then, that Katherine says to Erik, 'The angel told the shepherds about the birth of the baby Jesus.' For this kommunicative act to be successful, Katherine will have had to manipulate the nativity scene that Erik is looking at in such a way that she gets Erik to see the angel talking to the shepherds, telling them something like, 'Christ is born.' Taking the analogy to the extreme, we can see Katherine take hold of the angel and move it to where the shepherds are, and saying with the voice of the angel, 'Christ is born.' Another thing we talked about on Wednesday was that many aspects of the perspektive do not have to be exactly the same in order to maintain the homeostasis. So, in this kommunicative act it is not crucial whether the angel said, 'Christ is born,' or 'Baby Jesus is born,' or whether the angel looked 60 degrees to the right or 65 degrees, or if the angel flew at 10 miles an hour or 20. These details make up all of the possible worlds that maintain the homeostasis of that slife in each of the Arkadians."

"What if they do not share the same perspektive?"

"Let us see. Suppose that between Erik and Katherine a kontent of that nativity scene is not shared; that is, the slife is not equivalent. Let us say that the nonequivalence is that to Katherine, the Virgin Mary is a virgin, but that to Erik, she is not. Say that Katherine tells Erik, 'She is called the Virgin Mary because she was a virgin; the baby Jesus was conceived in an immaculate conception.' At that moment a discrepancy is produced, so the kommunication will not have been a success. However, the word 'virginity' has activated a konceptual connection that existed in Erik's kognitive system, and that connection is transferred to the current slife, so that this kontent can be added, as if it were a coat of paint, to the Virgin Mary. Therefore, a manipulation of that slife has been objectified, the discrepancy disappears, and the perspektives that maintain the homeostasis of the slife are the same."

"Should a successful kommunication be based on perspektives already possessed?"

"No. The perspektives can be obtained by the recipient by rearranging kontents already possessed. The kommunication can be successful even if the recipient experiences the required slife during the kommunication."

"Examples, please"

"Let us look at a situation in which Katherine says to Erik, 'Cowards usually lie without looking straight in the eyes.' Here Katherine wants to evoke in Erik a slife in which we can see particular kontents. For one thing, we have 'cowards.' Imagine that the word 'cowards' evokes in Erik a series of memograms gathered from slifes in which, to simplify, the leader of the neighborhood gang called him or one of his friends a 'coward.' What happened in these slifes was that he or one of his friends refused to do things that they had been dared to do: Erik was labeled a coward when he refused to confront the members of a rival gang, when he did not jump off a ten-foot high fence, when he did not lie to his parents, etc. These slifes that gave rise to memograms in which the set of memories of the attribution of 'coward' connected by konceptual connections, make up what the word 'cowards' evokes. Then we have the expressions 'lie' and 'not to look people straight in the eyes' that provokes a peculiar situation in Erik. Let us leave 'lie' for later, assuming that Erik understands such an expression, and let us focus on 'not looking straight in the eyes.' Simplifying, Erik recognizes the words but has never heard the complete construction. In this situation, what Erik's kognitive system does is to evoke a series of memograms based on the expression 'look people straight in the eyes.' This expression does not have an intense konceptual connection; instead, it evokes situations related to 'looking' and 'eyes,' which correspond to the slifes in which Erik looked at the person with whom he was talking. That is, it evokes slifes normally evoked by the expression 'look at your interlocutor' for which he does have a konceptual connection. Finally, the particle 'not' evokes the situation opposite to that of 'look at your interlocutor.' Consequently, the sentence, 'Cowards do not look people straight in the eyes,' evokes in Erik a slife in which the kognitive system tries to establish or reveal some connection between the 'coward' slifes and those of 'not looking at your interlocutor.' But Erik has not detected the kontent 'not looking at your interlocutor' in the 'coward' slifes, so he cannot understand what Katherine is trying to say with that sentence, regardless of whether or not he accepts that such a perspektive may exist. In a way, then, we could say that Erik cannot understand Katherine because their virtual worlds are not equivalent. Suppose, then, that Katherine adds, 'Cowards do not look people straight in the eyes because that is where the strength of the individual resides.' Once Erik has heard this, he has a slife in which the konceptual connections of 'eyes' and 'strength' are activated, the perspektives of which he does share with Katherine. In this new slife, Erik transfers the association between 'strength' and 'eyes' to the association between 'look' and 'cowardice,' and he can finally understand what Katherine is saying."

"Does he understand it completely?"

"Just like in all the other areas of Arkadia, kommunication is not an all or nothing affair, but a continuum that ranges from total incomprehension to an almost perfect sharing of the perspektive. The degree of comprehension, or incomprehension depending on how you look at it, corresponds to the degree of differences between the virtual worlds of each individual, and of their ability to manipulate their memograms."

The church bells rang.

"All of the relevant past slifes always have to be evoked?"

"That is right, although it may appear to you to be an excessive, extravagant, and pointless process, kommunication necessarily involves evoking all the relevant past slifes. However, most kommunication occurs along paths that are already well trodden by the two interlocutors, and that make, like I said on Monday, a kind of 'floor' upon which kommunication takes place. This floor is what underlies expressions like:

Hello, good morning, how are you, fine, please, good-bye....

In many cases these expressions are taken as kommunicative contexts, just as human beings do not always pay attention to all of the objects that we perceive. At times, when human beings do not observe what we are doing, our minds are elsewhere, yet the brain does not stop pedaling the bicycle, driving the car, or piloting the airplane. Something like that happens to the words in Arkadian kommunicative acts. The 'hellos,' 'How's it going,' and similar expressions evoke general kommunicative contexts, and not precise perspektives; in a way, they 'prepare' the kommunication."

"How do you know that these words have this function?"

"Words evoke. The first 'hello' was possibly anchored by Katherine in a slife that her father evokes when he came to pick her up at school, but thousands of 'hellos' later, it merely evokes the kommunicative context of greeting someone."

"If meaning is evokation in Arkadia, then words will have only one meaning/evokation. However, we human beings can kommunicate with each other using words with different meanings without creating any kommunicative difficulty."

"That is roughly correct. Situations exist in which the evokation model appears to have problems in explaining kommunication. In human beings, normal conversational exchanges like, 'The door is open,' can have lots of different meanings. It may contain the implicit meaning of, 'Go close it,' or a request, 'Could you please close it?' Or it could be a reproach such as, 'You forgot to close the door again,' or a metaphorical meaning like, 'You can leave whenever you want,' or the ironic sense of, 'Anyone who pleases comes right on in.' Similarly, if someone says, 'Long live my mother!,' or, 'Hooray for our team!,' that person says it thinking more about a way to encourage, to express happiness, than wanting to transmit a message through the meaning of the words. To put it another way, in theses cases, what has meaning is the act of uttering words, not the words themselves. The same purpose can be achieved by giving a kiss, throwing flowers, carrying a person on your shoulders. In fact, conventions supposedly regulate and condition the multitude of possible interpretations of a single sentence, depending on the context, the people involved, reference knowledge, etc. and that everyone follows these norms in any kommunicative context. Furthermore, these norms are autonomous from other linguistic norms, since the conventions can be flouted, or they can intentionally be used in a personal way."

"I guess that is what I meant."

"Then, you will understand that these aspects apply to Arkadians in a similar way. Arkadian language is evokative and not symbolic, showing greater freedom and flexibility than what we human beings have, since language is just another kommunicative instrument, without particular restrictions other than evoking slifes in other people."

"What do you mean?"

"Remember that Arkadian words are polysemic, or polyevokative, and that they serve their purpose not only through their form, but through how they are anchored in a specific slife context. To say, 'I am going to kill you,' to a child who has broken a vase is not the same than saying it to a soldier at whom we are pointing a gun, or to a computer that does not work. Or to say, 'Taxi!,' in the street, while we are looking at a picture drawn by a child, or while doing a crossword puzzle with the clue 'Four-wheeled public transport with four letters.' Consequently, since a specific semantic function lacks for each word, for an Arkadian is simpler to use words along with another type of kommunicative tool in order to evoke the desired slife."

"Let us move on to specific examples."

"Consider the following three cases:

(1) I hereby name you honorary member.
(2) I pronounce you husband and wife.
(3) I promise.

These sentences are not what human beings would call transmissions of messages. Their intention is not to inform anybody, but to perform an 'act.' When human beings utter these sentences, their intention is not to transmit a message but to 'do something' with the words. With these sentences, individuals perform acts that could be performed with equivalent sentences or with another type of action, like saying, 'Welcome to the club,' or giving an diploma instead of saying, 'I hereby name you honorary member,' or nodding instead of saying, 'I pronounce you husband and wife.' A kommunicative act is thus any situation in which an Arkadian attempts not only to evoke a slife, but to carry out an act with the very fact of kommunicating, just like when someone gives someone else a kiss, the idea is not just to put two pairs of lips together, but to demonstrate our affection."

"So?"

"The explanation for these kommunicative acts is not complicated in Arkadia, since these sentences are formulas that are used in different slifes with a specific structure. At one point in their lives, all Arkadians learn to use words to carry out a social kontent that requires their active participation. If an Arkadian becomes, for example, a justice of the peace, he or she will learn that 'I pronounce you husband and wife' ends the marriage ceremony, but it could have been any other formula, gesture, or action. Therefore, these words are used as complex formulas that evoke, in a particular slife context, a specific action that in some cases is 'marrying two people,' or in others 'naming an honorary member,' etc. In short, it can be said that the Arkadian uses these expressions to kommunicate with the objective of getting the other person to do something, and to achieve the objective a series of words and typical expressions are used that evoke, due to their being anchored in particular types of past slife, precise situations, such as 'giving personal guaranties about a future action.' Again, since words are not symbolic, no problem exists for them to be specified as evokations of particular slifes in which the formulas were originally anchored."

"I am not fully convinced. We human beings can use words in a way that is contrary to their normal use, even if it is just once, and yet the kommunication will usually not fail. But Arkadians cannot use words with a meaning opposite their conventional sense, can they?"

"As I said yesterday, a way of understanding conventional use exists in Arkadia. An Arkadian lives and grows up in a community, and thanks to the homogeneity of the community, and the great wealth of slifes, the Arkadian adopts some slifes that give shape to equivalent virtual worlds, or worlds that overlap the true world. In the long run, the use of language to evoke these slifes creates a basic corpus of uses, a nucleus if you press me, and in this way the later uses that voluntarily deform the meaning are recognized by fellow Arkadians as an altered use."

"Examples, please."

"Let us suppose that 'thank you' is usually said when one Arkadian does a favor for another. The words 'thank you' are therefore used in kommunicative contexts in which somebody is 'thankful.' If instead of using it in this situation it is used in the opposite situation, when someone does something that is not appreciated, the words 'thank you' can be used to evoke in the other person the superimposition of the situation that was hoped for, a favor being done, with the one the emitter has experienced, something negative. In this way, the emitter shows the recipient that the slife evoked is not appreciated."

"But if I tell my mother 'I am hungry,' she will know that I want her to cook me something, even though I have not said it, right?"

"That case is explained in the same way. The scene created by your 'I am hungry' has a continuation in which your mother cooks something for you. I repeat. The emitter uses any tools available to situate the recipient in a position that brings to mind a given slife, with a derived perspektive. Wrapping up all the implications in the kommunication is not necessary: the perspektive already contains them."

"When you say implications, to what are you referring?"

"Let us take your situation to Arkadia. Let us suppose that in a conversation Erik says to Katherine, 'I am hungry,' and Katherine responds, 'There's nothing in the fridge.' In this dialogue a series of implications exist, the most important being that Erik is asking Katherine for something to eat. How has this implication been transmitted? It has not been. The sentence said in that context, with a slife background between the two of them that most likely has produced similar situations, evokes in Katherine a slife that is something like, 'If Erik is hungry, we should cook something for him.'"

"What happens when Erik asks Katherine for Roko's telephone number, and Katherine responds, '323–5790?'"

"In such a case, transmission of data appears to occur, and not the evokation of some slife. Likewise, when the doctor tells Erik's father that he suffers from Dullman's syndrome, and his father can mention the syndrome at home or in the bar without knowing what he is talking about."

"Exactly!"

"But no transmission occurs. The evokation may not occur and yet still not compromise the ultimate purpose of the kommunication. For example, if an Arkadian sees on a control panel the written warning, 'In case of fire, push the vermilion button,' and the Arkadian does not know what vermilion means, but only one button on the panel exists, the message will fulfill its objective, whether the Arkadian understands it or not, merely because one possible perspektive exists."

"Okay, but that is an exception."

"Not really. This is a situation that should be considered much more frequent than what you may think. I would say that a large proportion of community activities in Arkadia function despite the fact that the equivalent slifes are not always evoked. I compare it with the ability that human beings have to use a computer without knowing the electronic operations that are carried out by one's orders."

"So?"

"We are talking here about one particular type of kommunications: *surrogate kommunication*."

"What's that?"

"To put it briefly, surrogate kommunication is the transmission of the 'sound' or 'form' of the words and sentences. Surrogate kommunication works like the human transmission of telephone numbers, or the giving of calling cards by one person to another. In this kommunication, the Arkadians reproduce the acoustic image of the word, or the expressions. Katherine can learn to multiply by learning the times table by memory. Once she has learned it, she can kommunicate to others the result of the multiplication, understand a question about multiplication, or even correct her classmates. However, she need not understand what multiplying is. Similarly, a crazy man can make other people think that he is a doctor by correctly using medical jargon, although he does not understand what he is saying, or an Arkadian can speak and recognize the correctness of a sentence or a word and not understand what is being said."

"You say that this happens frequently?"

"Much more frequently than you would think. This leads us to the issue that often the kommunicative acts undertaken by Arkadians fail without them realizing it, and without it having much of an effect on the future of the speakers, or ones that depend on them. The examples are so numerous that it would take all day, but if you like I will give you one of them."

"Go ahead."

"Imagine that a soccer coach is talking to his or her players, and he or she says something like this:

I do not want you to be a pusillanimous team, shirking responsibility all over the field, and ceding to the excesses of the other team, which tends to exaggerate its playing and demonstrate minimal citizenship. The game must be diverted from the terrain of passion. You should not display interest in bodily contact. We must rely on our skills of discernment, and oblige the opposing team to reflect on these skills.

Let us suppose that none of the players understood what the coach said, but they do know what he or she wants, which is that they play a particular kind of soccer. Then they go out on the field and play that kind of soccer, and they win. When they go back to the dressing room, the coach comes up and says, 'Thanks for understanding me!'"

"I know what you mean."

"This kommunication also occurs all those times in which two individuals who have known each other for a long time seem to have agreed about something but then something happens and both of them say honestly, 'I did not say that,' 'You misunderstood me,' or, 'I thought that we had agreed,' etc."

"From what you are saying I deduce that the perspektives of the two kommunicators do not have to be part of the knowledge of the Arkadians, that is, they do not have to overlap with the world of K, right?"

"Yes, and that is a good thing to point out. The virtual perspektive does not have to be knowledge, to intersect with the true world, the omniscient world of K. For example, if two Arkadians believe in astrology and they say, 'Frank is a Taurus and Kati is a Gemini, so their marriage will not work,' their view of that virtual world can be considered equivalent. Even if from K's point of view, the property of 'being Taurus' (and astrology for that matter) is not true, in this fictitious world that these two Arkadians share, the kontent of 'being a Taurus' does exist. Thus, for example, when these two Arkadians look at an astral chart, they panceive it as a real characterization of the cosmic forces, while another Arkadian, in whose world astrology is a big hoax, panceives it as a bunch of nonsense."

"Do conventions or rules exist regulating the kommunication between two Arkadians to assure the success of that kommunication?"

"Human communication is conditioned by the tacit agreements and the reference knowledge held in common by the two individuals involved in the communication. For example, the emitter will, unless evidence appears to the contrary, calculate the discourse according to several parameters: the person will tell the truth, evaluate the knowledge of his or her audience and adapt the discourse to it, etc. In general, these considerations are also valid in Arkadia. The difference is that in the case of Arkadian kommunication, the conditioning factors are not data that must be kept in mind, and upon which the interlocutors agree. In Arkadia, kommunication occurs only when the interlocutors share the

slife perspektive. The Arkadian kommunicative act does not require the computation of data, but the activation of the slife context that is relevant to the
kommunicative act. These contexts are activated thanks to slifes that anchor
conventions of kommunication that condition the possible evokations. Among
them, we can emphasize two conventions that are present in all kommunicative
contexts and that allow us to clarify the presuppositions and implications that are
kept in mind in a kommunicative act and what they correspond to:

> *Maxim of Equivalence*: Kommunication takes place on the basis that the
> interlocutors can share the same perspektive.

To kommunicate is to activate, to visit, the same virtual landscape as our interlocutor and see what the speaker wants us to see in that landscape. That is why
any Arkadian who embarks on a kommunicative act has to assume that the
success of the kommunication depends on the people looking at the same part of
the virtual world. Therefore, this condition is concerned with what we could call
commensurability of the virtual worlds, or the guaranty that the Arkadians who
are going to kommunicate have lived enough, or have had comparable enough
slifes, so as to have available to them a compatible virtual world, the relevant one
for the kommunicative act. This principle indicates a fundamental difference
between human beings and Arkadians. Human beings, once they have acquired
linguistic competence, can understand any sentence containing words and combination rules with which they are familiar. Arkadians need one more condition to
be fulfilled: the people involved must share an equivalent perspektive. If they
talk about soccer, then they have to have accumulated a set of slifes related to
that sport, and about its place in the social fabric, the virtual worlds of which
have the same kontents. The more common the world that joins them, the easier
it will be for two Arkadians to understand each other. This can occur, obviously,
without necessarily having physical proximity. Two people who share an equivalent perspektive can understand each other perfectly, despite their being a consid-
erable distance apart. In consequence, when Arkadians talk about something like
the 'concept of freedom,' or even the 'concept of society according to so and so,'
what is necessary is that they share equivalent perspektives."

"And the second?"

"The second convention on which kommunication is based is the following:

> *Maxim of Competence:* Kommunication takes place on the basis that the
> two interlocutors share the same kommunicative competence.

In other words, the interlocutors must have learned to use the same tools in an
effective and compatible way: language, kommunicative conventions, etc. In
short, the kommunicators assume from the outset that the virtual perspektive can

be the same, and that they know how to use kommunicative tools in the same way."

"Where does this lead us?"

"Arkadian kommunication has the advantage of not requiring complicated principles to be put into effect, or costly assumptions to be activated during the kommunication, or laborious inferences to be made and checked with the other person. Keep in mind, in any case, that I am not going into questions like whether the 'noise' or the 'channel' are appropriate for transmission. I am taking for granted that no interference exists, which would be the case if Katherine wanted to irritate Erik and did not listen attentively, or if Erik were drunk and did not articulate well. I only want to show that the success of the kommunication depends on the ability of both people to use the tools, but above all to share the same slife virtual world."

"Summarizing, how is it guaranteed that the kommunication will be successful?"

"Not much can be guaranteed. The same thing happens with knowledge; Arkadians can never have a complete guaranty that they understand each other. For an Arkadian, to kommunicate is to get the other person to have a slife similar to the one that he or she is having. Thanks to the representative power of language, we human beings find out what other persons think when they tell us. However, Arkadians would only be able to guarantee the success of the kommunication if they could enter the virtual world of the other persons and see their perspektive, but that is impossible. Therefore, Arkadians lack the guaranties that would allow them to assume that the other person is adopting an equivalent view of the virtual world. As the second convention indicates, for kommunication to be successful, each Arkadian has to be competent in the use of kommunicative tools, including linguistic and non-linguistic ones, and know their conventional uses. We have, first of all, the language of that community, which is comprised of elements similar to human languages, like phonology, syntax, and the lexicon, although, as we said, it cannot be broken down into modules, or systems. Instead, these disciplines study functional specializations of panception. These instruments are basic, like they are in human beings, but they are not the only ones. Their importance and centrality means that it has been forgotten that kommunication is packed with other strategies and tools. Any linguistic, paralinguistic, or non-linguistic tool can be used to make the other person evoke the desired slife. Arkadians approach any kommunicative act with a great interest in the kommunication being successful, for they are kommunicative beings. So they will do anything to achieve the goal of making what they want to say understood. Any indication is valid to make progress toward comprehension. Thanks to this circumstance, two Arkadians can find themselves for the first time in a strange situation and they can evoke the same slife quickly. Thus, they can use other kommunicative tools like body language, including physical contact, eye contact, gestures with the head, body position, movement, responding to the other person's movements. Other tools exist of a more social type, like fashion, clothes, commercial items, protocol, rituals, and games, that can also be used as tools."

He looked at me.

"Do you understand what I am telling you?"

I nodded. He went into the house again and came back carrying a tray with what appeared to be a bottle containing a greenish liquid and a twig from a bush. He filled two glasses with the liquid and gave me one of them.

"You have to try this herb liqueur made by the Arkadians from the island of Gor."

The aperitif was just what the doctor ordered; its slight alcoholic content was enough to make me believe that I was beginning to understand.

"Delicious."

"I am glad you like it."

"I am puzzled by the fact that in today's discussion we still have not mentioned the word 'information.'"

"That is true. I have not mentioned the 'object' of a kommunication, or what is to be transmitted, at all. Arkadians have been asking themselves for years what it is that they transmit in a kommunicative act. They have considered meanings, propositions, thoughts, ideas, beliefs, attitudes, emotions, and many other things."

"What is information in Arkadia?"

"I will find it difficult to answer that one. Not even human beings have agreed upon a definition of information. In general, human approaches to the concept of information with a view to its possible definition follow the path of describing it as 'things' that are received by an individual and that have some kind of interest for the recipient."

"What a definition!"

"Etymologically, the term 'information' is a noun formed from the verb 'to inform' that was borrowed from the Latin 'informare.' While the original Latin word means 'to give shape, model,' the word 'to inform' has come to be used in a figurative sense, in the sense of 'sending a message.' However, the concept of information still has not been made explicit."

"Nowadays information is everything."

"True enough, but no agreed-upon definition exists. Some authors describe information as 'news or facts about something,' and some dictionaries describe it as 'knowledge, communicated or received, that refers to a particular fact or specific circumstance.' Others have come up with a more amusing definition, like 'Information = knowledge *minus* human body.' In general, however, information is assimilated with the concept of meaning or sense, the concept of knowledge that is transmitted from one organism to another. That is, neither you nor I know Chinese, so if a Chinese person says something to us in the street, we most likely will not understand what is being said, and therefore we cannot say that an informative act has taken place. Only when we understand the message can we say that we have received information. But others say that is not necessary. One thing is information, which can be in any message, and another thing is its interpretation or revelation. Whether a paleontologist is nearby or not, the dinosaur imprint contains information about the dinosaur."

"Do general properties about information exist on which everyone agrees?"

"Yes, generally information is considered to be 'something' that has causal power, that is true or false, that can be measured, that consists of something about something, and can answer the following question: what is this message about? This excludes those messages that are chance events, like the fact that rain drops falling on a porch cannot be understood as a message in Morse code, although some falling rain drops can be eventually interpreted as 'It is raining.'"

"To what does 'information' correspond in Arkadia?"

"To kommunicate is to situate the recipient in the slife that the emitter is trying to stimulate. So, the object of the kommunication is not a 'thing' but an 'act.' Thus, information can be understood in Arkadia as coinciding with its etymology: information would have the original Latin meaning of 'to shape' because it shapes the virtual world of the kommunicator. Its noun form should disappear since nothing is transmitted."

"Is that possible?"

"I do not know whether it is or not, but no transmission exists, only interaction. And this interaction consists of the emitter of the message 'shaping' the virtual world of the recipient. This 'shaping' is metaphorical, but I think it is the best way to understand what happens. Just like an individual can grab another person by the shoulders and make the person look at some part of the nearby landscape, an Arkadian can intervene in the kognitive system of the person listening and make him or her look in a particular direction. Through the use of tools, language, and other types of kommunicative codes, like prosody and gestures, the emitter 'enters' the virtual world of the recipient and performs operations that, thanks to the conventionality of some codes, to the homogeneity of the slife background of each Arkadian, and to the kognitive architecture, manage to activate the relevant part of the virtual world in which the recipient lives. So, we could say that in a kommunicative act, when the recipient has received a message, and has understood it, that person has not apprehended informative material, because no such thing exists. The material in that individual's kognitive system is the same, except that it is more or differently organized."

"Does no way exist to measure or evaluate the information of a kommunicative act?"

"If we understand that 'to shape' is a way to reorganize, then I would say that a way exists to measure the informative capacity of an act of kommunication what we could call the 'informativity' of a specific kommunication. In this sense, the informativity of a kommunicative act would be the magnitude of manipulation, or organization, of the recipient's virtual world that the act is capable of bringing about. The informativity would be a property of the kommunicative act, and not of the codes, or the signals, that are used in it."

"So kommunication does not serve to enrich the virtual world of the interlocutor."

"The base material, or what comprises the virtual world, and which has been constituted from slifes, cannot be increased or diminished through kommunication. In order for the kontents to enter, the Arkadian must have the slife for himself or herself. It is as if we were to say, 'You feel an electric shock if you touch the two poles of a live wire.' If Erik has never felt an electric shock, then the semantic associations of the kontent will not be established until he does feel it."

"A quite solitary perspective is all they can hope for."

"Not really. Even though the virtual world does not increase through kommunication, a kommunication can change the virtual world in such a way that it is enriched in its organization or magnitude. We can say that after kommunication takes place no augment in 'slife material' occurs, but a change appears in the organization of the virtual world."

"So, we cannot determine the information contained in a text or oral discourse, right?"

"Exactly. The informativity is not a property independent from whoever is using it. In a string of signs, in an icon, in a dinosaur imprint, nothing happens independent from the kognitive apparatus of whoever is using it that is 'information.' This does not mean that informativity is a subjective property, because in the future making an analysis of the slifes experienced by Arkadians will be possible. It will also be possible to measure the changes that have been brought about by the signs or the manipulations of the emitter in the recipient, although imagining it now may be hard for us. This implies that the modification of virtual worlds that takes place in a kommunicative act can never be pre-established. The elements conditioning how a sentence modifies the virtual world of the recipient are, no doubt, so complex that they cannot be calculated in advance. We must keep in mind the use of kommunicative tools in the exact context: what words, gestures, and other kommunicative tools are used and in what way. Also, we have to consider the slife background of the recipient, that person's attention to the process, his or her motivation at the time of kommunication, and all the other conditions that can normally affect the kommunicative act."

The sun hides behind a cloud, the first one of the day. A light breeze picks up that brings the sound of sirens from the port and the smell of the sea.

"I am still not quite convinced. This thing about eliminating information is quite strange to me. Arkadians live in a world based on information, like human beings do, because they have television, radio, internet. All is information. When people are watching TV or listening to the news, what they are hearing about is information, information in a pure state, and that is undeniable. What about kommunicative acts in which 'data' is transmitted?"

"Let us take the following case:

(5) 'What time does the train leave,' asked Katherine; 'At ten after eight in the evening,' replied the station master.

"Exactly. How can you say that in this exchange no transmission of information occurs? The recipient of the message has received 'informative data' that she did not have before, something that may change her behavior, right?"

"In a way you are right, but no information exists, and I have already given you the reason why no transmission of data occurs in these cases. It is hard, I know, to make such an abrupt separation between human beings and Arkadians in a subject as familiar as this one. But the fact is that what the station master operates in Katherine is a modification of her virtual world. Only when this modification is superimposed on a perspektive of the true world will Katherine be capable of interaction with the world in the direction that her interlocutor intended. This change will consist of a train, in Katherine's virtual world, leaving the station at a particular point in her temporal context. For this change to be effective, Katherine will have learned to evoke slifes according to the temporal axis used by the station master. When Katherine receives the message about the time her train leaves, what happens is the following: the station master that has informed her enters Katherine's virtual world and modifies it, so that what evokes 'the next train' is associated with an aspect of the temporal context correlated with the use of conventions regarding the use of objects, like clocks. If Katherine had not learned to use clocks in her community, then hearing, 'it leaves at ten after eight,' would not be of any use to her. For the modification of the station master to be effective, Katherine should have learned the rules that allow her to deduce a position of the hands on a clock face, when the short hand points to the '8' and the long hand points to the '2.' She should also have learned that for trains to leave at some time, they have to wait for that moment begin to move. And nothing of this is a piece of information."

"If you say so."

"The train leaving at ten after eight is not data; it is not something that exists in the world independently from the capability of this data to transform the virtual world of the recipient in order to change the willingness of the recipient to do some things and not others. Let us suppose that the station master says, 'Twenty hours and ten minutes,' instead of, 'Ten after eight in the evening,' and let us suppose that Katherine has not learned about the use of the 24-hour clock.

Has information been transmitted? No. Not because she 'does not understand what it means.' If at that moment someone explains to Katherine what the 24-hour clock is all about, then we could say that she has the necessary elements to understand what it is all about, but Katherine may still not understand the message because she has not been able to evoke the desired slife, that is, incorporating the temporal axis to the slife that she is having at that moment. For her to understand, she must have experienced slifes in which the 24-hour clock is superimposed on a regular clock, until the overlap is finally quite complete."

"I am not convinced yet."

"Let us explore some more informational possibilities. What time does the station master mean? The time according to that area's time zone? And what does that time mean? Is not it different from Greenwich mean time? The time according to whose watch?, the station master's or the engineer's? If the train usually leaves at ten after eight and thirty seconds, then the information is no longer information because it is not true. This detail may appear trivial, but it just may be that the time lag resulting from the train leaving an hour or a fraction of a second late is of great importance in determining, for example, the future of the Arkadian universe. For that matter, what does it mean for a train 'to leave?' That it starts moving, that it is moving too fast for a passenger to get on, or that it leaves the station? Also, what does 'the next train' mean? The next one as of the question being asked, when the question is over, or during the conversation? All of these considerations are an implicit part of the virtual world, and can therefore be easily modified. However, they are not implicit in the data-sentence, and to be considered information they would have to be. Consequently, to extract information from a sentence like 'at ten after eight,' it would be necessary to address everything we know about the Arkadians, from the way their brains keep track of time to the railroad conventions, and including the use of technological instruments. Because the station master's sentences can be transformed into a modification of her virtual world, including her future virtual world, Katherine can make use of them; if not, no real information exists."

"Does not she 'know' something new, something that she did not know before the station master told her, 'it leaves at ten after eight in the evening?'"

"No, in a strict sense, she does not. Her virtual world has not been 'enriched' with new kontents; they have been organized in a different way. The change in the relationship between the virtual world and the true world allows her to do things or understand things that she could not before. However, it is not that the station master 'has transmitted something to her.' That is another basic difference as compared to human beings. In a figurative sense, it is as if the station master entered Katherine's virtual world and set her clock at ten after eight in the evening."

I got up and went over to the balustrade. The swallows were already there. I took a deep breath, noticing the orange blossom mixed with other odors that I did not recognize.

"If such thing as information, or meaning, do not exist how do you explain lies in this mess?"

"As I said on Wednesday, Arkadian language cannot be characterized according to the two values of truth: truthfulness or falsity. However, in the kommunicative context, lying does exist, and it is crucial. Arkadians, as human beings, sometimes say of each other that 'they are not telling the truth.' In Arkadia lying has an explanation different from the human one:

Lie: Any kommunication through which the emitter intends to evoke a slife in the recipient, the perspektive of which is *opposite* to that of the emitter.

So, if Erik says to Katherine, 'Unicorns exist,' Erik is trying to evoke in Katherine a slife the perspektive of which describes a virtual world that not only does not coincide with Erik's virtual world, which does not contain unicorns, but that is the opposite perspektive, a slife in the perspektive of which unicorns exist."

"Is that simple?"

"Of course not. Complications exist with such a notion. Like just about everything in Arkadia, we have to evaluate this characterization in a continuous way instead of in an absolute way, since the human concept of 'opposite' has to be assessed in each context and it does not always have the same characterization. Thus, Erik's father may ask him, 'Did you drink a lot last night?,' and Erik may answer 'No' because he imagines that if his father had seen him he may think that he had drunk a lot. However, since Erik cannot be sure of exactly what perspektive opposite that of 'drinking a lot' is, this lie is a partial lie."

"Could anything help us intuit what 'to comprehend' means in Arkadia?"

"Yes. The aspect that characterizes Arkadians, and separates them from human beings, is that to komprehend a discourse, an utterance, a text, is not to understand its words, but to experience a slife, adopt a view of the virtual world. Arkadians understand each other not because meanings hang from the words, or because words are connected to a little box where the meaning is held. They understand each other because when they say each word they dominate and penetrate all the slifes in which this word has been used, uttered, heard, etc. While they talk, the words take the Arkadians to perspektives of their virtual world, moving from one to another, and from one time to another. Consequently, comprehension is not something that can be defined in relation to the transmission of something called knowledge or information, but instead comprehension should be characterized in relation to the modifications to which the recipient is subjected in the kommunicative context. Erik can manipulate Katherine's virtual world through words because the words are anchored in kontents of the kognitive system, and also thanks to her ability to evoke these kontents. Never because the words mean something."

"Then words cannot take them beyond what they know, right?"

"Yes and no, and this points to the peculiarity of the Arkadians. We could say that in order to komprehend, Arkadians have to be in disposition to understand."

"What does it mean to be in disposition to understand?"

"It means that an Arkadian can understand a message, an idea, when he or she possesses the relevant kontents. If the virtual world of an Arkadian does not contain the objects, properties, and associations that make up the perspektive of a slife, then no matter how much is said or explained, that person will not be able to understand what the emitter wants to evoke with his or her sentences. In order for a kommunicative act to be successful, it has to work with raw materials, since life is that material of which the knowledge of Arkadians is made. No kommunicative tool, including language, is enough by itself to take Arkadians to the desired perspektive. If an Arkadian does not have at his or her disposition the kontents of a given perspektive, trying to take her or him there is pointless, regardless of the time invested or the tools used."

"But, from a human point of view, this appears trivial, because we already know that we cannot understand another person if that person does not have our concepts, right?"

"No, because humans appear to transmit new knowledge with words. Language allows us to communicate new ideas and thoughts, to communicate with someone who does not have our concepts and to whom we can transmit them. It allows us to teach and to learn. Arkadians, however, are left to their virtual worlds and to their kommunicative capabilities."

"Then, can we explain how Arkadian societies transmit knowledge from the older generation to the young people?"

"If you understand that ideas, knowledge, are slifes, then the teachings that each individual of a generation has acquired cannot be transmitted to the coming generation, unless they are linked to the slifes of that generation. This may appear radical, and I have had a lot of discussions about it with Arkadians, but it is the best explanation that I can find. The learning of one population is not transmitted to its descendants."

"Examples, please."

"If the Arkadian society had gone through a world war fifty years ago, it would be approaching a key moment in which the direct slifes of the war would be close to be inexistent. Therefore, the new generation would be unable to understand what the old generation means by something like the 'pain of war.'"

"But that means that Arkadians cannot learn from their history."

"Exactly. Historical memory is a fallacy in Arkadia. Let us suppose that a young Arkadian of today is told that the war is terrible, and that the citizens accepted it because they believed the lies told by the authorities about the need to fight. If such an Arkadian has not experienced slifes in which he or she has learned that war is terrible, then the discourse about the war will be useless. Without such slifes, the adolescent will turn into an adult that has war attitudes toward the Meteks, the Arkadian enemies *par excellence*, even if he or she believes to be different from Second-World-War citizens. This attitude will respond to a reasoning that the Arkadian himself will develop: 'Yes, the past war was useless, but the current situation is different, because the Meteks are dirty, they sell drugs, steal, and rape; they are different from us. We must fight them.' When the set of slifes that enabled people to understand war disappears, war attitudes will return. So, a logical derivation of the theory of slife is that after a while, when the slife memory of the historical facts has become a more or less surrogate explanation, the circumstances that lead to historical events cannot be stopped. War attitudes are repeated, and, no doubt about it, they always will be."

Non-Professor O prepared his pipe. For once, I observed each of his gestures, which were deliberate, awkward, and amused. The smell of the tobacco reached me all of a sudden. Aromatic and sweet.

"All of what you say still sounds very strange to me, because I cannot see how my view of society fits in. For example, to what does culture correspond in Arkadia?"

"We cannot talk about the kulture of an Arkadian country, of a society, unless it has become incorporated in the slifes of its components. In other words, no traditions and customs exist independent from the individuals who embody them. What human beings call 'tradition' is nothing more than a slife. Thus, if in some human populations burping after a meal is good manners, while in others it is impolite, for Arkadians 'burping after a meal' would be inscribed as figure/ground within a type of social slife of their community. In some of them, it would have 'positive' connections, while in others it would have 'negative' ones. Just as a word does not represent but instead evokes, 'burping after a meal' does not point to 'something' in the community; it evokes a type of slife in each Arkadian."

"How is kulture preserved in Arkadia? For human beings, the kulture of a country has been maintained in books, but if I have understood correctly what you are saying, no way describes, preserves, transmits, these things in Arkadia other than slifes."

"Exactly. Customs and traditions must be understood as a set of slifes instantiated in a population. Therefore, the kulture of a community will be maintained or transmitted from generation to generation if the conditions, the situations, that make up the typical slifes of what we understand to be knowledge remain. Arkadians themselves could cease to understand their ancestors if the slifes that instantiate traditions were to suffer a slife discontinuity, that is, if each new generation had to learn its traditions from, for example, books. Kulture is in the life of the Arkadians, not in their books. Someone who has read about the customs of a community does not have the kulture of that community, no matter how much empathy is felt for an Arkadian of that community. And a child of that community who has not experienced any of those slifes does not have it either. Customs, and belonging to a kulture, come from the repetition over the years of kultural type of slifes. So trying to transmit the kulture of a people by explaining it is pointless, unless the recipient has the elements necessary for comprehending the slife that is to be transmitted."

"If what you have said so far is true, then Arkadian schools must be condemned to failure because students cannot learn through lessons or books. If I have understood correctly, if Erik attends a class about the history of Europe, after the lesson he has not learned anything about Europe! And if Katherine reads the biography of Albert Einstein, at the end of it she has not learned anything new about Einstein, right?"

"But if you ask Erik about European history after the class he will tell you things that he could not have answered before, and the same will happen if we ask Katherine about Einstein."

"How is that possible?"

"Remember that on Wednesday we said that learning implies that the Arkadian can do things that he or she could not do before, or can panceive new things that were not panceived before. Arkadians do learn something after going to class or reading a book if the lectures and the texts have modified some perspektive of their virtual world."

"Once again, how?"

"Basically, the lectures and the texts help them to look at their world in a different way, moving the kontents around, or focusing in on different contexts. If the Arkadian has never seen a sword, nor felt the violence of a battle, then understanding or learning something from the story of a fencing contest is impossible. You cannot explain what a sneeze is to an Arkadian who has never sneezed."

"This is no sneezing matter!"

"Indeed! However, if Erik has a virtual world in which the kontent Europe exists along with other relevant kontents, like war, he will be able to modify his basic virtual world by reading about European history, and then he will be able to answer questions about the subject."

"Yes, but will he be able to say things like, 'World War II lasted from 1939 to1945?'"

"In many cases, the capability to respond to such questions is due to the words having the nature of surrogate kontent, in the same way that an address book contains telephone numbers without understanding them."

"What about geography, voyages, far-away lands? What about books with texts, essays, history, chronicles. Do not Arkadians learn things from them? How do university students learn? With human beings, thanks to lessons, books, and magazines we can learn something about the world. Millions of human beings have gone to school and learned about the past of their community, about the plants and animals that live in on the planet, about social and political systems around the world, about art and literature. Universities everywhere have trained engineers, doctors, lawyers, and they have done it through books and lectures."

"Not even with lectures and textbooks does an Arkadian incorporate anything genuinely new to his or her background. This is the hardest thing to accept, but that is the way it is. Nothing of what is in a book or a lecture augments the slife background of the listener or reader; it only modifies it. The kontents can be manipulated, though, integrating figure/grounds in diverse contexts to achieve a different view, a new view of that world that already existed in a virtual way. While this does not seem like much, it is a lot. With it, the Arkadian is capable of learning, of panceiving, and of acting upon new kontents in his or her virtual world. However, lectures or books do not provide knowledge, they just organize what is already there."

"I insist, the human school is based on the transmission of knowledge through language. So the Arkadian school must be useless, because what children do in school is done through language."

"I will say it again. In Arkadia, learning is not based on a supposed transmission of knowledge, as if it were goods that can move from place to place. Learning at school is not based on acquiring and apprehending, only on modifying the virtual world of each student. The slifes of each individual are what make up the virtual world to which books and lectures can be incorporated as organizers of kontents. Each piece of knowledge corresponds to a type of slife necessary for each discipline."

"How in the world is it possible for an Arkadian to learn history? The past is the past, and we cannot recreate it: Civilizations, weapons, diseases that no longer exist, episodes in the life of a monarch, the chronicle of a battle. In these situations, the person that attends a class does not know anything about how the events occurred, and when the class is over it can be said that the person has learned something, right?"

"Arkadians cannot apprehend history, in the human sense of the word, by listening to lectures or reading books about history. After reading about the battle of Waterloo, they have not detected kontents that are in the books and incorporated them to their virtual world. This does not mean, I repeat, that Arkadians cannot learn about that history by reading books or going to history class. But for this to happen, they need a base of slifes upon which to transfer what is said to them. They have to have the kontents of 'battles,' 'emperors,' 'countries,' etc."

"They do not learn anything about natural sciences at school either? How can you say that nothing is transmitted, if they will probably never see an asteroid, a cell, or an atom? What they know after going to school does not come from what they knew before."

"But that is the way it is. I will give you this piece of information, all

Arkadian science textbooks are full of images, diagrams, and other panceptual aids. This is not because the drawings help in the learning, but because they make it possible to determine the necessary slifes, or the memogramatic evokations required, so that the biological kontents can be transmitted. In other words, a picture is worth a thousand words in Arkadia, too. All those elements that allow for a better recreation of slifes, like photos, and diagrams, are so much the better, and the photographs and drawings allow the Arkadians to better evoke those kontents that are lacking. The further away, slifely, that a kontent is, the more important those aids to evokation become. They do not have to be pictures; if sound and movement are added, like in videos, all the better, and if visits to the zoo are organized to understand what a tiger is, what they are told about tigers will be better understood."

"So, they know mathematical formulas, they know about physiology, they know about so many things before a teacher teaches it or before they see it in a text? As much as you insist, I cannot accept that those children already have the necessary knowledge. It cannot be that when a professor teaches them about 'chlorophyll synthesis' this knowledge falls upon some previous knowledge."

"Again, that is how it is. A child does not learn from nothing, directly incorporating the concept, in human terms, of a text or what a teacher says. Instead, the child learns upon slifes already experienced, and only if the concept can be incorporated into memograms with a structure comparable to the kontent that is to be transmitted, will the child be able to acquire it."

"I cannot believe that an Arkadian of six years old has already experienced all the slifes that will allow him or her to learn at school."

"I have repeated that the vast majority of memograms and kontents that the Arkadians use are acquired early in life, in the first six years. In this time, Arkadian children have experienced slifes involving dogs, cats, turtles, birds, lions, mathematical problems, the construction of toy houses, and countless other slifes that make up the structure of their basic virtual world necessary for later scholastic learning activity. Much of this learning will broaden their memogramatic base, and that is where figures, drawings, games, and other school activities will come in handy, because they allow the necessary slifes to be established, or the existing ones to be broadened, in order to be more effective. But as complicated as the new learning may be, like second-degree equations, the basic structure into which this concept is incorporated is already established. Although grasping it is difficult for you, the child incorporates these signs and their combinations into slifes, and sets of slifes, in some cases quite varied, that allow the child to conceptually handle the formulas. Therefore, when the child is not in the position to learn, because he or she does not have the required memograms, he or she cannot learn. For each new modification a substantial change must occur in the slifes themselves. Any knowledge has to call upon some previous slife structure, or has to be able to become established through previous slife structures."

"Even maths?"

"Yes, let us take the case of mathematics. The real comprehension of a mathematical idea, excluding the delegated repetition of formulas and theorems, has to do with a previous structuring of the virtual world in such a way that it potentially contains the view that the theorem or the formula wants to evoke."

"How is that possible?"

"Say that we explain the commutative property to Erik, according to which the 'order of the elements to be added does not affect the product.' Then, if he understands the formulation it is because he has experienced such a kontent."

"What would this kontent consist of?"

"The memograms that make possible the comprehension of the laws of math, physics, biology, etc. are of a diverse nature, and their structuring may or may not be shared by all Arkadians. Thus, the commutative property may have been established by Erik in a slife in which the figure/ground focused in on a situation that made him realize that it did not matter if somebody gave him a bunch of candies altogether or one by one, or the mint gumdrops before the strawberry gumdrops. And he experienced it again when he had to count his money and he realized that it did not matter if he counted the nickels and the dimes together or separately. Let us suppose, therefore, that Erik experienced this slife, and he recorded it in the form of memogram, but he did not think much about it, believing that it was just like any other sensation. Then, when his math teacher wrote the principle on the board and explained it, Erik remembered the slifes and not only could understand the principle but also give it a name, the commutative law in this case. From then on, Erik has the original figure/ground available as an element to transfer to other situations in which he finds himself. Similarly, to learn what 'the force of gravity' means, Arkadians have to apply this kontent to a slife, or set of them, such as the now trite slife of an apple falling on someone's head. The slife of 'an apple falling' allows the learning of the 'gravity' kontent as a modification of the already existing slife background. Another type of common slife is the pie that is used to help students understand the concept of fractions. The student does not have to stick with this kind of slife; any other type can also be used. For example, abstract concepts, like that of infinity, may be associated with a slife of 'an object disappearing into the darkness' or 'very, quite far away, further away than anything else.' The rest of the knowledge that is taught in any discipline applies the same strategy to a greater or lesser degree."

"Learning at school then would be working with each student's own world."

"Exactly. The possibilities of learning are associated with the slifes that the student has experienced, his or her capability to apply educational kontents to the slifes or to create associations with slifes that might be remotely similar —like atoms being similar to a model consisting of plastic balls— in order to understand the new kontent. In this sense, a child does not learn anything new that was not already implicitly known. That is why models and examples are so crucial."

Non-Professor O looked at me curiously. I smiled at him.

"Okay, what role do the school and education have in Arkadia?"

"School is essential. First, because it is the catalyst of an independent process —the teachings that the Arkadians acquire for themselves— and second, because it provides the necessary stimulus and the appropriate instruments to continue incorporating new slifes, and new elements in the slifes, and to organize the pre-existing ones in a richer way. In other words, the purpose of the teachers is not to create new, completely original slifes, but to manipulate the virtual worlds of the students by managing to reveal in them those memograms, those kontents that they want to evoke, or to provide them a new and different view of the ones they already have."

"But school still serves no purpose, because the teachers cannot direct the Arkadians, since they all live in their virtual world."

"Categorically no. As I told you on Wednesday, each Arkadian has knowledge in the form of a virtual world, but that does not mean that they live in different worlds, nor that Arkadians build their personal knowledge through their capabilities and as they go through life. Arkadians live in virtual worlds, but their kontents are, in large part, shared by K, that is, they are true worlds. Therefore, Arkadians, do not build their realities; instead, they discover the realities belong to everyone, in their time and in their way. Applying this to education, you should not think that each Arkadian goes around building a personal world. The school can evoke many kontents in Arkadians, either through new slifes or through identification of the slifes from their slife background that may be relevant."

"What should school be like, then?"

"School should have been designed taking into account the kognitive architecture, making the most of the fact that each Arkadian goes to school just as she or he goes through the rest of life, interacting with it, getting the most out of it. Therefore, school should not be understood as a center for the transmission of knowledge, but as a catalyst of that knowledge that is appropriate for dealing with the world and society. The student will not learn anything if the learning does not involve the right slifes, and the school should make it possible for these slifes to occur and for the student to discern them well and make the most of them."

"All of this reminds me of a friend who says that pedagogy should avoid the transmission of knowledge, to base itself instead on children building their concepts, interacting with the world by way of playing. Does my friend have Arkadian ideas?"

"Not exactly. I am familiar with similar theories, and their pedagogy has interesting practical propositions that would improve Arkadian school a great deal, but the problem is that the Arkadian kognitive structure is based on slifes. These theories are right to consider that education gives too much weight to surrogate learning on top of other activities. Approaching Arkadian education with an open mind is preferable, for example expecting the child to take an active role, and to follow the steps and the phases progressively, trusting the child's natural process. However, the explanatory model of these approaches cannot be transferred to Arkadians. Kognition is based on slifes, while cognition is based on concepts. Arkadian language is evokative, while human language is symbolic. Therefore, the meeting point of Arkadians with these approaches of active, contextual, and practical educational strategies responds to different motives. According to your friend's theories, the concept of contents/container will be better understood by a human who sees practical examples. In contrast, the slife contents/container is nothing but a practical example, or a set of practical examples. Moreover, some Arkadian slifes must be distanced from what is practical and contextual. For an Arkadian, the understanding of 'multiplication' consists of having a series of slifes, but the Arkadian will always require the times table, because it is crucial surrogate learning. We cannot exclude surrogate learning."

"If you say so."

"Secondly, in contrast to these approaches, Arkadians do not build their personal and nontransferable knowledge."

"But they live in virtual worlds, right?"

"Yes."

"So?"

"They live in virtual worlds, but you have to take into account that these worlds in large part are true worlds and are shared by many Arkadians. The only difficulty is that they are slife-dependent, not language-dependent, and that is why texts and lectures are not what is needed."

"I see."

"Finally, some people defend the idea that we human beings have a cognitive development that is normally respected in children, or at least they think so. But Arkadians do not have a kognitive development that occurs in phases. For one thing, Arkadians acquire thousand and thousands of slifes in the first years of life in order to be able to establish thousands and thousands of different konceptual connections among different memograms. Each of these slifes, and each one of the connections is particular and different from the next. Therefore, at the present time, when we can just barely glimpse these kontents and slifes, thinking that with a few concepts borrowed from human beings we will get somewhere is ridiculous."

"So I say!"

"A large part of the kontents have to be acquired by the child, and these acquisitions will be invisible to the educator; the school can only become a catalyst of these kontents."

"Because it cannot transmit kontents."

"Exactly. Therefore, and because of all this, if we were to apply your friend's strategies to Arkadian school, education would improve, because many of the propositions would have the effect of preparing the terrain for original slifes. However, the improvements would just be a small part of the picture, the most visible consequences, like the fact that the best way to learn is through playing, or in the relevant contexts of the kontent. Hundreds of additional elements are involved in the education of Arkadian children through slifes. For an Arkadian, all slifes are crucial, and all slifes can embody what human beings call concepts. Also, slifes have many more elements, concepts, that pedagogical experts have not been able to characterize and never will be, because the person is not consciously aware of them. Not only playing and the manipulation of a few toys are crucial, but also all types of interaction with the surroundings, with the doors, the stairs, voices, songs, colors, furniture. Consequently, these approaches would help or complement the strategies that are used by Arkadians for learning, but they would be incomplete."

"Then what?"

"The moral of the story is that the school has to set its objectives and make use of the appropriate strategies for obtaining them."

"This is very easy to say, but very difficult to apply. You should be more precise."

"You are right, but we do not have time to go into this issue with all what should be included. However, I can say a few things."

"Namely?"

"Understanding school as a transmission of knowledge is not correct, nor should we think that school just has to stimulate the natural learning process of the child."

"What do you mean by this?"

"Arkadians have a particular kognitive structure, and it is a plastic one, since it is capable of penetrating reality regardless of its characteristics. The appropriate thing, then, would be to incorporate into the Arkadians a wealth of slifes that are like the ones that they will have to face."

"Meaning things like learning outdoors?"

"No. Learning outdoors is not necessarily better for Arkadian children, nor keeping them far away from computers."

"Why?"

"Because nothing about the surroundings is more or less appropriate. If the world that the Arkadians are going to live in is a technological world, full of machines, books, televisions, no point exists of sending them out to the country, unless panceiving kontents of that world is going to be useful for them. The more active the child is, the better; the richer the slifes, even better, and the more interaction occurs, the best."

The sun unexpectedly appeared from behind a cloud, illuminating the slopes of Kuo in green and coloring the walls of the houses an intense orange. Then, immediately afterwards, the sun went down, as a betrayal.

"Oh, no! I have many issues left to discuss with you!"

"Tomorrow."

"Are you going to say anything else than 'tomorrow' when I ask you for more time?"

"Yes."

"When will it be?"

"Tomorrow."

Eight

SATURDAY
On How Living Dissolves the Mind

I woke up earlier than other days. I felt a strong premonition that this was going to be my last and my most important day in Arkadia. I could barely think about anything else while I got ready, to the point that I was dressed and waiting before the rabbit appeared at the door. But he did not appear. I had to go myself alone to the terrace. I did not want to waste my time.

"I think that it is about time that you answered a question that I have been asking myself all week."

"Go ahead, Alice."

"I will tell you through a slife. It is Thanksgiving Day. As usual, we play grandfather's games after the meal. He takes a card from the deck, and the rest of us have to divine which card he is looking at. Today I won. Now everyone is taking a nap. If I go to sleep, I will wake up in a terrible mood. I open the photo albums. How odd. Those dresses, those shoes, those hairstyles that I used to like so much now look so strange and ugly. I cannot understand how I could have gone around like that. I have a silly idea. Could we play grandfather's game with a photo instead of with a card? Would we be able to transmit that sensation of strangeness?"

"Is that the question?"

"Not exactly. What I want to ask is: What kind of mental life do Arkadians have?"

"From what we have learned up to now, you should already guess what the answer is, but I can see in your face that you do not quite get it."

"Right."

"I find it curious to talk about the mental life of Arkadians, because as similar as they appear to be to human beings, this is the aspect that requires a special look."

"You do not say."

"Let us see. The mental state par excellence of human beings is thought, which has the particularity of being a state that contains 'something about something.'"

"What are you referring to when you say 'something about something?'"

"One can think about an 'apple' without the thought being an apple. This issue of 'something being about something different from itself' is called 'intentionality' and it is the difference that is normally established between mental states and any other type of state of the world. Thus, for example, any state of the world, like a chimney, the sun, a mountain, is not 'something about something': a mountain is a mountain and nothing else. Thanks to the intentionality of thought, we human beings can have beliefs about nearby things, like the apple that is in front of us, or things that are beyond the reach of our senses, like the milk in the refrigerator, things that are far away in space, like the moon, things that happened in the past, like man's visit to the moon, things that will happen in the future, like the upcoming Olympic Games, and things that do not exist, like unicorns."

"So?"

"Let us continue. Suppose that Eric and Catherine are arguing about whether or not unicorns exist. Let us name the thing that they are arguing about by way of the sentence 'Unicorns exist.' Eric and Catherine somehow share the meaning of that sentence as the object of their disagreement, and this is expressed with the sentence 'Eric thinks that unicorns do not exist' and the sentence 'Catherine thinks that unicorns exist.'"

"Right, what about it?"

"Well, the content of a thought like 'Unicorns exist' is said to correspond to a 'proposition.' A proposition is something that is enunciated in a sentence that asserts something and can be true or false. Normally, a proposition is what comes after the form expression 'think that,' like Eric thinks that 'unicorns exist,' the proposition being in this case, 'Unicorns exist.' This assertion, or whatever you want to call it, is something independent from the language in which it is stated. So, the proposition, 'Unicorns exist,' is the same as, 'Los unicornios existen,' or, 'Les unicornes existent.' A proposition is something like a nucleus, but it is at the same time comprised of elements. Concepts are generally accepted as propositions' constituents, just as the words 'exist' and 'unicorns' are what constitute the sentence 'Unicorns exist.' Therefore, in order to grasp the proposition 'Unicorns exist,' both Catherine and Eric should have, among other things, the concepts 'exist' and 'unicorns.'"

"Let us get to the point."

"The notion of propositions in Arkadia is both much more complex and much simpler than in the world of human beings. In the first place, propositions have no place in Arkadia because Arkadians do not have the right medium with which to represent them. As I have said on other days, Arkadian language can trick you. Unfortunately, language in Arkadia does not appear to be like in the human world, where words refer to objects in the world and the combination of words allows us to say, to represent, states of the world. Therefore, Arkadians cannot enunciate something that may be true or false. The peculiar nature of Arkadian language is its evokative structure. Words do not represent; they do not stand for what they refer to in the human world; instead, they evoke the slifes and kontents in which the words are anchored. Consequently, and in the absence of other mechanisms, propositions cannot be fixed by language in Arkadia. No sentences lead univocally to the slifes that are to be transmitted. And in the absence of a method of representation that is univocal and universal, Arkadians cannot determine what proposition they are discussing, what thing they are talking about."

"In the real world a 'fact' corresponds to 'Unicorns exist' or to 'Unicorns do not exist,' right?"

"Do not fall into the language trap. You, as a human, use language to characterize a state of affairs, be it real or possible, but Arkadians cannot do that with language. They do it through slifes, and language is only a part of these slifes. Facts cannot be described with language, only evoked: 'Water boils at 212 degrees Fahrenheit,' 'The sun rises in the east' or 'Pregnancy lasts 9 months' are not representations of facts in Arkadia, unless we describe the perspektives of the Arkadians that say so. Consequently, the thing that Erik and Katherine are arguing about is not characterized by whether unicorns exist or not; instead, this sentence takes them to the slife in which the point of view is specified and in which, if the conceptual competence of the slife 'Unicorns exist' is instantiated, we can say that this perspektive of Erik's intersects with K's point of view."

"To what does a thought correspond in Arkadia?"

"In order to understand what a thought is in Arkadia, you have to move to the context of a slife, its kontents, its associations, and its configuration as figure/ground."

"So?"

"The content of a thought is the perspektive derived from a slife, or a set of slifes, with a particular figure/ground."

"A thought cannot be a slife. Even human beings can have a slife without having thoughts, cannot they? Does Katherine have a human thought when she is eating an ice-cream, going to the toilet, or driving a car?"

"In a way, she does. Let us see. The translation from human thought to Arkadia slife is not complete and exhaustive. All human thought is translated into a perspektive, although not all perspektives would be considered a thought by human beings. Because of the wealth of each slife, and the complexity of the processes involved, we are still far from being able to create a translation manual between slifes and thoughts, not even for the simplest human thought. But, who knows, some day we may have the elements to do that."

"I do not follow you. What are we referring to by the 'thing' that Erik and Katherine are arguing about? Is 'unicorns do or do not exist' an idea or isn't it? Is it something that people can discuss?"

"No proposition or an abstract idea is floating around the heads of Erik and Katherine; instead, it is something that is rooted in the slife background of each of them. To be more exact, 'Unicorns exist' corresponds to a perspektive of their virtual worlds that was born of a set of specific slifes, and from all the slifes that have been experienced afterwards and have become associated with one another."

"How can they discuss about 'Unicorns exist' if such a thing depends of a slife background?"

"In one slife a specific kontent was noted and a specific figure/ground was created, with a derived perspektive, that contains all that is relevant in the discussion about 'Unicorns exist.'"

"'Unicorns exist' is an abstract idea."

"By contrast, in Arkadia everything that counts as a thought, in the human sense of the word, has to be seen as forming a part of some slife or of some connection between past slifes. If we then see in it, from the human point of view, an abstract element, a proposition, that is something that we human beings have put there."

"How can an abstract idea be created in a slife?"

"As I told you, the kontents of slifes do not appear because of a series of elements in the world, nor because the kontents pre-exist in the kognitive system waiting for something to activate them. They appear through interaction between the world and the kognitive system. The slife that Erik experiences of contents/container before a glass of water is not produced because Erik notes information in the surroundings, nor because an element within his kognitive system is potentially describable by 'contents/container relationship waiting to be activated.'"

"How is a slife described in order to compare it with a thought, such as 'Katherine believes that unicorns exist.' Does she imagine a unicorn in front of her? A herd of them? Does she imagine a day at the unicorn races? And what is the difference between the slife of imagining unicorns, and the slife described by human beings with the sentence 'Unicorns exist?'"

"I would say that in the case of the proposition 'Unicorns exist' we are referring to a perspektive through which, among many other things, Katherine is prepared to accept the presence of unicorns. However, if you want to look at the details about how this proposition is rooted, we would have to look for one or more slifes in which Katherine's unicorn is situated as figure/ground that connects konceptually with horses, elephants, elm trees, as opposed to fictional kontents, like dragons, fairy godmothers, Bug Bunny, etc."

"I do not know. Le us move to other related aspects of thoughts. For example, what happens in cases when we human beings hear that someone says, 'I think that this person is courteous,' in a situation in which someone let us go into the elevator first?"

"The trait of courteousness would not be an interpretation of the slife, but a kontent of the perspektive, with the same rank as any other kontent, like the scent of that person's cologne. Again, these more conceptual processes have no place outside of the parallel action of the other senses. That is, you will not find a place where the kognitive system says, 'what has been given me by the senses is a courteous action.' Instead, this conceptual process is situated at the same level and is connected to all the other kontents so that the slife contains the kontent of 'courteousness.' No 'courtesy' data is separated from the other aspects of the slife. We could say that the Arkadian kognitive system comes out into the world and impregnates that scene with the impacts of courtesy that have been seen in the past, in such a way that the kognitive system perceives the courteousness directly from the scene, in addition to the shapes and colors."

"But what is courtesy?"

"'Beauty' and 'courtesy' are kontents, elements that have been created in the development of one or many slifes. When Katherine thinks, 'This painting is beautiful,' she is not calling upon something floating in her head. She does not decide that the painting fits with something that is a concept of 'beautiful.' What she does is connecting the panception of this painting with all the other paintings that she has seen, and especially those that have produced what we could say artistic pleasure. She does not have a concept of beauty in the abstract sense, but all of her life, all the relevant memograms, each one well-structured, with a multitude of particularities, are activated as a context of the slife in which she is panceiving the painting. Therefore, nothing is in the property 'beauty' except a slife, or set of slifes, that were felt in a particular way and that were recorded in that way, in a set of slifes that she had in the past. So, in order to think, Arkadians have to re-live, or go through the original moment again, or the set of memograms that are relevant in that situation. No thoughts exist apart from living; instead, if an Arkadian thinks about beauty, the slife context that is activated are all the memograms in which beauty is activated by way of evokation, which is to say that the slife of beauty is re-lived. So, when we say, 'Katherine thinks that unicorns exist,' we include what we call 'thought' in the context of a situation. We do not need for the Arkadian to write the sentence 'Unicorns exist' in a different place, the mind, from where it is happening. The Arkadian does not have the interior space in which to reflect about what happens outside; it happens in the current world, or the past world. When Katherine thinks, in the human sense of the word, she is in the world, either in the current situation or evoking a past slife."

"Yet despite all these individual particularities, two Arkadians can think something equivalent, right?"

"Yes. Here, as with our examination of kommunication, we can suppose that two slifes are equivalent if the virtual worlds that maintain the homeostasis of both slifes, what we called their perspektives, are equivalent. So, two Arkadians can have an equivalent thought because they have slifes with equivalent perspektives."

"Then Arkadian 'thoughts,' if such a thing exists, do not exist independently from the Arkadians. No abstract thought is prior to the appearance of the Arkadians, or surviving beyond their disappearance, that corresponds, for example, to the 'contents/container' relationship."

"Exactly. The 'contents/container' relationship, or the idea 'Unicorns exist,' do not exist independently from the Arkadians, and not because the proposition is about whether or not they exist, but because the relationship 'contents/container' or 'Unicorns exist' is part of the virtual world of all Arkadians, or the world of K, which is the same thing."

"And if Erik loses the slife 'Unicorns exist,' or something from it, then the thought is lost?"

"Yes, it is. The kognitive system of an Arkadian is like an organized file folder of all the situations that have been experienced, and all the knowledge is integrated in each one of its slifes, and in the connections among them. If, for some reason, the kognitive system could not evoke the slife, because it was no longer able to integrate the different parts of the brain involved in the original slifes, the memograms would stop being kognitively relevant; the thought would have been lost, even though the brain preserves the memograms."

"Okay, I will accept what you say about the description of a thought not being exactly the same as in human beings. However, a thought is one thing, and quite another thing is 'to have thoughts' or 'to reason.' When we human beings talk about 'thinking,' we are referring to things like 'I am thinking about buying a car,' 'I like to daydream about what I will do on my vacation,' or 'I am solving a problem.'"

"When Arkadians are carrying out one of these activities, what they are doing is experiencing a present slife and manipulating past memograms, creating new scenes by the combination of evokations. Therefore, to think, to reason is to live re-living. Even when we say that an Arkadian is reflecting verbally, that individual is experiencing a slife, or a chain of slifes. When such persons are talking to themselves, what they are doing is evoking their past with words, lighting up memograms and manipulating them. To think in discourse is thus an interactive activity involving language and the spontaneous activation of the memograms. The relevant thing is that thanks to language, Arkadians can control this process."

A light breeze picked up. The village was calm, not even a sound from the port.

"Can we translate a thought to a slife?"

"Yes, but with great difficulty. Different basic problems make the translation process difficult, and they have to do with differences between how we characterize human beings and Arkadians."

"What are these differences?"

"Let us look at the first one:

Thoughts are separate from the world: Catherine's thought that 'Paris is the capital of France' does not contain the city of Paris, but simply refers to it.

This is not the case in Arkadia."

"How is Paris going to be contained in a slife?"

"The first day I said that a slife corresponds to a complex whole that includes the world or a part of it and the kognitive system. The kontents of a slife only make sense when they encompass both the world and the kognitive system. The kontents are not in the kognitive system, nor are they in the world; they appear through the conjunction of the kognitive system, the slife past, and the world. The world provides the objects, the kognitive system provides everything necessary to shape the relevant kontents in the slife. Without the world, the kognitive system can do nothing, and has nothing; without the kognitive system, the individual cannot shape reality nor establish interesting associations. Kontents, and therefore slifes, can only be characterized considering both elements. Remember once more the analogy of phantom limbs. A phantom limb is created through the conjunction of a real limb, flesh and bone, with the brain. When the limb is lost, the patient can still sense the limb; the patient feels it as if it were present. In the same way, if we want to describe Katherine's slife when she looks at the apple on the table, we cannot say that the kognitive system represents 'an apple on the table.' Instead, we have to include properties and elements of the world and activities of the kognitive system. Just by looking in Katherine's head we will not be able to discover Katherine's thought that 'an apple is on the table'; instead, we will have to analyze the world-kognitive system complex. Consequently, slifes cannot be understood as separate from the world, because they are part of the chunk of world in which the original slife was created. No two media exist, the kognitive system and the world; the slife is the only one."

"But Arkadians have memories, and they can remember that they thought an apple was on the table, with no need for the apple to be there when they remember."

"True, but remember that memograms include the imprints left by the slife. Since they are imprints of the original slife, and not representations, the memograms also have to be understood as one part of the world-kognitive system unit. When they are activated, the parts of the brain are activated that were activated when the person had the slife, so it is like reliving the original slife. In one way or another, if we want to describe the slife that is the memory of the original slife, we have to fill the empty space left by the world after it impregnated the kognitive system."

He stopped talking for a moment and looked at me.

"Do you follow me?"

"More or less."

"Let us take a look at the second difference:

Thoughts represent states of the world: The thought described by the sentence 'Catherine believes that Paris is the capital of France' represents a relationship between the city of Paris and the country of France.

Again, a slife is not a representation of the situation that the Arkadian lives through. The kognitive system shapes reality, instead of creating a representation, outline, or copy of what is happening in the world. When Katherine looks at the apple in the fruit bowl, she has no image or representation of the apple, the dish, and the table. What she experiences is the panceptual activity of kognitive system. In the case of a phantom limb, when the patient describes the missing limb, he or she is not examining a copy or a representation of the limb; instead, they just feel it. Remember the strategy that my grandfather uses to remember telephone numbers. A telephone number can be preserved without it being represented anywhere, since remembering the movements necessary to dial that number on the telephone is enough. While the movements correspond to a typical telephone, that is, as long as the numbers are arranged in the same way and the same finger movement is required, then the telephone number will be remembered, since the conceptual competence of the movement 'satisfices' the telephone number. The movement is not a representation of the number. So, if somebody changes the telephone and the numbers are arranged differently, then my grandfather will lose the ability to call that number. Similarly, the kognitive system does not represent reality; it only shapes it and discerns it. As long as the discrimination satisfices the conceptual competence of its kontents, it will not be necessary to represent the situation."

He stopped again, and looked at me hard.

"Are we doing all right?"

"I guess so."

"Let us look at the third difference between human thought and Arkadian slife:

> *Thoughts are either true or false*: The thought described by the sentence 'Catherine believes that Paris is the capital of France' can be true or false.

This condition, as we have seen, is fulfilled in the case of slifes, although it is not objectively expressed in the same way. To be able to say that Katherine has a true slife, we must call upon a kind of true world, a virtual world in which an omniscient being like K would live. This world corresponds to all the kontents that can be revealed in the real world from the perspective of the Arkadian kognitive system, or, the world as seen by the omniscient being K. In those areas in which an overlap exists between the Katherine's perspektive and K's perspektive, her slife can be considered true. Okay?"

"If you say so."

"I also said that Arkadians do not have incontrovertible criteria regarding the verisimilitude of a belief. To be able to determine the truth of this virtual world in which the Arkadian lives, we must be able to transform their slifes into elements that can be true or false, that can be compared with something of the world that confirms them or denies them. In the human world, this appears to be achieved through language, but in Arkadia that is not possible. Arkadian language does not describe reality because it lacks the ability to represent the states of the world, so it cannot characterize slifes or the world, and it therefore cannot determine the truthfulness or falseness of a slife. However, Arkadians have what we call omniscient guaranties, or K guaranties, that determine the verisimilitude of a slife, and whose values are continuous, not absolute, which is to say that they determine greater or lesser verisimilitude. By trusting these guaranties, Arkadians can attribute verisimilitude to a perspektive."

Another pause, and another look.

"How are we doing?"

"Well...."

"Let us look at the last fundamental difference between human thought and Arkadian slifes:

> *Thoughts form part of inferential relationships*: Catherine can make an inference between the thought, 'Paris is the capital of France,' and the thought, 'Paris is in France.'

This condition can be established in the case of the Arkadians, but not because slifes are represented in some kind of language of thought. In Arkadia, inferential relationships can exist between two slifes, keeping in mind the specific figure/ground, their konceptual connections, and the capability for transfer among different slifes. For example, the slife:

(1) Which hand has more fingers, the left or the right?

is inferentially related to the slife of:

(2) Both hands have the same number of fingers.

through the slife:

(3) Hands have five fingers.

In general, all Arkadians can make this inference. As we saw, because the perspektive *1* is included in *x*, the relationship can be expressed objectively. It may occur that the same Arkadian that can carry out the operation from *1* to *2*, will not be able to carry out a similar one that responds to the same human inferential rules. I am referring to getting from:

(4) Which weighs more, a kilogram of straw or a kilogram of lead?

to:

(5) Both weigh the same.

through the slife:

(6) All kilograms weigh the same amount.

In fact, some Arkadians say:

(5*) A kilo of lead.

and this is because the inferences that they make are based both on their kognitive capability and their slife background."

"So they do not reason logically?"

"They do not reason following or applying the rules of logic. Their being able to resolve a reasoning problem according to a rule of logic does not mean that we should deduce that they will solve all the reasoning problems in which that rule of logic applies. To reason in Arkadia means being able to transfer the appropriate past figure/ground to a new situation that has not been experienced before. So if the figure/ground corresponds to a rule of logic, it can be used to solve similar problems, but not all of them. As always, it depends on a myriad of factors."

"Then how do Arkadians reason?"

"By applying the transfer capability of their kognitive system to their slife background. This, like any other kognitive capability, has to be anchored in the nature of the slifes and the application of transfer mechanisms."

"Can they, for example, resolve syllogisms?"

"Yes, they can resolve syllogisms, but not all types of syllogisms and not all the contents of one type of syllogism. As I just said, logic does not describe the Arkadian way of reasoning, since they learn to reason through the combination of capabilities of their kognitive system and their slife background. For this reason, their ability to resolve syllogisms is not based on the learning of rules of logic, but on the application of figure/grounds to situations. As is the case with other capabilities, they will be progressively more successful in different types of syllogisms, and for different contents of syllogism. In this sense, we can state that their reasoning respects the rules of logic, but that, as we know, is because they are capable of adapting *satisficingly* to the rules, not because they apply them."

"Examples, please."

"Let us see how Erik resolves a syllogism:

Premise 1: All planets revolve around a sun.
Premise 2: The earth is a planet.
Conclusion: The earth revolves around a sun.

Let us say that Erik has not learned the rules for resolving a syllogism, since what I want you to keep in mind is the natural way, the way determined by the kognitive system, of reaching the conclusion. Erik's strategy is to adopt a view in his particular world for each sentence and see if they agree. Thus, the first sentence evokes a slife that focuses on, as figure/ ground, the relationship between a planet and a sun in a model of the solar system that they had in school, and the surrogate slife that such a slife will apply to 'all planets.' The second sentence can evoke a slife in which the kontent 'Earth' is situated as figure in the ground of the kontent 'planet.' How does he reach the conclusion? Not spontaneously. An Arkadian must know what is being asked with these sentences, and so he or she must have seen cases of syllogisms in order to detect that what is being asked is to relate in a reasonable way the terms that are not repeated in the premises. The conclusion corresponds therefore to an overlap of the premises, and the sentence used tries to evoke the terms that are not repeated. Thus, in the conclusion, the two sentences of the premises overlap, and Erik has a slife in which the Earth is focused on as figure in the ground of the relationship with the kontents sun. Finally, the reading of the conclusion evokes a slife whose perspektive is equivalent to the slife in which the two sentences overlapped, and then Erik asserts that the argument is correct. In any case, just because an Arkadian resolves one type of syllogism, it does not mean she or he will resolve all the syllogisms of that type."

"Could you identify more differences?"

"Yes, a crucial one. Human thoughts have a special quality, our 'awareness,' or consciousness of the content of the thought, just as an awareness of the color red, of the sound of a bell, or the taste of tea. In all of these cases something is specific, an activity carried out by the individual that seems a realization of what he or she is thinking, and that is beyond the information of the senses: a mind that observes what is happening in the body and the world."

"I think I know what you mean."

"Well, for you to understand how this particularity is different in Arkadia, I am going to use an experiment that is impossible to carry out, but which we can talk about. To begin with, will you accept that a thought may correspond to a slife and its derived perspektive?"

"I will accept that."

"Let us suppose, then, that the slife, to make things simple, is what may be evoked in Katherine by the sentence, 'An apple is on the table.' Let us suppose that, with the help of a wonderful and sophisticated technology that you have available, you disconnect in Katherine's brain all those areas that are concerned with thinking."

"If you insist."

"Yet, despite your having done so, Katherine continues to have the same slife, and therefore, the same thought, and this is because in a slife nothing happens but the activity of the senses, everything that we have called panception."

"But wait a minute, let us say that Katherine closes her eyes, is not she still thinking, 'An apple is on the table?'"

"That she closes her eyes does not change anything, for she is still connected to the world with her senses active and functional. The areas of the brain that process those senses are active. Though her eyes are closed, the impact of the apple is still functional, since the imprint activates the memories of apples, what is preserved in the memograms. Consequently, the slife derives a perspektive in which the apple appears, and this kontent is also a recreation of the apple that she just saw."

"What if all access to her senses was cut off?"

"Then she would not have slifes."

"Excuse me?"

"In fact, she would no longer 'be there.' The key is the deactivation or disarticulation of the connection among the senses and the cerebral cortex. Without this functional connection, no kognitive activity is possible."

"We human beings have something, a mind, that goes beyond the senses, and if Arkadians are like human beings, they should also have minds, right?"

"Not necessarily. The mind as understood by human beings is an entity that is beyond the mere perception of the world. Somehow, human beings know that we do not need to be connected with the world in order to think; we can disconnect ourselves superficially, closing our eyes for example, and begin a discourse process. In an extreme case, even if the senses were completely disconnected, as meditation experts appear to do, thought would remain intact. But in Arkadia things are not like that. To think is to experience a slife in the same way as panceiving the world. If Arkadians evoke a memogram, they live it as if they were living the original moment again, although with reduced intensity because the chunk of original world is missing."

"What do we do then with the sensations of, for example, 'red,' 'pain,' or 'fear?' What I mean is, does Katherine have the same sensation of the color red as Erik does? Does an out-of-tune clarinet sound the same to Katherine as it does to a professional clarinet player?"

"As I have just said, Arkadians, like human beings, have subjective sensations, something that can be described as a perception or awareness of what is happening, a state that has a subjective component. The essence of this something is a quality of what is being experienced."

"Of what does this awareness consist in Arkadia?"

"Just as the quality of a thought is a present view through the past, the quality of 'red' or of 'sweet' is the consequence of superimposing all the slife background of that Arkadian for those kontents with which the sensation is felt. The awareness of 'red' or of 'Nikole's beauty' is not something independent of that slife past. As I said on Monday, when Katherine as a newborn baby looks at this apple, she does not see anything clearly, just vague shapes and colors. However, after a few months, Katherine has subjective sensations that are the consequence of looking at the apple through the whole past of apples and reds. Therefore, the sensation of 'red,' the awareness of 'red,' is the consequence of an impact in the kognitive system seen through a slife past. Similarly, when baby Katherine looks at 'Self-Portrait with Pipe and Bandaged Ear' by Van Gogh, she does not see anything specific, only vague shapes and colors. After a few months, Katherine sees specific areas of color and shapes. As she gets older, Katherine sees new things, especially after studying the history of art. The subjective sensation of the shape of a pipe is the consequence of the overlapping of all past slifes and their kontents of pipe shapes. It is not something inherent to the present of the panception; instead, that pipe is looked at literally through her slife past."

"I am not sure if I understand."

"Allow me to use an analogy. We could say that a banknote for one hundred eukos, the currency in Arkadia, has no volume. But if you pile up a thousand hundred euko bills, the money will have volume, and the volume is the consequence of piling up the bills. In the same way, we cannot explain the quality of the color 'red' that is panceived without making reference to a specific slife past of 'reds.'"

"And pain?"

"The same thing. The quality of a pain is a slife past seen from the current electrochemical phenomenon."

Non-Professor O stopped talking. He took a bottle out of his pocket. It was Tuesday's perfume. He opened it, splashed some liquid on his hand, spread it around and then gave me his hand.

"Smell it."

"How strange! It is as if I had traveled through time. For a moment I have felt you as I was sensing you on Tuesday. And I have realized that I no longer sense you as I did on Tuesday, even if I thought so."

"That is what happens to Arkadians. They cannot be aware of kontents that they have not experienced in the past, nor how they have changed. An Eskimo, for example, can differentiate between varying shades of white snow, and will be aware of them, while for any non-Eskimo this would be impossible, even though their eyes and their brain work the same way. And an expert chess player panceives in any game of chess a configuration that is derived from the arrangement of the pieces on the board, of which the expert is aware, while non-experts cannot be aware of it no matter how much it is explained to them. This is due to their respective pasts, and not only some contemporaneous activity of their kognitive systems."

"Can this awareness be seen, or analyzed, or reproduced?"

"No, for the time being that is impossible. But when we do have the necessary elements, we will be able to include the contents/container relationship, pain or the color red in the characterization of a slife. We will be able to describe that what we are calling the awareness of red is, for a given kognitive system and slife past, the attention to a type of kontent, in such a way that the attention to this type of kontent provokes a situation that is the subjective sensation of what we call awareness of 'red.'"

The smoke from his pipe came straight to me. Today it had a lot more nuances that it did the first day; I could pick up hints of honey and a light aroma of young mahogany. I looked up at the sky. It was clear, not a single cloud. The slopes of Kuo were such an intense shade of green that it almost hurt.

"Then, that Katherine needs her past to be able to think would mean that telepathy is not possible in Arkadia, right?"

"Exactly. Since all present slifes are a look at the world through the past of the individual, a human thought translates in Arkadia into experiencing the present through the past. The shape of the apple on the table is seen the way it is because it is seen through all the apple shapes that have been seen in the past. Therefore, Erik having telepathy with Katherine would mean that Erik is having Katherine's current slife, panceiving all the kontents of the situation through all of Katherine's slife past, which is frankly quite difficult to achieve."

"Could telepathy exist if somebody were able to transmit his or her perspektive, that is, the virtual world that complements his or her slife?"

"No, because the virtual world cannot be transmitted. It can be shared when kommunication is successful, but no transmission is possible."

"This also means that the way we saw things in the past is lost forever, right?"

"More or less. The sensations depend on the weight of all the previous sensations, and thus those that have had a continuity in time can no longer recover the original quality. For that reason, childhood is in the distance, separated from each individual forever, since that person, that slife brain that panceived as a child is no longer there, and therefore cannot see the world like it used to. However, an exception exists. The sensations that have not been reproduced maintain the original quality. If at some point in my childhood I ate a kind of muffin that I have not had since, that muffin will preserve its original flavor.

But if I have eaten lots of the same muffins, or substances that interfere with that flavor, the original flavor will end up being lost. The present is a present seen through the past, but the past can also be a present in the future."

"What I do not see is how we can explain the behavior of the Arkadians, their decisions, their reactions, if we cannot base our explanations on mental states. In our world, when we want to explain why somebody has done something, like why someone bought a new car, or why that child started to cry, why a family goes on a trip to France instead of Italy, we talk about 'wishes,' 'beliefs,' 'fears'; we say things like 'he bought a new car because he was envious of his neighbor's new car,' or 'she started crying because she was afraid to go to school,' or 'he decided to take his family to France instead of Italy because he wanted to see the Louvre.' And that requires a mind, doesn't it?"

"Yes, it does. The psychological explanation in human beings introduces 'reason,' 'motives,' 'wishes,' 'feelings,' etc., that is, mental states that have causal power. That is why human beings are said to be rational creatures. Human actions are carried out because of reasons or feelings that shed light on the behavior of a person and help us to explain it. But do not think that by saying this about the human world we have said everything. To say that reasons are the cause of behavior is problematic. If we consider the fact that we are part of the physical world, then the reasons have to be causes, but the reasons are not physical causes. Physical causes, described by empirical laws, are contingent, while logic or reason is not. As opposed to the empirical laws, a rational law is discovered by reflection, and it is true by definition: it is not an empirical principle revealed by slife. A given rational law can be broken or not remembered by the person: sometimes persons may not do what they want, or not accept what they believe. If they were empirical laws, then they could not be broken, for we would always have to behave in the same way. An apple always falls from a tree, unless something holds it up, while we human beings can give a spare coin to a beggar or not give it without any intervention in our decision by the world of physical laws. Consequently, in contrast with the natural sciences, the elements that comprise an explanation of human conduct are established *a priori*. However, in Arkadia we do not have to make this distinction."

"How is that possible?"

"Imagine the following situation:

Catherine is eating in a restaurant. During the meal, an alarm goes off. All of the clients look at each other, and look at the waiters, but nobody does anything. Suddenly, the cooks run out of the kitchen and rush toward the exit. A second later, everyone in the restaurant gets up and runs out.

If we wanted to explain what had happened, from the outside, we could say the following:

Catherine thinks that she heard an alarm. Catherine knows that alarms are used to warn about dangers. Catherine does not want to endanger her life. Catherine knows that sometimes alarms sound for no reason. Catherine sees no sign of worry on the part of the restaurant personnel. Catherine calms down. Catherine sees the cooks running out of the kitchen. Catherine knows that when a serious and imminent danger occurs people flee. Catherine decides to flee.

"I get it. In the explanation you have used several references to reasons, beliefs, and wishes."

"Exactly. In the explanation I have indicated psychological causes like, 'Nobody wants to endanger their life,' 'When faced with imminent danger, you should flee,' and also knowledge about the world like, 'An individual knows that nobody wants to endanger their life,' 'The people who work in an establishment know the meaning of its alarms,' 'A cook has no reason to run out of the kitchen except to flee,' 'If someone is running away, probably a good reason exists.' But language is a trap; do not trust it when we are talking about Arkadians. What we say about them has to be submitted to a precaution that you must not forget."

"Okay."

"If we suppose that the same thing has happened to Katherine, we also have to make use of some types of laws. In Arkadia we do not have to talk about psychological laws, but slife laws, whose application does not require that we call upon reason or desires in the sense of psychological states separate from the slifes."

"What does it mean to say that 'Do not put your life in danger' is a slife law?"

"From the human point of view, to consider that 'to hear an alarm' is an imminent danger means playing with an enormous advantage, that of language. Let us try to explain the situation that we have devised for Arkadia. Let us suppose that many of Katherine's slifes correspond to the reference knowledge that Catherine has about restaurants, alarms, cooks, etc. Let us suppose that Katherine has seen people running away from fires on TV. One day, for example, she saw a show with people running from a fire in the city hall of the Island of Gor. If the 'hearing the alarm' and the 'seeing the cooks running' contexts are linked, determining the explanation by reference to situations that she has recorded in her memograms is possible. Therefore, one can say that the cause is not a singular mental cause, but the relevant memograms that are transferred to the new situation. Do you follow me?"

"I am not sure."

"If we look at the slifes that gave rise to the relevant memograms, and we can establish an analysis of their occurrences, we will see inscribed there rational and psychological aspects forming part of the slife like just any other panceptual aspect. The 'cause and effect' slife background, in which Katherine learned about a relationship between billiard balls, allows her to understand that the cause of the cook fleeing is that danger exists."

"I am far from convinced."

"Let us suppose that in a slife a figure/ground is established that can be described as follows:

(7) In Katherine's virtual world a kontent can be described as 'Alarms have the function of warning about danger,' which is rooted in school slifes in which she was taught that alarms warn about danger, and that people should vacate the place in which they are as soon as possible.

(8) In Katherine's virtual world a kontent can be described as 'Alarms often sound for no apparent reason,' which is rooted in slifes in which she has heard alarms sound in public places even though no danger existed.

(9) In Katherine's virtual world a kontent can be described as 'People tend to flee from danger as soon as possible,' which is rooted in slifes in which she has learned that as soon as a danger appears, people run away.

"So?"

"In the restaurant, perspektive (7) was activated as soon as the fire alarm sounded. However, perspektive (8) was also activated, so at the beginning nothing happened, but as soon as she saw the cooks run by, perspektive (9) was activated, (8) was voided, and (7) took over the situation again, prompting Katherine to get up and run. In other words, the threat is based on a panception of the situation, and the action counts as a slife based on old slifes."

"Are not we failing to explain the main point, that a danger is perceived and that people want to flee from it?"

"No, because that is already included in all the relevant past slifes."

"Wait a minute, situations arise in which the past does not count. If some-one threatens us, we feel fear, and we will try to flee. This is because we respond immediately to threats, because of the mental causes present at that moment."

"False. In Arkadia Katherine flees not because she is obeying a psychologi-cal law, but because her past is always active. Fear does not make her flee, something floating around her head, but 'the-fear-in-the-slife' and the transfer of past slifes in which fear-in-the-slife exists. In these past slifes a panceptual element corresponds to what human beings call the feeling of fear, but it has the same rank as the color or shape of an object."

"And if we say that Katherine has given her spare change to a beggar because she felt pity?"

"The feeling does not move; instead, its structured past does. When we explain why the human Catherine gives her change to a beggar, we say that she does it because she feels pity. This 'because' points to a relationship not indicated by an empirical law but by a rational law, that does not depend on the slife, but on a discipline that we can call 'rationality.' But in Arkadia the 'because she feels pity' responds to, or is analyzed, in a set of memograms that prompt Katherine to give something to a beggar, according to the structure of her current slife. Let us suppose that the original slife is one that Katherine experienced while playing ball in a park. She saw a child looking at her with a sad expression, and Katherine realized that the child wanted to play but was too shy to ask. This 'feeling of pity' or whatever you want to call it, is not something that was floating around her head by itself, but was just another aspect of the slife, like colors, or shapes. Without the slife, they do not exist."

"Why does this eliminate the need for psychological laws?"

"It does not eliminate the need for psychological laws; it just puts them at the same level as any other type of kognitive process of the slife. What it eliminates is the empirical-rational opposition. If the restaurant-alarm slife activates the old slifes involving alarms because of its transferable structure, this can have an empirical characterization. This is so because, to simplify, the memogram has a characterization, a complex one, true, but one that is also empirical. Therefore, if the old slifes with alarms bring about a decision to flee, the cause can be characterized empirically, since the connection between memograms and the current slife can be established, and the result of the fleeing too. When it comes time to explain her behavior in detail, we will have to reveal in her those memograms that determined her attitude. Without them, she would not have acted that way."

"So, if we find the catalogue of slifes-causes, we will have all the psychology explained."

"Even if such a task is extremely long, complicated and difficult to achieve."

"Why?"

"Because the slife in which she sees people in danger flee is a complex structure, and the slife in which she sees the cook running away is also a complex structure, and the relations between them are not simple. They reveal a complex structure in each of the slifes; the revelation also involves many more unconscious and automatic processes than conscious ones. Not merely 'because that happened to me, I will do this,' but 'because that, that, that, and that happened to me, I will do this, this, this, and this.'"

"So coming up with an explanation for each situation is not easy."

"Exactly. The complete causal explanation of any situation will always be extremely complex, because all the slifes have multiple causal connections, so we would almost have to refer to all slifes since the moment of birth. To simplify, we can say that on a given day Katherine experienced a slife whose figure/ground was 'people fleeing' from danger, and another which was 'alarm-danger,' and that both, structured in the Arkadian brain, are activated in the slife that she experiences in the restaurant. She understands the situation by reference to these slifes, and then acts in accordance. The explanation does not require that we avoid the empirical, and at the same time we can make a generalization about those connections and characterize a behavior by using shortcuts like saying, 'Katherine has fled because she felt fear.'"

"Say that Erik wants to light a match, and when he does it he gets burned, and, according to our point of view, he concludes that 'lighting matches is dangerous'. How can this situation be described in Arkadia?"

"Let us suppose that this situation comprises the following steps, as described by you:

(10)   Erik wants to light a match.
(11)   Erik remembers where the box of matches is.
(12)   Erik sees the box of matches.
(13)   Erik lights a match.
(14)   Erik burns himself and feels pain.
(15)   Erik thinks that lighting a match is dangerous.

What is happening in (10)? To put things in ridiculously simple terms, what is happening is the following. To begin with, (10) does not just appear out of nowhere, but is the product of a previous situation. Let us suppose that someone offers Erik a cigarette, and at that moment he experiences a slife in which he remembers himself smoking. The memory has pleasurable elements, and is followed by a slife in which he imagines himself smoking. He returns to the original slife, adding the new kontent that prompts a modification of that slife so that it becomes another one in which Erik is smoking; what we human beings would call desire. In Erik's case, a new aspect is added to the panception, as if another object from the world were added. What happens is that Erik is looking at the cigarette, and the slife demands that it be lit, because Erik knows that he has to light the cigarette in order to smoke it. He experiences then a slife whose structure is that of finding a box of matches. That is where the first stage ends. Let us go on to stage (11), in which we have described Erik as 'Erik remembers where the box of matches is.' At that moment, what happens is that Erik's kognitive system tries to evoke a memogram that will indicate to him where the matches are. When he finds that memogram, Erik has a memory of the original slife, or of a recreation of it, in which he sees, for example, the box of matches in a desk drawer. In stage (12), Erik 'sees the matches,' that is, he opens the drawer and experiences a slife in which the object in the drawer is focused on and evokes all of those memories of objects in which the term 'box of matches' has been anchored. Remember that some of these memories may not correspond with what other Arkadians, K, or we would call 'box of matches,' but, as we said, if these konceptual connections maintain conceptual competence, then we can get along with Erik. In (13), Erik picks up the matches and proceeds to light one, thanks to a series of past slifes in which the gestures for lighting matches became well established, and the only thing that Erik does is to reproduce those gestures. In (14), a part of the combustible material that lighted the cigarette sticks to Erik's finger; he gets burned and feels pain. This pain appears in the slife, although it is just another panceptual element, like the color of the flame. Finally, when we characterize Erik in (15) as 'Erik thinks that lighting matches is dangerous,' what Erik has done is focus on all the slifes in which he lit a match as related to the accident, the burn, that has happened to him as ground."

"What advantages do we gain with these explanations?"

"This way of characterizing Arkadians allows us to do something that we cannot do with human beings, and that is to understand the 'because' of their behavior without having to set up an opposition between empirical laws and rational laws. We can then explain why Arkadians behave in a rational way without having to call upon non-material causes. This is where we find the best distinction for studying the Arkadians. Their behavior is not directed by reasons, but by reasons-in-slifes, how they are characterized and how they are transferred. Everything that we have to say about Arkadian behavior will be defined by the structural characteristics of each situation, and the way in which they are associated slifely."

"However, it seems to me that you are cheating, because it does not matter if we remove those rational laws if in reality they are included in the original slifes. Suppose that Katherine sees a guy kicking a dog, and she thinks that it is a bad thing to do, a 'bad deed'."

"Again, in each slife we can include as many kontents as we want, and among the relations that we establish aspects that characterize associations which human beings call psychological or rational. In one of Katherine's slifes an association is fixed in which kicking a dog. This is seen as a bad thing, but is explained just as are all the other panceptual elements that have an abstract or kognitive nature. The kognitive system establishes that association as it does any other type of relation, like contents/container, behind/in-front, large/small, friendly/dangerous. The association exists because of the intrinsic characteristics that 'unpleasant,' 'avoidable,' 'reprehensible' may have, and because of the consequences that may result from 'sounding off the Arkadian who kicked the dog' or 'praising the taking care of the injured dog.' You will say that these consequences connect two situations, the panception of the kicking and the sounding off, that are not connected empirically but rationally. But precisely because Katherine has seen the sounding off of similar situations, she connects these two complex situations, and this behavior adapts smoothly to the kognitive structure of the Arkadian."

"Katherine can also find something 'bad' spontaneously, for the first time, right?"

"False again. Since infancy, Katherine has learned from her family and social setting lots of kontents regarding social and moral behavior of which she may not be aware, but which are still present."

"But 'bad' is a moral term, not a panceptual term."

"False once more. Arkadians do not behave altruistically or meanly because they apply a law or a rule, but because in their particular slifes, on a specific day, they learned that 'to do such and such is good' and the good thing that was done is what human beings would call a good deed. Therefore, this particular slife, and those that are associated with it, is the cause of the current altruistic act, and not a general law. The causes of an action are not some 'laws of rationality,' but specific events, from the past, and that were subjected to processes that conditioned their occurrence. These conditioning factors can be counted as examples of laws of rationality."

"Then rationality does not exist in Arkadia without having experienced a life."

"Exactly. But do not believe that a life, by itself, by the mere chance of being in some place provides the moral and rational kontents. As I said on Monday, the kognitive system is born with a strong capability of conditioning the slifes of an individual. It does not come with the kontents 'good' and 'bad' but it comes with the necessary tools to bring about such kontents. And such kontents can potentially be described from a physical point of view."

"I do not get that last part about how they can potentially be described from the physical point of view."

"What I mean is that the slife is a structure potentially describable in the language of physical substances, as opposed to mental substances."

"Excuse me?"

"Let us see. Among human beings two positions attempt to account for mental phenomena. Some people are of the opinion that nature, including the human body, is material and therefore governed by the principles of physics. They understand human beings in a special way in that they are composed of one material substance and another non-material, or mental substance; an individual would essentially be a combination of mental and material substances. This is what is known as dualism. But, as occurs with the empirical-rational opposition, dualism is far from having done away with the body-mind problem, since how to identify, how to explain the interaction of the two substances remains to be seen. To put it a different way, if the mind is an immaterial substance, lacking the physical properties such as spatial localization and shape, how can it be the cause of effects in the material world, how can it make objects move, and at the same time be causally affected by the world, like when we feel pain from a stubbed toe?"

"That is what I ask."

"The other human position is known as materialism. Materialists sustain that everything that exists is either material or physical in nature. Minds are in one way or another composed of physical substance. As with dualism, up to the present different routes deal with the 'one way or another' detail, but even the most popular position, that the mind is superimposed on the brain, is problematic. Even if materialism is accepted, the problem of the particular relationship between what is mental and what is physical remains, since even physical minds have special properties, like what we have called intentionality, or consciousness, that require explanation, and are not easily accessible by the materialists. The simple proclamation that the mind is not made of mental substance, but is material, like the rest of the world, is not enough to explain the mind's traits that appear distinctive, if not unique."

"So?"

"If all human thought is described in the case of Arkadians as a complex activity of the brain, complex but activity nonetheless, and like a part of the world, then describing it in physical terms is possible. We do not have to explain the concept of 'beauty' as something mental, but as a situation that an individual lives through at a given time, or as the set of situations or connections among elements of different situations. We do not have to explain the thought 'Unicorns exist in Pluto' as something immaterial, but as a situation experienced by an individual. We do not have to explain the idea of 'freedom' as something that floats around in a person's head, but as a situation experienced by an individual. In short, mental states are part of the slifes, and the slifes are states of the Arkadian brain and the world, physical states that are highly organized and describable for the time being only in terms of kontents and their distinctiveness, like a storm being a physical state that is described in meteorological terms, and whose characterization has to be done from the perspective of a third person."

"But pain is not something physical."

"When an Arkadian gets burned with a match, he or she feels the burn and thinks something along the lines of 'how unfortunate,' but that is a 'body-that-feels-in-the-world' and not a 'mind-that-feels-what-is-happening-to-its-body.' The pain is a specific panceptual characteristic describable in terms of states of a brain, and of a slife past. The causal properties of pain are the causal properties of pain-in-that-slife that depend on the causal properties of all the pains that have been felt in the past. That is, nothing is floating around the Arkadian's head, pain, that makes that individual decide not to light another match; instead, the specific slife is associated with other slifes that have been followed by others, and thus the kognitive system can transfer these structures to the new situation. On other occasions, depending on the structure of the slife, that pain may prompt her or him to burn herself or himself again, if she or he wants, for example, to demonstrate how courageous she or he is. Pain in a pure state does not exist.

What we human beings describe as the thought 'how unfortunate' is not a sentence in a language of thought, but a slife whose figure/ground is the same Arkadian with panceptual characteristics associated with other Arkadians who have experienced unfortunate situations, and that new slife has a reality in the kognitive system that can be described in the language of material substances and their distinctiveness."

"How then is the mind related to the body?"

"If the thesis is that only to live re-living the slifes exists and that slifes can have a physical description, then we have a direct road to considering that the mind, as separate from the body, is a superfluous concept. We do not need to refer to entities separate from a specific situation to account for the behavior or kognitive competence of an Arkadian. For one thing, everything that human beings explain as mental is explained in the case of Arkadians by their relation with a slife, or a set of them, that has a physical reality, which is the structure that remained in the brain after the original slife, and the subsequent manipulation of that memogram. The human concepts of 'love,' 'beauty,' and 'loyalty' are not mental entities, but a set of situations experienced at some point in the past that remain connected as a potential unit. The beliefs, desires, thoughts are views of the virtual world of each Arkadian, and not sentences in a language of thought, images floating inside the brain, or properties emerging from physical activities. The views are constituted by the dense weight of a slife life. Slifes correspond to phenomena that are physical, and complicated, that can be described as the apprehension of a series of kontents and their structuring in the form of figure/ground. Each slife can be characterized physically, by the description of its kontents, and those kontents, even the most abstract ones, are explained through the analysis of what we have called panception. In consequence, what is mental no longer makes sense as a substance and as explanation, and the mind is no longer necessary. No 'mind' floats around, but a structured past of slifes view, analyze, and decide in the present situation. True, a central axis exists, a self, although this self, as we will discuss later, is nothing more than the superimposition of the centrality and unification of all past slifes."

The breeze had become more intense, along with the cold. The sky was painting itself orange. The town was getting quieter, and I began feeling anxious.

"Does this mean that we can describe the elements that define a particular Arkadian?"

"Yes, but as I said, the description, although possible, will be complex. To describe in a precise way all the elements that comprise a single slife is in itself a task beyond the expectations of any current scientific discipline. In each slife, which occupies only a tiny fraction of a life, an infinite number of relations exist with an incredible quantity of different slifes, and with each one of them relationships are established that substantially change the slifes themselves. That is why the road to explaining all thoughts from the slife perspective is an extremely long one. Also, we currently lack the necessary elements for carrying out this demanding task. To discover how a thought like, 'A quark is a basic element of the atom,' or, 'Freedom is a human right,' can be characterized is complicated. It being incredibly complex does not mean that it is impossible. Just as we could examine a mammal embryo and work out something that corresponds to the stomach, or the heart, K can identify the patterns in a slife that correspond to the impact of a contents/container relationship. My impression is that as we further our investigations and get closer to revealing the mysteries of slifes, and as we progress toward a better understanding of kontents, we will be able to discover the mechanisms of kognition. Consequently, we can assume that in the distant future the descendants of today's Arkadians will have identified each and every one of the particularities that are noted in their slifes. And when that moment arrives, it will be possible to characterize each slife down to the tiniest physical detail. From there, we will be able to explain Arkadian behavior by making reference to the slifes that are behind it, without having to call upon any distinct immaterial substance to explain the intentional, rational, and psychological properties."

"Let us suppose that we can analyze each and every one of Erik's memograms. Suppose we have that kind of sophisticated technology available and we are capable of identifying all of his nerve connections. Could we use this description to derive the virtual world in which Erik lives?"

"No. One thing is to physically identify each and every one of the elements that appear in the characterization of that Arkadian brain, but to read there where the imprints come from would be quite another, and more difficult thing. We cannot know to what memories of kontents those connections belong, because the semantics of cerebral engrams is contextual; it depends on what happened originally, since those same neural patterns can encode any imprint. What a neuron remembers today depends on what was noted when it was activated. Nothing of what is recorded in a neuron or a group of neurons is in itself a representation of anything, but is the impact of something from the surroundings or the body. Therefore, knowing the neurons does not explain what they record, what they 'remember'; we need to know what is happening in the body, the surroundings, the visual field, the audio field, etc. Furthermore, the original imprints may no longer exist and may be now a combination of the originals. If this is the case, to analyze the new ones may be pointless, because the slife history has to be followed in order for the new structure to evoke a color, a place, or a voice. Without the history, the same structure may evoke a different smell or color, a different form or shape. All of this leads us to derive the following thesis:

Semantigram Thesis: The perspektive of a given memogram is the result of its slife past.

From this we can deduce that in order to read the biography of a given individual in that person's memograms, we must attend each one of his or her existential moments from birth, or even before that, and observe and record absolutely all the elements that the brain notes, and how the elements are related with each other, and also record the subsequent modifications of all those traces. For this, the visual field of each situation has to be known, the temperature of the objects in contact with the body, the sounds noted, and those that remain as background noise, the emotions stimulated, etc. This represents an extremely high degree of complexity, and it would be almost impossible to manage it all at the same time."

"Yes, but suppose that we could do it, that we could reproduce the analysis of memograms in an android, for example. Would we have a clone of the person? Would they be indistinguishable from each other?"

"I will say it again: An Arkadian is literally the slife past that the person has experienced throughout life. This past is recorded in memograms. Therefore, if we reproduce the memograms of an Arkadian, we will reproduce the Arkadian. But grasping just how complex that would be is difficult for us. As I described to you, the neural connections that are included in a memogram do not specify the situation in the world with which they were connected. These connections were established at a given moment and their signifikance depends on the situations with which they connected. No fixed correspondence exists between the current state of the brain and the world with which it was connected. In addition, a memogram is the trace of a slife, but this memogram has been enriched through time with konceptual connections with new memograms. So, even if we could characterize a memogram in a specific moment, we could not determine of which kontent it is a trace. To be able to make the android reproduction the only conceivable thing would be to make a copy of the individual's body and mind and find a way for each one of its neurons to be recorded along with the setting and the position of the individual, in other words, reproducing the individual's life step by step. It would probably be easier to reproduce the universe."

"Okay, but what I want to know is if the android would be the same as the Arkadian. Would they feel the same? Would they be the same person?"

"If all that is recorded could be reproduced in an android, I think that person should be understood as being the same person: we would not be able to differentiate between them. Only at the moment of creation, because later they will each have experienced slifes in which the spatial-temporal localization would be different, and then they would also be different."

"If that is true, what happens when Arkadians suffer amnesia and do not remember anything about their past, including their name, to whom they are married, what their parents look like, etc.?"

"I told you on Monday that if an Arkadian suffers a temporary amnesia, that person will not lose his or her knowledge. The person knows how to do the same things as before, how to ride a bike, how to multiply, how to work out a syllogism. The person maintains the capability of what we have called the slife flavor of the slifes; that is, she or he perceives the color red from a unit and appreciates its 'qualities.' Only the sense of self has been lost, the sensation of who the person is, what her or his past was like."

"What would happen if we disconnected Erik from his past?"

"If we were to disconnect Erik from his slife past, he would no longer exist as Erik. This means not only that nothing of what he experiences at that moment would have the same signifikance, neither the subjective sensation, such as the taste of a cherry or the sound of clarinet, nor the sensation of Erik as 'Erik,' with a biography, but also that he would barely be able to experience anything at all. Losing his slife past as a context would make Erik incapable of panceiving hardly anything. Therefore, if we were to disconnect Erik from his slife past, we would convert Erik into a baby that is just a few minutes old. The 'Erik' of the past would no longer exist."

"But, if I understand what you are saying, then a huge difference exists between Arkadians and human beings: Arkadians are not free because if what happens to them at a given moment depends so much on what they have lived in the past, then as complicated as the individual history of each Arkadian may be, it would be possible to predict what that Arkadian will do, right?"

"You are right that free will is crucial and that the theory presented here could be in conflict with the indeterminate nature of human thought. What I have mentioned up to now about the Arkadians has been explained by the same science that explains the human world, and especially in this area, all the physical changes have to be explained in terms of physical causes. Immaterial causes have no place in Arkadia, and for that reason the behavior of the Arkadians has to be explained through empirical laws. Consequently, if all decisions made by Arkadians are determined by the laws of physics, then Arkadians are not truly free. However, no matter how difficult it is, I want to convince you that no problem exists in combining these principles with the idea that Arkadians do have their free will, and that they are not automatons."

"How is that possible?"

"To put it briefly, the free will enjoyed by the Arkadians depends on the unique character of each slife, understood as the combination of an individual, with all of that individual's history, and a situation."

"What?"

"Let us imagine a situation in which Erik is reflecting on whether or not he should continue a relationship he is in. He goes over his past, and what novels, films, his friends say about such matters. After weighing the pros and cons for quite a while, Erik experiences a slife in which he sees that the best thing would be to end the relationship. The question you are asking corresponds to: does the explanation of this decision through a sophisticated analysis of the slifes, kontents, relations, and organization eliminate the notion of free will?"

"I think so."

"My impression is that the question no longer makes sense if we understand that *that* moment, that situation, that slife is unique, and that nobody has experienced that specific slife, with that structure, in the past, nor will anybody experience it in the future; not even K has experienced it until now. The complexity and wealth hidden behind every slife history, every personal history of an Arkadian, make each new moment unique, even for K. In the first place, we have the complexity of the slifes, the immensity of the elements that comprise each slife, the magnitude of the relations that can be established between the different elements and slifes. For each situation that is as complex as that, no computation is possible other than the one performed by the Arkadian herself or himself. So many factors have to be considered, that only the reproduction of the situation, the slife, will allow for the unknown to become clear."

"Is such computation inconceivable? In a few years we may have all the information about Arkadians and their kognition, and we may have computers with astronomical capacities. Would not it be possible to calculate the decision that Erik will make?"

"It would be impossible to reproduce the sequence of circumstances that leads to an Arkadian decision in a way that would allow for the determination or reproduction of someone's decision at a given moment. Even if we were K, it would be this way, because chance also plays a role in each moment. Maybe in the future the necessary elements and computers will be available to undertake this daunting task. More than the computational complexity itself, is the spatial-temporal particularity in which every individual lives in, beginning with the local setting and including the social and historical settings, which are the elements that configure the past, present, and future of this Arkadian. In short, we can say that each moment of an individual's life is unique, in both the physical and metaphysical senses of the word. No other moment in the past or future will be the same or equivalent. Therefore, the individual, that sensation of self that shapes that individual, is free in that it is K's hand that writes the present. In each slife no regularity, no pre-established relationship, and no law, comprise that slife and the decision to be made. Erik is the first in the world to go through that situation, to exemplify the properties of that situation, for that slife. Consequently, Arkadians are free in that they are unique and in that their vital moments are original, and have never occurred before and never will again. Nobody, not even K, can know what may happen in the following moment."

"Is that the way that starts at birth?"

"In a way. You could say that the more complex the slifes of an organism are, and the more elements they contain, the freer the organism will be, since the degree of determination will be less. That is why animals, who have less rich slifes, are less free, but only less free."

"Does a self exist taking the decisions?"

"Yes and no, no and yes. We cannot say that an immaterial self exists that decides at each moment, regardless of what a particular situation determines. The impression that it is a self, like a 'soul,' that decides is an illusion. This does not mean that Katherine cannot justifiably feel that she is the one who decides whether to go to Crete or Finland for vacation, whatever that self may be, and that she blames her actions on reasons of a psychological or moral nature, and that she considers herself a free agent, able to choose among different actions. This sensation of self as a unit that perceives, thinks, and acts is the consequence of the unity of all the slifes that Katherine has experienced, and the repetition over the years of that unity. It is not something that is outside the slife, like something that observes what is going on and then decides. No. The Arkadian self is in the middle of the slife, forming part of it."

"Then what does not exist is what we human beings call the 'soul' or the self."

"Let us take this in parts. We could call the 'autobiographical I,' the self that allows Katherine to talk about herself and say, 'I went on vacation to Crete four years ago,' 'I used to be impulsive,' and 'I have fallen in love twice,' etc. This self may have appeared in the following way. In the first stages of life, Katherine lives in a world for which she does not need to remember her past. She just lives. But, at some point in her childhood, her parents got out the photo album and started looking at it with her older brother. Katherine went up and saw the photos. Her parents talked about the vacations, and Katherine remembered the vacations. Her older brother interacted with their parents and talked about things he did and said. Katherine wanted to interact as well, but she could not. At that initial point, Katherine did not know what to say. A series of memories had been stimulated in her, but she did not know how to manage them. She saw herself in a place, but it had a complicated name; she saw her parents and herself, but she did not know what to say, nor how, even though she wanted to. She did not like the situation. The next day, she asked her parents to show her the photos, and she started to say things. This is how Katherine learned to manipulate her memories. The past began to flesh out, and, within it, so did she. When an Arkadian has understood this, when the slife in which 'the self is remembered' has become a functional memogram, the basis for the autobiographic memory has been turned on forever. From that point on, as Katherine has more and more slifes, the self becomes the flavor that remains of 'Katherine's presence in all past slifes.' Later, the help provided by language will make the memory activities much stronger and more flexible so that she can be much more efficient in her precision of a given episode and be able to access it later and transmit it as she likes. Consequently, the 'autobiographical I,' which can also be called the 'narrative I,' the self that we can describe, say its likes and dislikes, what it has done in life, corresponds to the konceptual connection among all the occurrences in which Katherine appears as herself in the slife. When this 'autobiographical I' has been established as a konceptual connection, then it can be incorporated as figure/ground of some or many slifes, so that Katherine recognizes it as a kontent. This is also what differentiates Arkadians from animals, because it means they can separate the self from other kontents, and therefore they convert the self into another object, which allows for the end of egocentrism, and the emergence of 'other.' In other words, it allows for the appearance of 'self-consciousness.'"

"Why does that subjective sensation of an self that 'experiences the world' have to be 'conscious?' Why does the subjective sensation of self that allows Arkadians to say, 'I am the one that is panceiving this Mozart sonata from the third row, seat number twelve, and nobody else can feel it like I do,' exist?"

"In my opinion, which is absolutely hypothetical, the appearance of consciousness in Arkadians responds to a biological function that the kognitive system must have in order to be able to get along in the world. To be more specific, consciousness, understood as the subjective property of experiencing sensations, emotions and thoughts as a unified whole, would appear as a result of the need that decisions be taken in a unified and centralized way."

"What decisions are you talking about?"

"Basically, the centralization of decisions is required in situations in which no possibility exists of making automatic decisions. The majority of biological decisions do not require centralization and unification. You have to keep in mind that the occurrence of a slife involves the intervention of a huge number of processes to which conscious access is not necessary, because they are made automatically. A large part of the kognitive process, as we saw before, involves parallel activities in many areas of the brain. However, in situations that require the assessment of distinct variables whose combination is not calculable through pre-established natural processes, then consciousness appears as a process that can weigh the different variables and make a decision. And the conscious variables are the ones that are relevant for making the decision, although slifes are also comprised of many other variables. To sum up, consciousness would contain those elements of a slife that are necessary for making a decision that cannot be adopted through biological rules or pre-established principles."

"So, if we were not complicated, we would be neither free nor conscious, right?"

"More or less."

At that moment the sun set for the last time, although I did not yet know it. The anxiety that I had been feeling off and on all day was now at its peak. I got up from the chair and walked to the balustrade. Down below was the town. The breeze had disappeared. A strange silence reigned that made the church look unreal. Little by little, my anxiety was diluted by the cries of the swallows above me, and the calm of the afternoon. When the anxiety was just crossing the border to serenity, a glimmer of lucidity struck me. Arkadia did not exist, Arkadians did not exist. Non-Professor O had been talking to me about human beings, about the way he understands being human. That had been the rabbit's warning. I turned around and saw that something strange was happening. The house, the terrace, the volcano, and the sky that I saw before me were fading slowly, until I could see only what appeared to be the mocking smile of Non-Professor O. I wanted to speak, to move, but I could not.

Nine

SUNDAY
"Tap-Tapping" the Compass

I am back from Arkadia. I, Miss Common Sense, am supposed to have acquired a new way of looking at my perplexities. But I am not sure I have understood it, and even less sure whether it will dissolve my perplexities or not. Let me try.

1. The Slife Is the Unit of Knowledge, not the Concept

The first lesson is that my life is a never-ending succession of slifes. Through each one of those slifes I understand the world. How crucial or relevant such slifes are does not matter. Everyone counts. All I have learnt stems from one or a set of slifes, and from having experienced them in a particular way. True, a slife is no nothingness. Every one of my slifes is a universe full of contents that have been created in the interaction between my brain and the world. And every slife has been connected to many other slifes and past contents. And more. Many more. Slifes have power because they have meaning. Their meaning is rooted in the configuration of the contents that were created in the slifes. Knowledge is essentially slife-dependant. This may be the way out for my cheetah perplexity, that I told on Monday. According to Arkadia, cheetahs do not hunt gazelles, but gazelles-that-run-and-try-to-avoid-being-caught, because their slifes taught them so. And I am also a cheetah that understands the world through my past slifes in order to catch the bus, to pay for the ticket, to know where to stop. What matters is to have an organized past. Who knows.

2. Knowledge Is a Virtual World that Fills in Our Experiences

If the past thought was strange, what about this one. Now it appears that my knowledge is not a data base, nor an encyclopedia, nor an instruction manual. It does not even have a proper language to be written in. My knowledge appears a virtual world, that is, a world full of virtual objects, properties and events, with private landscapes, pasts, futures, and with even its own physical laws, psychology, biology. The most difficult thing to accept is that it is a virtual world, which means that it is the default world, the world that my brain could explore "with its eyes wide shut." Provided that it is the world that fills in my slifes, and only mine, it is a private world, a world that nobody can visit, and in which I have to live alone. A world I cannot even get fond of, because it is a world in perpetual motion. The world in which I live today is quite different from the world in which I lived in my childhood, and quite different from the world I will live in the future. For this reason, among many other, my knowledge can be completely different than that of my neighbors, friends, or enemies, regardless of our sharing the same language, of our knowing each other since childhood. For this reason, I can witness an event which will be unique in this and in many other worlds. However, this inflation of worlds does not exclude mutual understanding. My world can be, and in general terms is, a shared world. Even if I live in a virtual world, private and in motion, I share the majority of its landscapes with the majority of my neighbors, friends, and enemies. Moreover, my world can be truthful because I somehow "know" about the real world.

3. Knowledge Requires Being Lived

I should not only accept that my life is a never-ending succession of slifes. I should not only accept that my knowledge is a virtual world. I also have to accept that knowledge is not something that can be established beforehand; instead, it is something that needs a "past." Knowledge is not a thing, nor a final state; instead, it is the endpoint of a process, situated at the end of a set of slifes. Now knowledge appears to be a gift that comes from living, and without living, it does not exist. The ground it offers me to walk on, the objects with which it fills my eyes, the emotions that color my slifes, all of it has been born during my existence and because of my existence. Knowledge requires the presence of a history of experiences, and such experiences must be maintained. Only in this way is it possible to know, because every bit of knowledge is made of other bits of knowledge that are rooted in time. The millions of slifes that I have experienced are made of millions of particular memories of things whose existence required other particular memories to exist. I know, therefore I lived. Perhaps this explains why filling out computers with our knowledge is extremely difficult. They cannot live, therefore they cannot know. Maybe only when they live, when they have a past of experiences, they will be able to know. Strange, but curiously satisfying.

4. Conceptualizing Something Is not a Matter of Representation, but of Creation

Strange things are strange, but rarely extravagant. And this is just an extravagant thought. What is created by perception? What is handled by memory? The objects, the properties, and the relations that my perception models and my memory handles appear not to be "things" of the world, nor their representations or copies. No. The objects, properties, and relations are created in the close collaboration between the brain and the world. The world provides the objects and properties, and my brain provides everything that is needed to model them. Only this collaboration can create such objects and properties. Only through experience and the interaction with the world objects emerge in slifes. Objects, properties, or relations are extended along the virtual space that forms part of the world and part of the brain. Even if I try to examine the form of an object, the shade of a color, or the taste of a breakfast, I need both the world and the brain. For this reason, I should get rid of the idea that my mind has representations of things. And for this reason I should understand that my brain has only the traces of objects that maintain the memory of the brain-world intimacy. The artist's work can only be conceived if we consider both the artist and the clay. If the artist stops working, then the work ceases to exist, even if the artist keeps the memory of the gestures that modeled it. Only then.

5. Every Slife Is Prisoner of Its Time

Part of the cost of slifes as the unit of knowledge is that everything that I understand is trapped in one, or in many slifes, and in the complexity of its contents. Being trapped in time entails that such an understanding will always depend on the other elements of the slife. The meaning of a slife is the "figure in the carpet," and the whole carpet will always have to be where meaning is. Every one of my understandings, every object, property, relation that I know depends on the slife where it was trapped. Beauty, solidarity, chairs, countries, love, and any other understanding has to be obtained, regardless of how abstract it is, from a particular slife. For the same reason all I know about fate is prisoner of my Baghdad story, that I told on Tuesday, and of any other connections that such a story has established. For such reason, all my understandings about fate are contaminated by the form and content of the understanding that crystallized in the slife of the Baghdad story. For such reason, and not because I have some textbook about fate in some mental pocket, that in order to understand any future fate, Baghdad will have to come in my aid.

6. To Understand Is to Notice the Past that Explains the Present

Perhaps this thought is the least strange of all. Accepting that understanding something is noticing something in our past experiences that explains the present one is not difficult for me. I am convinced now that I understood Wednesday's proverb, "The fish is the only one who is not aware of the water," because I remembered my friend's anecdote about the sun going around the Earth. People believe that the sun goes around the Earth because it can only look that way; we are then a sort of fish who are not aware of the water, the water being that it can only look that the sun goes around the Earth. Accordingly, every one of my understandings, every object, property, relation that I know will depend on the past slifes that explained it. And this explanation can correspond to experience a slife that contains new contents which are understood thanks to past contents, or to a slife that manipulates past contents in a new way. In sum, beauty, solidarity, chairs, countries, love, and any other understanding is not explained by itself, but through who-knows how many past slifes.

7. An Abstraction Is an Understanding that Has Forgotten Its Past

What about this one! I do not know if I grasp it. Now I have to accept that if I am able to say that a clock is a clock, that a ball is a ball, that somebody is courteous, or that some painting is beautiful, is not because I apply some sort of mental gadget that allows me to characterize what I experience. No. I have no concepts that I have extracted from my experience, or that my brain has had it since birth. No. I have to accept that only a vast systematization of past concrete experiences underlie my ability to categorize, to abstract, to generalize. Yes. My concrete experiences are very rich, created by the tools that the brain possesses since birth and by the events that I have gone through. But concrete experiences nevertheless. Thus, if I say that a clock is a clock is because all the clocks that I have experienced in the past relive in my present experience, and allow me to say that what I see is a clock. Without those experiences from the past, I would not be able to see a thing as a clock. As simple as that. Fortunately, they appear without making themselves noticed, as if they were ghosts of the past, otherwise their weight would be unbearable.

8. A Metaphor Is an Understanding that Has not Forgotten Its Past

From there I come to more familiar grounds. Because one of the few things of which I am nearly convinced is that part of my understanding is metaphoric. My understanding consists of a constant transfer of meanings from some slifes to others, until they are forgotten. This explains why I do use some slifes to explain other unrelated slifes, without me noticing it. However, what I had not noticed is that every understanding, every meaning, is a metaphor in its origin; that all I now find self-evident was originally a metaphor; that everything I have understood stems from my applying some sort of explicit or implicit "like": my "reds" are made of thousands of slifes that stemmed from a "this is like what I experienced the other day." Why not! I find it possible for me to have forgotten the "likes" of my life, which might be the reason behind my finding a metaphor only as the last transference of slife meaning. To say that governments try to lift the economy is a metaphor because the transfer has yet to be consolidated, but to say that music lifts my spirits is not because the slife has forgotten its origins.

9. Words Are Evocative, not Symbolic

We come now to one of the strangest landscapes that I have seen in Arkadia. For

I have to accept that I do not master the language I speak because I learnt the objects, properties, or individuals to which words refer. Instead, my words reached my virtual world and lay their anchors in my virtual landscapes. As time passed, every word acquired the capability to switch on landscapes and objects in which it was rooted. To learn the word "straight" means that the word was anchored in "straight" slifes. The sacred moment happened when I understood that I could manipulate the word, and that such a manipulation could take me to any landscape of my virtual world, and take there whoever was listening to me. Hence, the search for the meaning of the peasant's "straight," of whom I talked about on Thursday, is a paleontologic work. I cannot reveal the meaning of the word, as if it were something different from the role that the word plays in slifes. Instead, the meaning of "straight" is at the end of a long journey through my virtual world, and the virtual world of the peasant, and the virtual world of anybody else. Such a journey can or cannot finish in the same place. For this reason, I should stop looking at words as symbols, because they stand for nothing, or at least they do not stand for things in a so-called external reality. Now I have to accept that words do not have meanings hanging from their forms, nor instructions that refer to objects or properties. Words do not stand for things. They have meaning because they evoke those landscapes that fill in the slifes I experienced with the relevant contents and, at best, that my friends, neighbors, and enemies also experienced.

10. Language Can Handle Truth, but It Cannot Tell It

In spite of whether I understand such a view or not, it is a view absolutely different from the one I had until today, which I still have. True, my view is the candid one, but at least it is mine. I still believe that words have a precise meaning, and that sentences have a meaning that is the outcome of combining the meaning of words. "The apple is on the table" has the meaning that an apple is on the table. That is it, and I am afraid that it will always be like that. The candid view is part of me, like the view that the sun appears in the east and slides through the sky toward the west. I still believe that a way exists to describe things and facts, that such descriptions can be evaluated instead of facts, and that we can say something true or false about the world. I cannot get rid of such a view. Yet I should think otherwise. I have to accept that language cannot describe facts and therefore I cannot tell whether something is true or false. Language can only evoke a point of view, a perspective of the virtual world. For this reason, facts cannot get into words. For such reason, I cannot say what I want, or what I say is not what I want. Yet even if I cannot tell whether something is true or false, my knowledge is truthful, and language can handle it. That is why I can still meet a friend in some place at a precise time. With a bit of luck!

11. To Communicate Consists of Manipulating Points of View, not of Transmitting Messages

I must now assume that to achieve successful communication whoever listens to me should adopt the same point of view, so that he or she sees the same things in his/her virtual world as the ones I see in my virtual world. I need to get into the virtual world of my listener. Once there, I have to employ whatever tools I can avail myself to manipulate his or her virtual world. This implies that every successful communication depends on the equivalence between virtual worlds, and on the ability to employ communicative tools, regardless of what I normally call the conventional or literal meaning of words. I do not know. I do not know if I am convinced in every case, even if I am convinced in the case of Albert and his orchestra, of whom I talked about on Friday. In order for Albert to transmit what he wants to his musicians, he needs to talk of "treasures" and "kittens." Albert wants them to feel the same slife as he is feeling. It may even be his only option. For perhaps in the future he can say something like "you, first violin, raise your *expressiveness* three degrees, and increase four your *arrogance*, and shorten two degrees of *virtuosity*." But Albert still cannot do so.

12. Information Is not a Thing, but an Act

Here we have one of the most curious outcomes of all the journey. My candid view entails that transmission of information occurs in any sort of communication. Now I should get rid of information. Nothing appears to be transmitted in a communication act. A communication act consists of mutual manipulation, but never of a transmission. We do not give information, as we give money, a gift, or virus. What sort of information did the orchestra conductor give the musicians? I do not know, maybe none. For this reason, then, I should give up information as a thing, and began looking at it as a fact, as an activity, as the outcome of the behavior. Communicating.

13. Words Are Incapable of Going Beyond Knowledge

This new form of viewing communication entails that the success of the communicative act between you and me depends on the possibility that our respective virtual worlds contain equivalent landscapes. Without this condition, communication cannot even start. What does not exist in a virtual world cannot be understood, and what cannot be understood cannot be communicated, regardless of how much we talk or insist on trying. This can happen between two friends or enemies, between two physically and temporally close speakers, or between a twenty-first century milk vendor and a priest of Ramses. For the same reason, understanding each other, sharing a language, a culture, or a time is so difficult.

Likewise, talking can be useless, unless based on a shared virtual world. If parents and their children do not understand each other because they do not share the same virtual perspective, then it will not help to try hard. If a friend cannot access our point of view, advising her or him is completely useless. Moreover, if nothing is understandable unless it is a part of our virtual world, then some people can see landscapes that they cannot share. History is full of individuals who have experienced new landscapes, and they have had many troubles in transmitting them. This includes the person who discovered agriculture, the person who invented tea, and the person who formulated the theory of relativity. Every idea has been completely new some time; this entails that it was, for a while, a landscape of one person. Provided that words cannot take us to that landscape, every new idea is born without understanding. Not that the rest of the world does not want to understand; instead, understanding is impossible for us. We are unable to see such a landscape. From such lack of understanding stems a desperate need for communication.

14. Texts Do not Codify Contents, but Readings

Another extravagant consequence that I shall take home with me is that books are empty. They are empty not in the sense that nothing is in them, or we have nothing to do with them, but empty because texts do not contain information. Texts are tools that can modify the virtual world of the reader; their content should be described in relation with the landscapes they evoke in its readers. Therefore, the knowledge transmitted in a book is not in a particular place, but potentially in each one of its readers, and globally in all of them. Books transmit knowledge insofar as they can evoke "truthful" virtual landscapes. This does not mean that the content of a text depends on the interpretation of the reader. A text is not in a secret code beyond the meaning of words, nor does it exist as the object of a possible interpretation by the reader. The content of a book is not interpreted, because it is not codified. Words are soldiers that invade us and from whom we cannot defend ourselves. At most, we can force them into a diversion, but as soon as we let down our guard they will come to evoke their landscape.

15. Imagination Is not Creative, but Re-Creative

This view of language and words has other peculiar consequences. If words cannot take us where we have never been, then books cannot take us where we have never been, and then literature is useless. This produced in me a great disillusion. Yet now I see that literature has kept its relevance for learning, and also it might have another valuable function. Literature would be the method of exploration of my virtual world. It could help me to travel in it, and discover landscapes that I did not notice, or landscapes that are composed of past landscapes. It could allow me to manipulate virtual objects and exploit them. For this reason, I can learn many things that have happened to me, and through them, to learn what some other people have experienced. Exploring my virtual world, I explore that of everybody. Every story, every novel, every play provides me with a part of the infinite landscapes that slifes offer. Moreover, provided that every slife is extremely complex, its richness will warrant the future relevance of literature, because the catalogue of possible slifes is vaster than the world of imagination. I will always have to understand others through my virtual world, through my slife background. Hence the re-creative character of literature. Hence its attractiveness.

16. Learning Is not an Acquisition, but an Adaptation

The virtual world, the nature of language, the way communication works entail that learning cannot be based on the transmission of knowledge. Instead, learning is a modification of my virtual world that changes the capabilities of my brain. Such a modification must be in some way beneficial for me, it must be an adaptation; otherwise it is useless. This view of learning has nevertheless a curious consequence, because now learning requires possessing the background contents and landscapes that provide the adaptation. However, I find it hard to accept that to learn I already possess much of the knowledge to learn. I find hard to accept that I cannot understand whatever may be beyond what I already know; that I cannot learn from "nothing." I find hard to accept that if my virtual world does not contain the objects, properties, and relations that fill some virtual landscapes, then no matter how much my teacher may talk, I will not be able to understand what he or she tells me. That regardless of how hard I may try to extract understandings of what people tell me, mastering language is not sufficient for me to be successful. Above all, I find hard to accept that knowledge is personal and non-transferable.

17. To Educate Consists of Conditioning Particular Experiences

If learning means that, then the education does not consist of transmitting knowledge from an individual to another, but of making the learner experience the slife that the teacher wants the learner to experience. Therefore, if I can only enrich my virtual world through slifes, and language cannot transfer information, and communication consists of manipulating points of view, then the school cannot be an unloading dock. Education, then, should be based on slifes, trying to make learners experience by themselves the landscapes that correspond to a particular piece of education. Why not! The critical point is to establish the elements that allow individuals to develop knowledge by themselves, to provide those tools by which they will be able to interact with the world and to develop their own knowledge that, in the best of cases, will have a common basis with their community and with the true world. But what a critical point!

18. Reason Is a Logic Without Truth

Since I was a young child, I have firmly believed in logic, perhaps because it was the universe of my first mentor. My faith was unshakable during a long time, and it kept the dream that some day I could correct stupid ideas, or resolve any argument regardless of how contaminated it was by prejudice, self-indulgence or bad faith. How candid! I believe now that never have I been able to share the analysis of an argumentation with anybody. I have never found a single interesting argumentation to be logically pure. I do not find strange that this happens so often. What I find curious is that complying with logical rules is not necessary. Not that we are careless or lazy reasoners. The fact is that we do not apply Logic. This appears to me more difficult to explain. Because one thing is that the background noise of discussions and arguments can blur our logic, and one very different is for logic to be unnecessary in our discussions. And the part of the problem that interests me is the rational ingredient of such noncompliance. How can we be rational and blind to truth at the same time? Yet this has an easy answer in Arkadia: what matters is not truth, but convenience. Probably, the last individual of the most logical species in Earth was gulped by a lion that was quite illogical.

19. The Cause of a Behavior Is not a Reason, but Its History

I am not sure whether I have finally understood this part of the journey, but I envision a figure in the fog. Everything that can explain an individual and his/her behavior, including his/her thoughts, beliefs, and hopes, can be explained through the same language that explains the behavior of planets. If every slife can be described as a complex activity, but activity anyway, of the brain and of the world, then describing it in empirical terms is possible. My desire of going to the beach is not a state that flies in my brain, but part of my slifes, and slifes are states of my brain and of the world. Granted, they are extremely complex states which can only be described in vague terms, such as a storm is a physical state that was described in vague terms two centuries ago. So all my thoughts, beliefs, and hopes are slifes composed of many past slifes, like a stew is the outcome of all the actions of the cook, and not of the waiter who serves it. For this reason, imagining that someone could draw the slife path that made me go to the coast on holidays is possible, even if I had planned to go to the mountains. The complete explanation of such a decision would be extremely complex, because all slifes have multiple connections, and we could call upon everyone of the slifes that I have experienced in my whole life. And that is a lot, even for me.

20. Free Will Is a Form of Singularity,
not of Indetermination

If the previous point is right, if all my slifes depend on their roots, then we have only one possible conclusion: my decisions are determined. Yet this does not exclude my freedom, in the sense that my next decision cannot be predicted. What a paradox! I am matter, and as such, determined by physical laws. Slifes and their contents are states which can be accounted for by empirical laws. Any change in my brain is a physical change, and it should be explained by physical causes. Yet I am free, provided that the richness of my past, of every moment of my life, is so high that it is not only a complex moment, but also unique. Perhaps when I was born my slifes were not sufficiently complex to be unique, but the more I lived, the richer my slife background became, the more unique I became. Every slife has many contents, and every new slife has more contents, and so on. It is not a question of computational complexity, but of singularity, of unique-ness, both in a physical and metaphysical sense. I am the first to be here, to embody this moment. No other moment in history has been like this, nor will any other moment be like this. Therefore, I can still think that I master my life, whatever "I" means. I am the master of my next move, whatever a decision is. I am free.

21. The Nature of a Sensation Is the Weight of Its Past

Why do pancakes taste *that* way? Why is the bluish greenness like *that*? Why does the "Mona Lisa" look like *that*? Nobody knows, but now I have a different way of understanding such a perplexity. The character of a sensation, its nature, depends on past sensations. When I watch the "Mona Lisa," what I believe to see in my mind is not a sneaky look at the world through my eyes, as if I were looking at the world through a window. What I see is seen through all the "Mona Lisas," and many other paintings and non-paintings, that I have seen until that moment, in the same way that the color of the Mona Lisa's skin is the product of all the layers that Leonardo da Vinci painted. Sensations would not be prisoners of the present, as things to be extracted or identified in the world; instead, they would be the outcome of all the past relevant experiences. Pancakes would have the superimposed taste of all the pancakes that I have tasted, and the Mona Lisa's form would have the superimposed form of all the Mona Lisas I have seen. For that reason, every conscious experience changes with time. The con-scious experience of the "Mona Lisa" that I had on my first visit to the Louvre as a schoolgirl was not the same as the one I had after I had visited the whole museum and came back to the painting, and it was not the same as the one that I had ten years later after having studied Art History and having seen many paintings. Because of the weight of all the "Mona Lisas," and of many other paintings that I have seen, that the "Mona Lisa" appears to me as it does. For the same reason, the "Mona Lisa" that I see now does not resemble the "Mona Lisa" that I may see in ten years, even if this will probably be closer to the first "Mona Lisa" that I saw. The "Mona Lisa" is different, despite the fact that my brain and my eyes will work more or less in the same way all my life.

22. A Thought Is a Look at the Present Through One's Whole Life

There we come to my grandad's dream, that I told on Saturday. How many times have I thought that mind-reading could be possible? A strong intuition has always told me that thoughts only have sense when they are translated into a sentence; and another strong intuition has told me that when they are translated into sentences they are not thoughts any longer. We have a way out of this paradox. A thought consists of the description of a slife and of its contents. To think is to experience a slife. No state, the thought, exists separated from living. For this reason, a thought is a look at the present through the past. To think that "An apple is on the table" involves connecting such an apple and such a table with all the apples and tables that I have seen, and organizing such an apple+all-the-apples-that-I-have-experienced and such a table+all-the-tables-that-I-have-experienced in a particular way. Such organization, and such apples and tables, are what I should call "thought." So the dream of my grandad will not come true. Telepathy does not consist of transmitting a sentence or an image, but of experiencing a present through a whole life.

23. To Reason Is the Word's Journey Through Its Virtual World

From there, we only need to make a small step to consider that "to think," in the sense of reasoning, is a manipulation of our past slifes through the present slife. Words are what allow us to do that. To think, to talk to oneself, consists of using words to awaken the past, traveling through the vast geography of our virtual worlds. When I think, the evocative power of my words takes me to landscapes of my virtual world that are near or far apart in time and space. When I think, I see things that were already noticed, and others which were not. Thinking is an intimate dialogue between language and the past. I like it!

24. The Mind Is the Present of a Past

There we are. At the end. An end that I am not sure I understand. I have to accept that if the nature of a sensation is the weight of its past, a thought is a way of living and re-living, the path of slifes is determined by empirical laws, then what I have called "mind" has no place any more. Nothing more, nothing less. I may understand that what matters is to take the mind toward perception and sensation. Because no place exists where I think and represent reality, where what I call "I" is sheltered. Only feeling-perceiving exists. No sensation exists, and then perception, and then cognition, and then emotion. The gestures that my brain uses to model reality are at the same time sensitive, perceptual, emotional, and cognitive, and every slife corresponds to millions of small brain gestures. Every gesture, be it cognitive, emotional, or perceptive, shares the same rank in the slife composition. I do not find beautiful some sky blueness after perceiving it; beauty impregnates the sky. I do not hear a bark because I infer that a dog barks; such a bark is part of the dog. The world does not get into my head, my "self" goes out. I am part of the world, I am world. The blues, the barks, happiness are sensations of my past, and I, my mind, is the tissue of such sensations. For this reason, I now prefer to see the world not as something beyond my eyes, but as part of me, or me as part of it. The blueness, the bark, are part of such a world and of the past that I have below my feet, even if I cannot see it. In short: living dissolves the mind.

25. No Fire Exists Without Smoke

I round up the number of aphorisms by acknowledging that, even if I have adopted a new point of view, I, Miss Common Sense, still have many doubts. My perplexities are too deeply rooted to be extracted in a single pull. They have been there for too many centuries. I guess that the way ahead is still very long. The Buddhist may strike again and time may eventually replant all of my perplexities. Even though that may be possible, I have a strong intuition. Regardless of what happens to my perplexities, its destiny is tied to Arkadia. Any other point of view may only be the red-hot coals with which we are condemned to juggle never-endingly.

BIBLIOGRAPHY

The Bibliography corresponds to a selection of key references that might help the reader to identify the sources behind the proposals made in the book. The book is nevertheless based on a general background in neurobiology, evolutionary psychology, epistemology, semantics, pragmatics, communication, and brain-mind theories.

1. Chapter One, "Monday"

Alston, William P. *The Reliability of Sense Perception*. Ithaca, N.Y.: Cornell University Press, 1993.

Anderson, Adam K. and Elizabeth A. Phelps. "Lesions of the Human Amygdala Impair Enhanced Perception of Emotionally Salient Events." *Nature*, 411 (17 May 2001), pp. 305–309.

Antonova, Irina, Ottavio Arancio, Anne Cecile Trillat, Hong-Gang Wang, Leonard Zablow, Hiroshi Udo, Eric R. Kandel, and Robert D. Hawkins. "Rapid Increase in Clusters of Presynaptic Proteins at Onset of Long-Lasting Potentiation." *Science*, 294 (18 October 2001), pp. 1547–1550.

Arbib, Michael A., Peter Erdi, and Janos Szentágothai. *Neural Organization: Structure, Function, and Dynamics*. Cambridge, Mass.: MIT Press, 1997.

Avrahami, Judith and Yaakov Kareev. "The Emergence of Events." *Cognition*, 53:3 (1 December 1994), pp. 239–261.

Baron-Cohen, Simon and Pippa Cross. "Reading the Eyes: Evidence for the Role of Perception in the Development of a Theory of Mind." *Mind and Language*, 7 (April 1992), pp.172–185.

Barsalou, Lawrence W. "Perceptual Symbol Systems." *Behavioral and Brain Sciences*, 22:4 (April 1999), pp. 577–609.

Bickhard, Mark H. "Scaffolding and Self Scaffolding: Central Aspects of Development." *Children's Development Within Social Contexts: Research and Methodology*. Edited by Lucien T. Winegar and Jaan Valsiner (Hillsdale, N.J.: Lawrence Erlbaum Associates, 1992), pp. 33–52.

Blackmore, Susan J., Gavin Brelstaff, Kay Nelson, and Tom Troscianko. "Is the Richness of Our Visual World an Illusion? Transsaccadic Memory for Complex Scenes." *Perception*, 24:9 (1995), pp. 1075–1081.

Bloj, M[arina] G., D[aniel] Kersten, and A[nya] C. Hurlbert. "Perception of Three-Dimensional Shape Influences Colour Perception Through Mutual Illumination."

Nature, 402 (23/30 December 1999), pp. 877– 879.

Calvert, Gemma A., Edward T. Bullmore, Michael J. Brammer, Ruth Campbell, Steven C.R. Williams, Philip K. McGuire, Peter W.R. Woodruff, Susan D.S. Iversen, and Anthony S. David. "Activation of Auditory Cortex During Silent Lipreading." *Science,* 276 (27 April 1997), pp. 593–596.

Castelo-Branco, Miguel, Rainer Goebel, Sergio Neuenschwander, and Wolf Singer. "Neural Synchrony Correlates with Surface Segregation Rules." *Nature,* 405 (8 June 2000), pp. 685–689.

Chapman, Barbara. "Necessity for Afferent Activity to Maintain Eye-Specific Segregation in Ferret Lateral Geniculate Nucleus." *Science,* 287 (31 March 2000), pp. 2479–2482.

Churchland, Patricia S., Vilayanur S. Ramachandran, and Terrence Sejnowski. "A Critique of Pure Vision." *Large-Scale Neuronal Theories of the Brain.* Edited by Chirstof Koch and Joel E. Davis (Cambridge, Mass.: MIT Press, 1994), pp. 23–60.

Clark, Andy. *Being There.* Cambridge, Mass.: MIT Press, 1996.

——— and David Chalmers. "The Extended Mind." *Analysis,* 58 (1998), pp. 7–19.

Crick, Francis and Christof Koch. "Consciousness and Neuroscience." *Cerebral Cortex,* 8 (May 1998), pp. 97–107.

Dalton, P[amela], N[adine] Doolittle, H[isanori] Nagata, and P[aul] A.S. Breslin. "The Merging of the Senses: Integration of Subthreshold Taste and Smell." *Nature Neuroscience,* 3 (1 May 2000), pp. 431–432.

Darian-Smith, Corinna and Charles D. Gilbert. "Axonal Sprouting Accompanies Functional Reorganization in Adult Cat Striate Cortex." *Nature,* 368 (21 April 1994), pp. 737–740.

Davis, Greg and Jon Driver, "Parallel Detection of Kanisza Figures in the Human Visual System." *Nature,* 371 (27 October 1994), pp. 791–793.

Dehaene, Stanislas. *The Number Sense. How the Mind Creates Mathematics.* New York: Oxford University Press, 1997.

DeLancey, Craig. "Real Emotions." *Philosophical Psychology,* 11 (December 1998), pp. 467–487.

De Sousa, Ronald. *The Rationality of Emotion.* Cambridge, Mass.: MIT Press, 1987.

Douglas, Rodney J. and Kevan A.C. Martin. "Neocortex." *The Synaptic Organisation of the Brain.* Edited by Gordon M. Shepherd (New York: Oxford University Press, 1998), pp. 389–438.

Driver, Jon, Gordon C. Baylis, and Robert D. Rafal. "Preserved Figure-Ground Segregation and Symmetry Perception in Visual Neglect." *Nature*, 360 (5 November 1992), pp. 73–75.

———, Charles Spence. "Multisensory Perception: Beyond Modularity and Convergence in Crossmodal Integration." *Current Biology,* 10:20 (October 2000), pp. R731–R735.

———, Greg Davis, Charlotte Russell, Massimo Turatto, and Elliot Freeman. "Segmentation, Attention, and Phenomenal Visual Objects." *Cognition*, 80:1/2 (June 2001), pp. 61–95.

Eimer, Martin, Daniel Cockburn, Ben Smedley, and Jon Driver. "Cross-Modal Links in Endogenous Spatial Attention are Mediated by Common External Locations: Evidence from Event-Related Brain Potentials." *Experimental Brain Research,* 139:4 (September 2001), pp. 398–411.

———, José van Velzen, and Jon Driver. "Cross-Modal Interactions between Audition, Touch, and Vision in Endogenous Spatial Attention: ERP Evidence on Preparatory States and Sensory Modulations." *Journal of Cognitive Neuroscience*, 14:2 (February 2002) pp. 254–271.

Elman, Jeffrey, Elizabeth Bates, Mark H. Johnson, Annette Karmiloff-Smith, Domenico Parisi, and Kim Plunkett. *Rethinking Innateness: A Connectionist Perspective on Development*. Cambridge, Mass.: MIT Press, 1996.

Felleman, Daniel J. and David C. Van Essen. "Distributed Hierarchical Processing in the Primate Cerebral Cortex." *Cerebral Cortex*, 1 (January 1991), pp. 1–47.

Freedman, David J, Maximilian Riesenhuber, Tomaso Poggio, and Earl K. Miller. "Categorical Representation of Visual Stimuli in the Primate Prefrontal Cortex." *Science*, 291 (12 January 2001), pp. 312–316.

Frith, Chris and Ray J. Dolan. "Brain Mechanisms Associated with Top-Down Processes in Perception." *Philosophical Transactions of the Royal Society of London, Series B: Biological Sciences*, 352 (29 August 1997), pp. 1221–1230.

Gao, Jia-Hong, Lawrence M. Parsons, James M. Bower, Jinhu Xiong, Jinqi Li, and Peter T. Fox. "Cerebellum Implicated in Sensory Acquisition and Discrimination Rather than Motor Control." *Science*, 272 (26 April 1996), pp. 545–547.

Gegenfurtner, Karl R. "Visual Perception: Reflections on Colour Constancy." *Nature*, 402 (23/30 Deember 1999), pp. 855–856.

Gelder, Beatrice de and Jean Vroomen. "Impairment of Speech-Reading in

Prosopagnosia." *Speech Communication*, 26 (October 1998), pp. 89–96.

Gibson, James J. *The Ecological Approach to Visual Perception*. Boston: Houghton-Mifflin, 1979.

Gilbert, Charles D. "Adult Cortical Dynamics." *Physiological Reviews*, 78:2 (April 1998), pp. 467–485.

———— and Torsten N. Wiesel. "Receptive Field Dynamics in Adult Primary Visual Cortex." *Nature*, 356 (March 1992), pp. 150–152.

————, Aniruddha Das, Minami Ito, Mitesh Kapadia, and Gerald Westheimer . "Spatial Integration and Cortical Dynamics." *Proceedings of the National Academy of Sciences*, 93:2 (23 January 1996), pp. 615–622.

Glenberg, Arthur M. "What Memory Is for." *Behavioral and Brain Sciences*, 20:1 (March 1997), pp. 1–55.

Goldstone, Robert L. "Effects of Categorization on Color Perception." *Psychological Science*, 6 (September 1995), pp. 298–304.

———— and Lawrence W. Barsalou. "Reuniting Cognition and Perception: The Perceptual Bases of Rules and Similarity." *Cognition*, 65:3 (January 1998), pp. 231–262.

Gordon, Robert M. *The Structure of Emotions: Investigations in Cognitive Philosophy*. Cambridge, England: Cambridge University Press, 1987.

Graham, Kim S., Karalyn Patterson, and John R. Hodges. "Episodic Memory: New Insights from the Study of Semantic Dementia." *Current Opinion in Neurobiology*, 9:2 (April 1999), pp. 245–250.

Harnad, Stevan, ed. *Categorical Perception: The Groundwork of Cognition*. New York: Cambridge University Press, 1987.

————. "The Symbol Grounding Problem." *Physica*, 42 (May 1990), pp. 335–340.

Hutchins, Edward. *Cognition in the Wild*. Cambridge, Mass.: MIT Press, 1995.

Jeannerod, Marc. "The Representing Brain: Neural Correlates of Motor Intention and Imagery." *Behavioral and Brain Sciences*, 17:2 (June 1994), pp. 187–245.

Johnson, Mark L. *The Body in the Mind*. Chicago: University of Chicago Press, 1987.

Jousmäki, Veikko and Riita Hari. "Parchment-Skin Illusion: Sound-Biased Touch." *Current Biology*, 8 (12 March 1998), p. R190.

Julesz, Bela. *Dialogues on Perception*. Cambridge, Mass.: MIT Press, 1995.

———— and Ilona Kovacs, eds. *Maturational Windows and Adult Cortical Plasticity.* Reading, Mass.: Addison-Wesley, 1995.

Kennett, Steffan, Martin Eimer, Charles Spence, and Jon Driver. "Tactile–Visual Links in Exogenous Spatial Attention Under Different Postures: Convergent Evidence from Psychophysics and ERPs." *Journal of Cognitive Neuroscience*, 13 (September 2001), pp. 462–478.

Kirsh, David and Paul Maglio. "On Distinguishing Epistemic from Pragmatic Action." *Cognitive Science*, 18:4 (October/December 1994), pp. 513–549.

Kosslyn, Stephen M., William L. Thompson, Irene J. Kim, and Nathaniel M. Alpert. "Topographical Representations of Mental Images in Primary Visual Cortex." *Nature*, 378 (30 November 1995), pp. 496–498.

Llinas, Rodolfo and Urs Ribary. "Consciousness and the Brain. The Thalamocortical Dialogue in Health and Disease." *Annals of the New York Academy of Sciences*, 929 (April 2001), pp. 166–175.

Macaluso, Emiliano, Chris Frith, and Jon Driver. "Modulation of Human Visual Cortex by Crossmodal Spatial Attention." *Science*, 289 (18 August 2000), pp. 1206–1208.

————, Chris Frith, and Jon Driver. "Multisensory Integration and Crossmodal Attention Effects in the Human Brain; Response." *Science*, 292 (June 2001), p.1791. http://www.sciencemag.org/cgi/content/full/1791a

MacKay, Donald G. *The Organization of Perception and Action: A Theory for Language and other Cognitive Skills*. New York: Springer-Verlag, 1987.

Maess, Burkhard, Stefan Koelsch, Thomas C. Gunter, and Angela D. Friederici. "Musical Syntax Is Processed in Broca's Area: An MEG Study." *Nature Neuroscience*, 4 (May 2001), pp. 540–545.

Magnuson, James S. and Howard C. Nusbaum. "Talker Differences and Perceptual Normalization." *Journal of the Acoustical Society of America*, 93 (April 1993), p. 2371.

Mark, David M. and Andrew Frank. "Experiential and Formal Models of Geographic Space." *Environment and Planning*, B, 23 (1996), pp. 3–24.

McKoon, Gail and Roger Ratcliff. "Inference During Reading." *Psychological Review*, 99:3 (July 1992), pp. 440–466.

Morrot, Gil, Frédéric Brochet, and Denis Dubourdieu. "The Color of Odors." *Brain and Language*, 79 (1 November 2001), pp. 309–320.

Nosofsky, Robert M. "Exemplar-Based Approach to Relating Categorization, Identification, and Recognition." *Multidimensional Models of Perception and Cognition.* Edited by F. Gregory Ashby (Hillsdale, N.J.: Lawrence Erlbaum Associates,1992), pp. 363–394.

O'Regan, Kevin and Alva Noë. "A Sensorimotor Account of Vision and Visual Consciousness." *Behavioral and Brain Sciences*, 24:5 (2001). http://www.bbsonline.org/documents/a/00/00/05/06/index.html

Pascual-Leone, Alvaro and Vincent Walsh. "Fast Backprojections from the Motion to the Primary Visual Area Necessary for Visual Awareness." *Science*, 292 (20 April 2001), pp. 510–515.

Pavani, Franceso, Charles Spence, and Jon Driver. "Visual Capture of Touch; Out-of-the-Body Experiences with Rubber Gloves." *Psychological Science*, 11:5 (September 2001), pp. 353–359.

Pessoa, Luiz, Evan Thompson, and Alva Noë. "Finding out About Filling in: A Guide to Perceptual Completion for Visual Science and the Philosophy of Perception." *Behavioral and Brain Sciences*, 21:6 (December 1998), pp. 723–802.

Peterson, Mary A. and Bradley S. Gibson. "Shape Recognition Inputs to Figure-Ground Organization in Three-Dimensional Displays." *Cognitive Psychology*, 25:3 (1 July 1993), pp. 383–429.

Quartz, Steven R. and Terrence J. Sejnowski. "The Neural Basis of Cognitive Development: A Constructivist Manifesto." *Behavioral and Brain Sciences*, 20:6 (December 1997), pp. 537–596

Radeau, Monique. "Auditory-Visual Spatial Interaction and Modularity." *Current Psychology of Cognition*, 13:1 (1994), pp. 3–51.

Rakic, Pasko. "Specification of Cerebral Cortical Areas." *Science*, 241 (9 July 1988), pp.170–176.

Ramachandran, Vilayanur S. "Visual Perception in People and Machines." *AI and the Eye.* Edited by Andrew Blake and Tom Troscianko (London: John Wiley & Sons, 1990), pp. 21–77.

————. *Phantoms in the Brain.* New York: William Morrow, 1998.

Rinberg, D[ima] and H[ananel] Davidowitz. "Insect Perception: Do Cockroaches 'Know' About Fluid Dynamics?" *Nature*, 405 (15 June 2000), p. 756.

Saldaña, Helena M. and Lawrence D. Rosenblum. "Visual Influences on Auditory Pluck and Bow Judgments." *Perceptual Psychophysics*, 54:3 (1993), pp. 406–416.

Salinas, Emilio and Terrence J. Sejnowski. "Correlated Neuronal Activity and the Flow of Neural Information." *Nature Reviews Neuroscience*, 2 (1 August 2001), pp. 539–550.

Schyns, Philippe G, Robert L. Goldstone, and Jean-Pierre Thibaut. "The Development of Features in Object Concepts." *Behavioral and Brain Sciences*, 21:1 (February 1998), pp. 1–54.

Seife, Charles. "Language Affects Sound Perception." *Science*, 290 (15 December 2000), pp. 2051–2052.

Sengpiel, Frank, Petra Stawinski, and Tobias Bonhoeffer. "Influence of Experience on Orientation Maps in Cat Visual Cortex." *Nature Neuroscience*, 2 (1 August 1999), pp. 727–732.

Shams, Ladan, Yukiyasu Kamitani, and Shinshuke Shimojo. "llusions: What You See Is What You Hear." *Nature*, 408 (14 December 2000), p. 788.

Sparks, David L. and Jennifer M. Groh. "The Superior Colliculus: A Window to Problems in Integrative Neuroscience." *The Cognitive Neurosciences*. Edited by Michael S. Gazzaniga (Cambridge, Mass.: MIT Press, 1995), pp. 565–584.

Spence, Charles and Jon Driver. "Attracting Attention to the Illusory Location of a Sound: Reflexive Crossmodal Orienting and Ventriloquism." *NeuroReport*, 11:9 (December 2000), pp. 2057–2061.

Steels, Luc. "The Artificial Life Roots of Artificial Intelligence." *Artificial Life*, 1:1 (January 1994), pp. 75–110.

Stein, Astrid von, Carl Chiang, and Peter König. "Top-Down Processing Mediated by Interareal Synchronization." *Proceedings of the National Academy of Sciences*, 97:26 (19 December 2000), pp. 14748–14753.

Stein, Barry E. "Neural Mechanisms for Synthesizing Sensory Information and Producing Adaptive Behaviors." *Experimental Brain Research*, 123:1/2 (January 1998), pp. 124–135.

——— and M. Alex Meredith. *The Merging of the Senses*. Cambridge, Mass.: MIT Press, 1993.

Stevens, Joseph C. "Detection of Very Complex Taste Mixtures: Generous Integration Across Constituent Compounds." *Physiological Behavior*, 62:5 (1997), pp. 1137–1143.

Thompson, Evan. "Symbol Grounding: A Bridge from Artificial Life to Artificial Intelligence." *Brain and Cognition*, 34:1 (Spring/Summer 1997), pp. 48–71.

Tong, Frank. "Brain at Work: Play by Play." *Nature Neuroscience*, 4 (June 2001), pp. 560–562.

Treisman, Ann M. and Nancy G. Kanwisher. "Perceiving Visually Presented Objects: Recognition, Awareness, and Modularity." *Current Opinion in Neurobiology*, 8 (April 1998), pp. 218–226.

Tulving, Endel and Hans J. Markowitsch. "Memory Beyond the Hippocampus." *Current Opinion in Neurobiology*, 7:2 (April 1997), pp. 209–216.

Ullman, Shimon. *High-Level Vision*. Cambridge, Mass.: MIT Press, 1996.

Ungerer, Frieredich and Hans-Jorge Schmid. *An Introduction to Cognitive Linguistics*. London: Longman, 1996.

Varela, Fernando, Evan Thompson, and Eleanor Rosch. *The Embodied Mind*. Cambridge, Mass.: MIT Press, 1991.

Vroomen, Jean and Beatrice de Gelder. "Sound Enhances Visual Perception: Cross-Modal Effects of Auditory Organization on Visual Perception." *Journal of Experimental Psychology: Human Perception and Performance*, 26:5 (October 2000), pp. 1583–1590.

Weisstein, Naomi and Charles S. Harris. "Masking and Unmasking of Distributed Representations in the Visual System." *Visual Coding and Adaptability*. Edited by Charles S. Harris (Hillsdale, N.J.: Lawrence Erlbaum Associates, 1980), pp. 317-364.

Whitaker, David and Paul V. McGraw. "Long-Term Visual Experience Recalibrates Human Orientation Perception." *Nature Neuroscience*, 3 (1 January 2000), p.13.

Zacks, Jeffrey M., Todd S. Braver, Margaret A. Sheridan, David I. Donaldson, Abraham Z. Snyder, John M. Ollinger, Randy L. Buckner, and Marcus E. Raichle. "How Does the Brain Parse Activities in the World into Discrete Perceptual Events?" *Nature Neuroscience*, 4 (1 June 2001), pp. 651–655.

Zangaladze, Andro, Charles M. Epstein, Scott T. Grafton, and K[rish] Sathian. "Involvement of Visual Cortex in Tactile Discrimination of Orientation." *Nature*, 401 (7 October 1999), pp. 587–590.

Zatorre, Robert J., Andrea R. Halpern, David W. Perry, Ernst Meyer, and Alan C. Evans. "Hearing in the Mind's Ear: A PET Investigation of Musical Imagery and Perception." *Journal of Cognitive Neuroscience*, 8 (January 1996), pp. 29–46.

Zeki, Semir. *Vision of the Brain: The Visible World and the Cortex*. Oxford: Blackwell Scientific, 1993.

2. Chapter Two, "Tuesday"

Baillargeon, Renée. "The Object of Concept Revisited: New Directions in the

Investigation of Infant's Physical Knowledge." *Visual Perception and Cognition in Infancy. Carnegie-Mellon Symposia on Cognition, vol. 23.* Edited by Carl E. Granrud (Hillsdale, N.J.: Lawrence Erlbaum Associates, 1992), pp. 265–315.

Barsalou, Lawrence W. "Structure, Flexibility and Linguistic Vagary in Concepts: Manifestations of a Compositional System of Perceptual Symbols." *Theories of Memory.* Edited by Alan C. Collins, Susan E. Gathercole, Martin A. Conway, and Peter E. Morris (Hillsdale, N.J.: Lawrence Erlbaum Associates, 1993), pp. 29–101.

―――, Janellen Huttenlocher, and Koen Lamberts. "Basing Categorization on Individuals and Events." *Cognitive Psychology*, 36:2 (1 August 1998), pp. 203–272.

Baylis, Gordon C. and Jon Driver. "Perception of Symmetry and Repetition Within and Across Visual Shapes: Part-Descriptions and Object-Based Attention." *Visual Cognition,* 8:1 (Spring 2001), pp. 163–196.

Bickhard, Mark H. "How Does the Environment Affect the Person?" *Children's Development in Social Context.* Edited by Lucien T. Winegar and Jaan Valsiner (Hillsdale, N.J.: Lawrence Erlbaum Associates, 1992), pp. 63–92.

Bloom, Lois. *The Transition from Infancy to Language: Acquiring the Power of Expression.* New York: Cambridge University Press, 1993.

Bloom, Paul. *How Children Learn the Meanings of Words.* Cambridge, Mass.: MIT Press, 2000.

Braitenberg, Valentino. *Vehicles: Experiments in Synthetic Psychology.* Cambridge, Mass.: MIT Press, 1984.

Brooks, Rodney. "Intelligence Without Representation." *Artificial Intelligence*, 47:1 (1991), pp. 139–159.

Churchland, Paul M. *A Neurocomputational Perspective.* Cambridge, Mass.: MIT Press, 1989.

Cooper, Lynn A. and Margaret P. Munger. "Extrapolating and Remembering Positions Along Cognitive Trajectories: Uses and Limitations of Analogies to Physical Motion." *Spatial Representation.* Edited by Naomi Eilan, Rosaleen McCarthy, and Bill Brewer (Oxford: Basil Blackwell, 1993), pp.112–131.

Davidoff, Jules, Ian Davies, and Debi Roberson. "Colour Categories in a Stone-Age Tribe." *Nature*, 398 (18 March 1999), pp. 203–204.

Donald, Merlin. *Origins of the Modern Mind. Three Stages in the Evolution of Culture and Cognition.* Cambridge, Mass.: Harvard University Press, 1991.

Dreyfus, Hubert L. *What Computers Still Can't Do*. Cambridge, Mass.: MIT Press, 1992.

Gelman, Rochel. "Structural Constraints on Cognitive Development." *Cognitive Science*, 14 (January/March 1990), pp. 3–9.

———. "First Principles Organize Attention to and Learning About Relevant Data: Number and the Animate-Inanimate Distinction as Examples." *Cognitive Science*, 14:1 (January/March 1990), pp. 79–106.

Goldstone, Robert L. "The Role of Similarity in Categorization: Providing a Groundwork." *Cognition*, 52:2 (1 August 1994), pp. 125–157.

———. "Perceptual Learning." *Annual Review of Psychology*, 49 (1998), pp. 585–612.

———, Douglas L. Medin, and Jamin Halberstadt. "Similarity in Context." *Memory and Cognition*, 25:2 (March 1997), pp. 237–255.

Greene, Joshua D., R. Brian Sommerville, Leigh E. Nystrom, John M. Darley, and Jonathan D. Cohen. "An fMRI Investigation of Emotional Engagement in Moral Judgment." *Science*, 293 (14 September 2001), pp. 2105–2108.

Greeno, James G. "The Situativity of Knowing, Learning, and Research." *American Psychologist,* 53:1 (January 1998), pp. 5–26.

Hilferty, Joseph, Javier Valenzuela, and Oscar Vilarroya. "Paradox Lost." *Cognitive Linguistics*, 9:2 (1998), pp. 175–188.

Hofstadter, Douglas and The Fluid Analogies Research Group. *Fluid Concepts and Creative Analogies*. London: Penguin, 1995.

Holyoak, Keith J. and Paul R. Thagard. *Mental Leaps: Analogy in Creative Thought*. Cambridge, Mass.: MIT Press, 1995.

Johnson, Mark L. *The Body in the Mind*. Chicago: University of Chicago Press, 1987.

Keil, Frank C. and Michael H. Kelly. "Developmental Changes in Category Structure." *Categorical Perception: The Groundwork of Cognition*. Edited by Stevan Harnad (New York: Cambridge University Press, 1987), pp. 491–510.

Lakoff, George. *Women, Fire, and Dangerous Things: What Categories Reveal About the Mind*. Chicago: University of Chicago Press, 1987.

——— and Mark L. Johnson. *Metaphors We Live by*. Chicago: University of Chicago Press, 1980.

Levinson, Stephen C. "Frames of Reference and Molyneux' Question: Crosslinguistic

Evidence." *Language and Space.* Edited by Paul Bloom, Mary A.Peterson, Lynn Nadel, and Merrill F. Garrett (Cambridge Mass.: MIT Press, 1996), pp. 109–171.

MacKay, Donald G. *The Organization of Perception and Action: A Theory for Language and other Cognitive Skills.* New York: Springer-Verlag, 1987.

Markman, Ellen M. "Constraints on Word Learning: Speculations About Their Nature, Origins, and Domain Specificity." *Modularity and Constraints on Language and Cognition: The Minnesotta Symposium on Child Psychology.* Edited by Megan R. Gunnar and Michael P. Maratsos (Hillsdale, N.J.: Lawrence Erlbaum Associates, 1992), pp. 59–102.

Maugham, W. Somerset. "The Appointment in Samarra." (Anthologized in: *Literature: An Introduction to Fiction, Poetry, and Drama.* Edited by X.J. [Josep Charles] Kennedy and Dana Gioia, New York: Longman, 7th ed., 1999).

Murphy, Gregory L. and Mary E. Lassaline. "Hierarchical Structure in Concepts and the Basic Level of Categorization." *Knowledge, Concepts, and Categories.* Edited by Koen Lamberts and David R. Shanks (Cambridge, Mass.: MIT Press, 1997), pp. 93–131.

———— and Douglas Medin. "The Role of Theories in Conceptual Coherence." *Psychological Review*, 92:2 (June 1985), pp. 289–316.

Needham, Amy and Renée Baillargeon. "Infants' Use of Featural and Experiential Information in Segregating and Individuating Objects: A Reply to Xu, Carey, and Welch." *Cognition*, 74 (September 2000), pp. 255–284.

Neisser, Ulrich, ed. *Concepts and Conceptual Development: Ecological and Intellectual Bases of Categories.* Cambridge, England: Cambridge University Press, 1993.

Nelson, Katherine. *Making Sense. The Acquisition of Shared Meaning.* New York: Academic Press, 1985.

————. *Language in Cognitive Development. Emergence of the Mediated Mind.* Cambridge, England: Cambridge University Press, 1996.

Nosofsky, Robert M. "Exemplar-Based Accounts of Relations Between Classification, Recognition, and Typicality." *Journal of Experimental Psychology: Learning, Memory, and Cognition*, 14:6 (December 1988), pp. 700–708.

————. "Exemplar-Based Approach to Relating Categorization, Identification, and Recognition." *Multidimensional Models of Perception and Cognition.* Edited by F. Gregory Ashby (Hillsdale, N.J.: Lawrence Erlbaum Associates,1992), pp. 363–394.

Peacocke, Christopher. *A Study of Concepts.* Cambridge, Mass.: MIT Press, 1992.

218   THE DISSOLUTION OF MIND

Reed, Catherine L. and Norman G. Vinson. "Conceptual Effects on Representational Momentum." *Journal of Experimental Psychology: Human Perception and Performance*, 22:6 (October 1996), pp. 839–850.

Rosch, Eleanor and Barbara B. Lloyd, eds. *Cognition and Categorization*. Hillsdale, N.J.: Lawrence Erlbaum Associates, 1978.

Ross, Brian H. "Category Learning as Problem Solving." *The Psychology of Learning and Motivation: Advances in Research and Theory, Vol. 35*. Edited by Douglas L. Medin (San Diego, Cal.: Academic Press, 1996), pp. 165–192.

Saffran, Jenny R., Richard N. Aslin, and Elissa L. Newport. "Statistical Learning by 8-Month-Old Infants." *Science*, 274 (13 December 1996), pp. 1926–1928.

———, Elizabeth K. Johnson, Richard N. Aslin, and Elissa L. Newport. "Statistical Learning of Tone Sequences by Human Infants and Adults." *Cognition*, 70:1 (1 February 1999), pp. 27–52.

Simon, Herbert. *The Sciences of the Artificial*. Cambridge, Mass.: MIT Press, 1981.

Smith, Linda B., Susan S. Jones, and Barbara Landau. "Naming in Young Children: A Dumb Attentional Mechanism?" *Cognition*, 60:2 (2 August 1996), pp. 143–171.

Spelke, Elizabeth S., Karen Breinlinger, Janet Macomber, and Kristen Jacobson. "Origins of Knowledge." *Psychological Review*, 99 (October 1992), pp. 605–632.

——— and Gretchen A. Van de Walle. "Perceiving and Reasoning About Objects: Insights from Infants." *Spatial Representation*. Edited by Naomi Eilan, Rosaleen McCarthy, and Bill Brewer (Oxford: Basil Blackwell, 1993), pp. 132–162.

Thelen, Esther, Gregor Schöner, Christian Scheier, and Linda B. Smith. "The Dynamics of Embodiment: A Field Theory of Infant Perseverative Reaching." *Behavioral and Brain Sciences*, 24:1 (January 2001), pp. 1–86.

Thompson, Evan. "Symbol Grounding: A Bridge from Artificial Life to Artificial Intelligence." *Brain and Cognition*, 34:1 (June 1997), pp. 48–71.

Varela, Fernando, Evan Thompson, and Eleanor Rosch. *The Embodied Mind*. Cambridge, Mass.: MIT Press, 1991.

Vilarroya, Oscar. "'From Functional 'Mess' to Bounded Functionality." *Minds and Machines*, 11:2 (May 2001), pp. 239–256.

Xu, Fei and Elizabeth Spelke. "Large Number Discrimination in 6-Month-Old Infants." *Cognition*, 74:1 (10 January 2000), pp. B1–B11.

3. Chapter Three, "Wednesday"

Ballard, Dana, Mary Hayhoe, Polly Pook, and Rajesh Rao. "Deictic Codes for the Embodiment of Cognition." *Behavioral and Brain Sciences*, 20:4 (December 1997), pp. 723–767.

Beer, Randall D. *Intelligence as Adaptive Behavior.* New York: Academic Press, 1990.

————. "Computational and Dynamical Languages for Autonomous Agents." *Mind as Motion: Dynamics, Behavior, and Cognition.* Edited by Robert Port and Timothy J. van Gelder (Cambridge, Mass.: MIT, 1995), pp. 121–147.

Bickhard, Mark H. "Representational Content in Humans and Machines." *Journal of Experimental and Theoretical Artificial Intelligence*, 5:2 (1993), pp. 285–333.

———— and Loren Terveen. *Foundational Issues in Artificial Intelligence and Cognitive Science-Impasse and Solution.* Amsterdam: Elsevier Scientific, 1995.

Braitenberg, Valentino. *Vehicles: Experiments in Synthetic Psychology.* Cambridge, Mass.: MIT Press, 1984.

Bredo, Eric. "Cognitivism, Situated Cognition, and Deweyian Pragmatism." *Philosophy of Education*, 1994.
http://www.ed.uiuc.edu/EPS/PES-Yearbook/94_docs/BREDO.HTM

Brooks, Rodney. "Intelligence Without Representation." *Artificial Intelligence*, 47:1 (1991), pp. 139–159.

Brown, John S., Allan Collins, and Paul Duguid. "Situated Cognition and the Culture of Learning." *Educational Researcher*, 18:1 (1989), pp. 32–42.

Ceci, Stephen J. and Antonio Roazzi. "The Effects of Context on Cognition: Postcards from Brazil." *Mind in Context.* Edited by Robert J. Sternberg and Richard K. Wagner (New York: Cambridge University Press, 1994), pp. 74–101.

Chaiklin, Seth and Jean Lave. *Understanding Practice: Perspectives on Activity and Context.* New York: Cambridge University Press, 1993.

Churchland, Paul M. *A Neurocomputational Perspective.* Cambridge, Mass.: MIT Press, 1989.

Clancey, William J. *Situated Cognition: On Human Knowledge and Computer Representations.* Cambridge, England: Cambridge University Press, 1997.

Clark, Andy. *Being There.* Cambridge, Mass.: MIT Press, 1996.

———— and Josefa Toribio. "Doing without Representing?" *Synthese*, 101:3 (1995), pp. 401–431.

———— and David Chalmers. "The Extended Mind." *Analysis*, 58:1 (1998), pp. 7–19.

Crammond, Donald J. "Motor Imagery: Never in Your Wildest Dreams." *Trends in Neuroscience*, 20 (January 1997), pp. 54–57.

Dennett, Daniel. "Cognitive Wheels: The Frame Problem of AI." *Minds, Machines, and Evolution.* Edited by Christopher Hookway (Cambridge, England: Cambridge University Press, 1984), pp. 129–151.

————. *The Intentional Stance.* Cambridge, Mass.: MIT Press, 1987.

Dreyfus, Hubert L. *What Computers Still Can't Do*. Cambridge, Mass.: MIT Press, 1992.

Fauconnier, Gilles. *Cognitive Mappings for Language and Thought.* Cambridge, England: Cambridge University Press, 1997.

Hendriks-Jansen, Horst. *Catching Ourselves in the Act.* Cambridge, Mass.: MIT Press, 1996.

Holyoak, Keith J. and Paul R. Thagard. *Mental Leaps: Analogy in Creative Thought.* Cambridge, Mass.: MIT Press, 1995.

Hutchins, Edward. *Cognition in the Wild.* Cambridge, Mass.: MIT Press, 1995.

Johnson, Mark L. *The Body in the Mind.* Chicago: University of Chicago Press, 1987.

Johnson-Laird, Philip N. and Ruth M.J. Byrne. *Deduction.* Hillsdale, N.J.: Lawrence Erlbaum Associates, 1991.

Lakoff, George. *Women, Fire, and Dangerous Things: What Categories Reveal About the Mind.* Chicago: University of Chicago Press, 1987.

———— and Mark Johnson L. *Metaphors We Live by.* Chicago: University of Chicago Press, 1980.

Landauer, Thomas K. and Susan T. Dumais, "A Solution to Plato's Problem: The Latent Semantic Analysis Theory of Acquisition, Induction, and Representation of Knowledge." *Psycohological Review*, 104:2 (April 1997), pp. 211–240.

Lave, Jean and Etienne Wenger. *Situated Learning: Legitimate Peripheral Participation.* Cambridge, England: Cambridge University Press, 1991.

MacKay, Donald G. *The Organization of Perception and Action: A Theory for Language and other Cognitive Skills*. New York: Springer-Verlag, 1987.

Millikan, Ruth. *Language, Thought, and Other Biological Categories*. Cambridge, Mass.: MIT Press, 1984.

Stabler, Edward. "How Are Gramars Represented?" *Behavioral and Brain Sciences*, 6:2 (September 1983), pp. 391–402.

Steels, Luc. "The Artificial Life Roots of Artificial Intelligence." *Artificial Life*, 1:1 (January 1994), pp. 75–110.

Stich, Stephen P. *From Folk Psychology to Cognitive Science. The Case Against Belief*. Cambridge, Mass.: MIT Press, 1983.

Tomasello, Michael. "Do Young Children Have Adult Syntactic Competence?" *Cognition*, 74:3 (14 march 2000), pp. 209–253.

Varela, Fernando, Evan Thompson, and Eleanor Rosch. *The Embodied Mind*. Cambridge, Mass.: MIT Press, 1991.

Wuethrich, Bernice. "Learning the World's Languages-Before They Vanish." *Science*, 288 (18 May 2000), pp. 1156–1159.

4. Chapter Four, "Thursday"

Bloom, Lois. *The Transition from Infancy to Language: Acquiring the Power of Expression*. New York: Cambridge University Press, 1993.

Bloom, Paul. *How Children Learn the Meanings of Words*. Cambridge, Mass.: MIT Press, 2000.

Clark, Eve V. *The Lexicon in Acquisition*. Cambridge, England: Cambridge University Press, 1997.

Clark, Herbert H. "Making Sense on Nonce Sense." *The Process of Language Understanding*. Edited by Giovanni B. Flores d'Arcais, and Robert J. Jarvella (London: John Wiley & Sons, 1983), pp. 297–331.

De Loache, Judy S. "Early Understanding and Use of Symbols: The Model Model." *Current Directions in Psychological Science*, 4:1 (1995), pp. 109–113.

Donald, Merlin. *Origins of the Modern Mind. Three Stages in the Evolution of Culture and Cognition*. Cambridge, Mass.: Harvard University Press, 1991.

Elman, Jeffrey, Elizabeth Bates, Mark H. Johnson, Annette Karmiloff-Smith, Domenico Parisi, and Kim Plunkett. *Rethinking Innateness: A Connectionist Perspective on*

Development. Cambridge, Mass.: MIT Press, 1996.

Glenberg, Arthur M., Marion Meyer, and Karen Lindem. "Mental Models Contribute to Foregrounding During Text Comprehension." *Journal of Memory and Language,* 26:1 (February 1987), pp. 69–83.

Graesser, Arthur C., Murray Singer, and Tom Trabasso. "Constructing Inferences During Narrative Text Comprehension." *Psychological Review,* 101 (July 1994), pp. 371–395.

Johnson, Mark L. *The Body in the Mind*. Chicago: University of Chicago Press, 1987.

Julesz, Bela. and Ilona Kovacs, eds. *Maturational Windows and Adult Cortical Plasticity*. Reading, Mass.: Addison-Wesley, 1995.

Lakoff, George. *Women, Fire, and Dangerous Things: What Categories Reveal About the Mind*. Chicago: University of Chicago Press, 1987.

—— and Mark Johnson L. *Metaphors We Live by*. Chicago: University of Chicago Press, 1980.

Langacker, Ronald W. *Concept, Image, and Symbol: The Cognitive Basis of Grammar*. Berlin: Mouton de Gruyter, 1991.

Markman, Ellen M. "Constraints on Word Learning: Speculations About Their Nature, Origins, and Domain Specificity." *Modularity and Constraints on Language and Cognition: The Minnesotta Symposium on Child Psychology*. Edited by Megan R. Gunnar and Michael P. Maratsos (Hillsdale, N.J.: Lawrence Erlbaum Associates, 1992), pp. 59–102.

Markson, Lorim and Paul Bloom. "Evidence Against a Dedicated System for Word Learning in Children." *Nature*, 385 (27 February 1997), pp. 813–815.

McKoon, Gail and Roger Ratcliff. "Inference During Reading." *Psychological Review*, 99:3 (July 1992), pp. 440–466.

Millikan, Ruth. *Language, Thought and Other Biological Categories*. Cambridge, Mass.: MIT Press, 1984.

Morrow, Daniel G., Steven L. Greenspan, and Gordon H. Bower. "Accessibility and Situation Models in Narrative Comprehension." *Journal of Memory and Language*, 26:2 (April 1987), pp. 165–187.

Nelson, Katherine. *Making Sense. The Acquisition of Shared Meaning*. New York: Academic Press, 1985.

——. *Language in Cognitive Development. Emergence of the Mediated Mind*.

Cambridge, England: Cambridge University Press, 1996.

Oshima-Takane, Yuriko. "The Learning of First and Second Person Pronouns in English." *Language, Logic, and Concepts: Essays in Honor of John Macnamara.* Edited by Ray Jackendoff, Paul Bloom, and Karen Wynn (Cambridge, Mass.: MIT Press, 1999), pp. 373–409.

Siegler, Robert S. and Eric A. Jenkins *How Children Discover New Strategies.* Hillsdale, N.J.: Lawrence Erlbaum Associates, 1989.

Slobin, Dan I. "Two Ways to Travel: Verbs of Motion in English and Spanish." *Grammatical Constructions: Their Form and Meaning.* Edited by Masayoshi Shibatani and Sandra A. Thompson (Oxford: Oxford University Press, 1996), pp. 195–219.

Sweetser, Eve E. *From Etymology to Pragmatics: Metaphorical and Cultural Aspects of Semantic Structure.* Cambridge, England: Cambridge University Press, 1990.

Tomasello, Michael, Ann C. Kruger, and Hilary H. Ratner. "Cultural Learning." *Behavioral and Brain Sciences,* 16:3 (September 1993), pp. 495–552.

Traugott, Elizabeth C. and Bern Heine, eds. *Approaches to Grammaticalization.* Amsterdam: John Benjamins, 1991.

Wellman, Henry M. *The Child's Theory of Mind.* Cambridge, Mass.: MIT Press, 1990 .

5. Chapter Five, "Friday"

Adams, Jeff. *The Conspiracy of the Text: The Place of Narrative in the Development of Thought.* London: Routledge and Kegan Paul, 1986.

Appleyard, J[oseph] A. *Becoming a Reader: The Experience of Fiction from Childhood to Adulthood.* Cambridge, England: Cambridge University Press, 1990.

Bach, Ken. *Thought and Reference.* Oxford: Oxford University Press, 1987.

———. "On Communicative Intentions." *Mind and Language,* 2:2 (May 1987), pp. 141–154.

Ballard, Dana, Mary Hayhoe, Polly Pook, and Rajesh Rao. "Deictic Codes for the Embodiment of Cognition." *Behavioral and Brain Sciences,* 20:4 (December 1997), pp. 723–767.

Brown, John S., Allan Collins, and Paul Duguid. "Situated Cognition and the Culture of Learning." *Educational Researcher,* 18:1 (January 1989), pp. 32–42.

——— and Paul Duguid. *The Social Life of Information.* Boston: Harvard Business

School Press, 2000.

Ceci, Stephen J. and Antonio Roazzi. "The Effects of Context on Cognition: Postcards from Brazil." *Mind in Context*. Edited by Robert J. Sternberg and Richard K. Wagner (New York: Cambridge University Press, 1994), pp. 74–101.

Chaiklin, Seth and Jean Lave. *Understanding Practice: Perspectives on Activity and Context*. New York: Cambridge University Press, 1993.

Clancey, William J. *Situated Cognition: On Human Knowledge and Computer Representations*. Cambridge, England: Cambridge University Press, 1997.

Clark, Andy. *Being There*. Cambridge, Mass.: MIT Press, 1996.

Donald, Merlin. *Origins of the Modern Mind. Three Stages in the Evolution of Culture and Cognition*. Cambridge, Mass.: Harvard University Press, 1991.

Gibbs, Raymond W., Jr. *The Poetics of Mind: Figurative Thought, Language, and Understanding*. New York: Cambridge University Press, 1994.

Glenberg, Arthur M. and David A. Robertson. "Indexical Understanding of Instructions." *Discourse Processes*, 28:1 (1999), pp. 1–26.

Gouzoules, Harold, Sarah Gouzoules, and Jennifer Ashley. "Representational Signaling in Non-Human Primate Vocal Communication." *Current Topics in Primate Vocal Communication*. Edited by Elke Zimmermann, John D. Newman, and Uwe Jurgens (New York: Plenum, 1995), pp. 235–252.

Hendriks-Jansen, Horst. *Catching Ourselves in the Act*. Cambridge, Mass.: MIT Press, 1996.

Hutchins, Edward. *Cognition in the Wild*. Cambridge, Mass.: MIT Press, 1995.

Johnson, Mark L. *The Body in the Mind*. Chicago: University of Chicago Press, 1987.

Kemmerer, David. "'Near' and 'Far' in Language and Perception." *Cognition*, 73:1 (1999), pp. 35–63.

Lave, Jean and Etienne Wenger. *Situated Learning: Legitimate Peripheral Participation*. Cambridge, England: Cambridge UniversityPress, 1991.

Newton, Natika. *Foundations of Understanding*. Philadelphia: John Benjamins, 1996.

Sperber, Dan and Deirdre Wilson, *Relevance: Communication and Cognition*. Cambridge, Mass.: Harvard University Press, 1986.

Steig, Michael. *Stories of Reading: Subjectivity and Literary Understanding*. Baltimore: Johns Hopkins University Press, 1989.

6. Chapter Six, "Saturday"

Barkow, Jerome, Leda Cosmides, and John Tooby, eds. *The Adapted Mind: Evolutionary Psychology and the Generation of Culture*. New York: Oxford University Press, 1992.

Bechtel, William and Robert C. Richardson. *Discovering Complexity*. Princeton: Princeton University Press, 1993.

Churchland, Patricia S. *Neurophilosophy*. Cambridge, Mass.: MIT Press, 1986.

Crick, Francis C. *The Astonishing Hypothesis*. New York: Scribners, 1994.

Cummins, Robert. *The Nature of Psychological Explanation*. Cambridge, Mass.: MIT Press, 1983.

Dreyfus, Hubert L. *What Computers Still Can't Do*. Cambridge, Mass.: MIT Press, 1992.

Gopnik, Alison. "How We Know Our Minds: The Illusion of First-Person Knowledge of Intentionality." *Behavioral and Brain Sciences*, 16:1 (March 1993), pp. 1–86.

Gregory, Richard. "What Do Qualia Do?" *Perception*, 25 (March 1996), p. 377.

Haugeland, John, ed. *Mind Design*. Cambridge, Mass.: MIT Press, 1981.

Hayes, Patrick J. "The Naive Physics Manifesto." *Formal Theories of the Commonsense World*. Edited by Jerry Hobbs and Robert Moore (Norwood: Ablex, 1985), pp.1–36.

Holyoak, Keith J. and Paul R. Thagard. *Mental Leaps: Analogy in Creative Thought*. Cambridge, Mass.: MIT Press, 1995.

Johnson, Mark L. *The Body in the Mind*. Chicago: University of Chicago Press, 1987.

Johnson-Laird, Philip N. and Ruth M.J. Byrne. *Deduction*. Hillsdale, N.J.: Lawrence Erlbaum Associates, 1991.

Julesz, Bela. *Dialogues on Perception*. Cambridge, Mass.: MIT Press, 1995.

———— and Ilona Kovacs, eds. *Maturational Windows and Adult Cortical Plasticity*. Reading, Mass.: Addison-Wesley, 1995.

Kahneman, David and Anne M. Treisman. "Changing Views of Attention and Automaticity." *Varieties of Attention*. Edited by Raja Parasuraman and D. Roy Davies (New York: Academic Press, 1984), pp. 29–61.

————, Paul Slovic, and Amos Tversky, eds. *Judgment Under Uncertainty: Heuristics and Biases*. Cambridge, England: Cambridge University Press, 1982.

Kolodner, Janet. *Cased-Based Reasoning*. San Mateo, Calif.: Morgan Kaufmann, 1993.

Llinas, Rodolfo and Urs Ribary. "Consciousness and the Brain. The Thalamocortical Dialogue in Health and Disease." *Annals of the New York Academy of Sciences*, 929 (April 2001), pp. 166–175.

MacDermott, David "A Critique of Pure Reason." *Computational Intelligence*, 3:2 (1987), pp. 151–160.

McClamrock, Ron. *Existential Cognition*. Chicago: University of Chicago Press, 1995.

McCloskey, Michael and Deborah Kohl. "Naive Physics: The Curvilinear Impetus Principle and Its Role in Interactions with Moving Objects." *Journal of Experimental Psychology: Learning, Memory, and Cognition*, 9:1 (1983), pp. 146–156.

Mithen, Steven J. *The Prehistory of the Mind: The Cognitive Origins of Art, Religion, and Science*. London: Thames & Hudson, 1996.

Nisbett, Richard E. and Lee Ross. *Human Inference: Strategies and Shortcomings of Social Judgment*. Englewood Cliffs: Prentice-Hall, 1980.

O'Regan, Kevin and Alva Noë. "A Sensorimotor Account of Vision and Visual Consciousness." *Behavioral and Brain Sciences*, 24 (2001).
http://www.bbsonline.org/documents/a/00/00/05/06/index.html

Peacocke, Christopher. "Intuitive Mechanics, Psychological Reality, and the Idea of a Material Object." *Spatial Representation*. Edited by Naomi Eilan, Rosaleen McCarthy, and Bill Brewer (Oxford: Basil Blackwell, 1993), pp. 162–176.

Pessoa, Luiz, Evan Thompson, and Alva Noë. "Finding out About Filling in: A Guide to Perceptual Completion for Visual Science and the Philosophy of Perception." *Behavioral and Brain Sciences*, 21:6 (December 1998), pp. 723–802.

Peterson, Mary A. and Bradley S. Gibson. "Shape Recognition Inputs to Figure-Ground Organization in Three-Dimensional Displays." *Cognitive Psychology*, 25:3 (1 July 1993), pp. 383–429.

Rakic, Pasko. "Specification of Cerebral Cortical Areas." *Science*, 241 (8 July 1988), pp.170–176.

Reber, Arthur S. *Implicit Learning and Tacit Knowledge: An Essay on the Cognitive Unconscious*. Oxford: Oxford University Press, 1993.

Rosenthal, Victor. "Does It Rattle when You Shake It? Modularity of Mind and the Epistemology of Cognitive Research." *Perspectives on Cognitive Neuropsychology.* Edited by Gianfranco Denes, Carlo Semenza, and Patrizia Biachi. (Hillsdale, N.J.: Lawrence Erlbaum Associates, 1988), pp. 31–58.

Schank, Roger C., Christopher Riesbeck, and Alex Kass. *Inside Case-Based Explanation.* Hillsdale, N.J.: Lawrence Erlbaum Associates, 1994.

Shallice, Tim. *From Neuropsychology to Mental Structure.* Cambridge, England: Cambridge University Press, 1988.

Shanker, Stuart G. "The Decline and Fall of the Mechanist Metaphor." *Artificial Intelligence: The Case Against.* Edited by Rainier Born. (London: Croom Helm), 1987, pp. 72–131.

Shapiro, Michael. *The Sense of Change: Language as History.* Blomington: Indiana University Press, 1991.

Tong, Frank. "Brain at Work: Play by Play." *Nature Neuroscience*, 4 (June 2001), pp. 560–562.

Tversky, Barbara and Elizabeth J. Marsh. "Biased Retellings of Events Yield Biased Memories." *Cognitive Psychology*, 40:1 (1 February 2000), pp. 1–38.

Westbury, Christopher and Daniel C. Dennett. "Mining the Past to Construct the Future: Memory and Belief as Forms of Knowledge." *Memory, Brain, and Belief.* Edited by David L. Schacter and Elaine Scarry (Cambridge, Mass.: Harvard University Press, 2000), pp. 11–32.

Winograd, Terry and Fernando Flores, *Understanding Computers and Cognition: A New Foundation for Design.* Norwood, N.J.: Ablex, 1986.

Zadeh, Lofti. "Fuzzy Logic." *Computer*, 21:1 (February 1988), pp. 83–93.

ABOUT THE AUTHOR

Oscar Vilarroya studied Medicine at the Universitat Autònoma de Barcelona. As an undergraduate, he worked as a research assistant in the Neuropsychology Section at the Hospital de la Creu i Sant Pau. After graduating, Vilarroya moved to the United Kindom, where he worked as research officer in Neuropsychology at the University of London, under the direction of Professor Christine Temple. Back in Barcelona, Vilarroya became interested in connectionist modeling and philosophy of mind. He completed his Ph.D. in Cognitive Science and Language at the Universitat Autònoma de Barcelona in 1998. Vilarroya has authored papers in major scholarly journals such as *Brain and Language, Cognitive Neuropsychology, Minds and Machines, Biology and Philosophy*, and *Cognitive Linguistics*, and is also one of the founders of the Centre de Recerca en Ciència Cognitiva. He currently is a lecturer in the Department of Psychiatry and Legal Medicine at the Universitat Autònoma de Barcelona, and is an active disseminator of science and medicine, appearing regularly in the Spanish press and radio media.

INDEX

The convention of employing the letter "k" to mark in the text all those terms used in a nonstandard way is omitted in the index.

VIBS

The **Value Inquiry Book Series** is co-sponsored by:

Adler School of Professional Psychology
American Indian Philosophy Association
American Maritain Association
American Society for Value Inquiry
Association for Process Philosophy of Education
Canadian Society for Philosophical Practice
Center for Bioethics, University of Turku
Center for Professional and Applied Ethics, University of North Carolina at
Charlotte
Center for Research in Cognitive Science, Autonomous University of Barcelona
Centre for Applied Ethics, Hong Kong Baptist University
Centre for Cultural Research, Aarhus University
Centre for Professional Ethics, University of Central Lancashire
Centre for the Study of Philosophy and Religion, University College of Cape
Breton
College of Education and Allied Professions, Bowling Green State University
College of Liberal Arts, Rochester Institute of Technology
Concerned Philosophers for Peace
Conference of Philosophical Societies
Department of Moral and Social Philosophy, University of Helsinki
Gannon University
Gilson Society
Ikeda University
Institute of Philosophy of the High Council of Scientific Research, Spain
International Academy of Philosophy of the Principality of Liechtenstein
International Center for the Arts, Humanities, and Value Inquiry
International Society for Universal Dialogue
Natural Law Society

Personalist Discussion Group
Philosophical Society of Finland
Philosophy Born of Struggle Association
Philosophy Seminar, University of Mainz
Pragmatism Archive
R.S. Hartman Institute for Formal and Applied Axiology
Research Institute, Lakeridge Health Corporation
Russian Philosophical Society
Society for Iberian and Latin-American Thought
Society for the Philosophic Study of Genocide and the Holocaust
Society for the Philosophy of Sex and Love
Yves R. Simon Institute

Titles Published

1.   Noel Balzer, *The Human Being as a Logical Thinker*

2.   Archie J. Bahm, *Axiology: The Science of Values*

3.   H. P. P. (Hennie) Lötter, *Justice for an Unjust Society*

4.   H. G. Callaway, *Context for Meaning and Analysis: A Critical Study in the Philosophy of Language*

5.   Benjamin S. Llamzon, *A Humane Case for Moral Intuition*

6.   James R. Watson, Between Auschwitz and Tradition: Postmodern Reflections on the Task of Thinking. A volume in **Holocaust and Genocide Studies**

7.   Robert S. Hartman, *Freedom to Live: The Robert Hartman Story, edited by Arthur R. Ellis.* A volume in **Hartman Institute Axiology Studies**

8.   Archie J. Bahm, *Ethics: The Science of Oughtness*

9.   George David Miller, *An Idiosyncratic Ethics; Or, the Lauramachean Ethics*

10.   Joseph P. DeMarco, *A Coherence Theory in Ethics*

11.   Frank G. Forrest, *Valuemetrics*[N]: *The Science of Personal and Professional Ethics.* A volume in **Hartman Institute Axiology Studies**

12.   William Gerber, The Meaning of Life: Insights of the World's Great Thinkers

13.   Richard T. Hull, Editor, *A Quarter Century of Value Inquiry: Presidential Addresses of the American Society for Value Inquiry.* A volume in **Histories and Addresses of Philosophical Societies**

14.   William Gerber, Nuggets of Wisdom from Great Jewish Thinkers: From Biblical Times to the Present

15.   Sidney Axinn, *The Logic of Hope: Extensions of Kant's View of Religion*

16.   Messay Kebede, *Meaning and Development*

17.   Amihud Gilead, *The Platonic Odyssey: A Philosophical-Literary Inquiry into the Phaedo*

18.   Necip Fikri Alican, *Mill's Principle of Utility: A Defense of John Stuart Mill's Notorious Proof.* A volume in **Universal Justice**

19.   Michael H. Mitias, Editor, *Philosophy and Architecture.*

20.   Roger T. Simonds, Rational Individualism: The Perennial Philosophy of Legal Interpretation. A volume in **Natural Law Studies**

21.   William Pencak, *The Conflict of Law and Justice in the Icelandic Sagas*

22.   Samuel M. Natale and Brian M. Rothschild, Editors, *Values, Work, Education: The Meanings of Work*

23.   N. Georgopoulos and Michael Heim, Editors, *Being Human in the Ultimate: Studies in the Thought of John M. Anderson*

24.   Robert Wesson and Patricia A. Williams, Editors, *Evolution and Human Values*

25.   Wim J. van der Steen, Facts, Values, and Methodology: A New Approach to Ethics

26.   Avi Sagi and Daniel Statman, *Religion and Morality*

42.   Clark Butler, *History as the Story of Freedom: Philosophy in Intercultural Context*, with responses by sixteen scholars

43.   Dennis Rohatyn, *Philosophy History Sophistry*

44.   Leon Shaskolsky Sheleff, *Social Cohesion and Legal Coercion: A Critique of Weber, Durkheim, and Marx*. Afterword by Virginia Black

45.   Alan Soble, Editor, Sex, Love, and Friendship: Studies of the Society for the Philosophy of Sex and Love, 1977–1992. A volume in **Histories and Addresses of Philosophical Societies**

46.   Peter A. Redpath, *Wisdom's Odyssey: From Philosophy to Transcendental Sophistry*. A volume in **Studies in the History of Western Philosophy**

47.   Albert A. Anderson, *Universal Justice: A Dialectical Approach*. A volume in **Universal Justice**

48.   Pio Colonnello, *The Philosophy of José Gaos*. Translated from Italian by Peter Cocozzella. Edited by Myra Moss. Introduction by Giovanni Gullace. A volume in **Values in Italian Philosophy**

49.   Laura Duhan Kaplan and Laurence F. Bove, Editors, *Philosophical Perspectives on Power and Domination: Theories and Practices*. A volume in **Philosophy of Peace**

50.   Gregory F. Mellema, *Collective Responsibility*

51.   Josef Seifert, *What Is Life? The Originality, Irreducibility, and Value of Life*. A volume in **Central-European Value Studies**

52.   William Gerber, *Anatomy of What We Value Most*

53.   Armando Molina, *Our Ways: Values and Character*, Edited by Rem B. Edwards. A volume in **Hartman Institute Axiology Studies**

54.   Kathleen J. Wininger, *Nietzsche's Reclamation of Philosophy*. A volume in **Central-European Value Studies**

55.   Thomas Magnell, Editor, *Explorations of Value*

56.   HPP (Hennie) Lötter, Injustice, Violence, and Peace: The Case of South Africa. A volume in **Philosophy of Peace**

116.   Jon Mills, Editor, *A Pedagogy of Becoming.* A volume in **Philosophy of Education**

117.   Robert T. Radford, *Cicero: A Study in the Origins of Republican Philosophy.* A volume in **Studies in the History of Western Philosophy**

118.   Arleen L. F. Salles and María Julia Bertomeu, Editors, *Bioethics: Latin American Perspectives.* A volume in **Philosophy in Latin America**

119.   Nicola Abbagnano, *The Human Project: The Year 2000*, with an Interview by Guiseppe Grieco. Translated from Italian by Bruno Martini and Nino Langiulli. Edited with an introduction by Nino Langiulli. A volume in **Studies in the History of Western Philosophy**

120.   Daniel M. Haybron, Editor, *Earth's Abominations: Philosophical Studies of Evil.* A volume in **Personalist Studies**

119.   Anna T. Challenger, *Philosophy and Art in Gurdjieff's Beelzebub: A Modern Sufi Odyssey*

122.   George David Miller, *Peace, Value, and Wisdom: The Educational Philosophy of Daisaku Ikeda.* A volume in **Daisaku Ikeda Studies**

123.   Haim Gordon and Rivca Gordon, *Sophistry and Twentieth-Century Art*

124.   Thomas O Buford and Harold H. Oliver, Editors *Personalism Revisited:Its Proponents and Critics.* A volume in **Histories and Addresses of Philosophical Societies**

124.   Avi Sagi, *Albert Camus and the Philosophy of the Absurd.* Translated from Hebrew by Batya Stein

125.   Robert S. Hartman, *The Knowledge of Good: Critique of Axiological Reason.* Expanded translation from the Spanish by Robert S. Hartman. Edited by Arthur R. Ellis and Rem B. Edwards. A volume in **Hartman Institute Axiology Studies**

127.   Alison Bailey and Paula J. Smithka, Editors. *Community, Diversity, and Difference: Implications for Peace.* A volume in **Philosophy of Peace**

128.   Oscar Vilarroya, *The Dissolution of Mind: A Fable of How Experience Gives Rise to Cognition.* A volume in **Cognitive Science**